To my darling niece Maura. You bring sunshine and flowers into all of our lives.

The NIGHT of Other DAYS

The Life and Work of Poet Seamus Heaney

With love Hugh Mulrooney,
Nov 2018.

HUGH MULROONEY

authorHOUSE®

AuthorHouse™ UK
1663 Liberty Drive
Bloomington, IN 47403 USA
www.authorhouse.co.uk
Phone: 0800.197.4150

© 2018 Hugh Mulrooney. All rights reserved.

No part of this book may be reproduced, stored in a retrieval system, or transmitted by any means without the written permission of the author.

Published by AuthorHouse 10/03/2018

ISBN: 978-1-5462-9684-3 (sc)
ISBN: 978-1-5462-9683-6 (e)

Print information available on the last page.

Any people depicted in stock imagery provided by Getty Images are models, and such images are being used for illustrative purposes only.
Certain stock imagery © Getty Images.

This book is printed on acid-free paper.

Because of the dynamic nature of the Internet, any web addresses or links contained in this book may have changed since publication and may no longer be valid. The views expressed in this work are solely those of the author and do not necessarily reflect the views of the publisher, and the publisher hereby disclaims any responsibility for them.

In memory of Catherine

To Margaret and my daughters Catherine,
Orna, Hilda, Anne and Clare.

CONTENTS

Introduction xi

PART ONE

Chapter 1	Christopher	1
Chapter 2	Patrick	11
Chapter 3	Margaret	26
Chapter 4	Absence	36
Chapter 5	Schooling	42
Chapter 6	Afterlife	48
Chapter 7	Space	59

PART TWO

Chapter 8	Water	65
Chapter 9	Mossbawn	78
Chapter 10	Earthmother	105

PART THREE

Chapter 11	Northern Ireland	121
Chapter 12	Poetry and Politics	134
Chapter 13	Poetry and Violence	144

Chapter 14	Integrity	155
Chapter 15	Voices	167
Chapter 16	Parables	187
Chapter 17	Seeing	196
Chapter 18	Contradictions	207
Chapter 19	Overview	213

Bibliography	225
Secondary sources	247

Books By Seamus Heaney Poetry:

Death of a Naturalist	DN
Door into the Dark	DD
Wintering Out	WO
North	N
Field Work	FW
Selected Poems	1965-1975
Station Island	SI
Sweeney Astray	SW
Sweeney's Flight	(with photographs by Rachel Giese)
The Haw Lantern	HL
New Selected Poems	1966-1987
Seeing Things	ST
Laments	Jan Kochanowski
The Spirit Level	SL
Opened Ground:	Poems 1966-1996
Beowulf	B
Electric Light	EL
District and Circle	DC
The Testament of Cresseid & Seven Fables	
Human Chain	HC
New Selected Poems 1988-2013	
Aeneid Book VI	
The Rattle Bag (edited with Ted Hughes)	
The School Bag (edited with Ted Hughes)	

Prose:

P	Preoccupations: Selected Prose 1968 – 78
GT	The Government of the Tongue
RP	The Redress of Poetry: Oxford Lectures
FK	Finders Keepers: Selected Prose 1971-2001
SS	Stepping Stones (with Dennis O'Driscoll)

Plays:

The Cure at Troy
The Burial at Thebes

INTRODUCTION

This book is written for readers who wish to enjoy the poetry of our beloved Seamus Heaney. He wrote beautiful lyric poetry and rich thought-provoking prose in words of everyday speech. He held audiences enthralled as they listened to his lectures and broadcasts. He was also a spokesman during the time of the Northern Ireland 'troubles'. He filled many roles in his lifetime and he gave of himself in an unstinting way. In 1995 King Carl XV1 of Sweden presented Seamus with the Nobel Prize for Literature and ten years later he was honoured with a visit to his Wicklow home by Emperor and Empress Michiko.

This book attempts to bring his poetry to ordinary readers who will find their lives enriched by its beauty and its truth. I am particularly interested in readers from outside of Ireland. Seamus Heaney lived and worked in an Ireland which was disappearing. The work of his father on the family farm and the domestic life of farm- home were making way for the post-war advances in mechanisation, industry and commerce. I record all of those changes as they are described in Heaney's work. There were massive changes in political life too and violence became a daily reality. The history, sociology, religion, myth and literature of Ireland are explored to give a detailed account of the background to Heaney's work. He was born in 1939 and he died in 2013.

My work crosses a line which is sometimes used to define poetry as the sole preserve of the academic. I want to reach ordinary readers. A huge corpus of academic research exists and I have made extensive use of it but my work is not written for academics. I am a teacher, in his eighties, who worked for six years alongside Seamus Heaney in Carysfort College of Education, Dublin.

I want to open Heaney's world to the general reader. My work will be of significant value to readers who are not familiar with Ireland's history, geography, literature and myth.

His complete poetic work is contained in twelve separate books published over his lifetime. I have made extensive reference to these and to his prose writings, especially to 'Finders Keepers'. The background on his life is referenced from that wonderful book 'Stepping Stones', which records his written conversations with the poet and author Dennis O Driscoll. It is a book of nourishment and richness which provides great insight.

Seamus Heaney lived and wrote about a world that is gone and he has left us a wonderful record of the calendar customs of a peaceful rural Northern Ireland. But the times were far from peaceful. For over thirty years, violence shattered that peace and Heaney looked to history and myth to find answers. His answers did not meet with universal approval but the situation was complex and deeply rooted in history. I try to give a brief, balanced account of that history. I have the non-Irish reader very much in mind, because even among the Irish there is not a consensus. Conviction and bias play their part and sometimes win the day. The history of Northern Ireland is a complex one and I have relied on the work of two eminent historians to get a balanced view.

The reason for reading Seamus Heaney's poetry is simply the pleasure and nourishment we get from it. It is within the grasp of every reader. But the poetry is multi-layered and it has been studied by academics the world over. Countless books and articles have been written on his work. This book is not an academic work although I gratefully acknowledge the many references to scholarly studies. My aim is to reach readers who wish to be nourished by the beauty and profundity of Heaney's work. Seamus believed that a very wide readership exists for lyric poetry, people who are not of the academic fraternity but who will gain immense pleasure and sustenance from his work.

Seamus Heaney has given his readers some idea of what they will find in his poetry. 'The ideal reader is one who would feel a strangeness- but also an attraction- in the sheer phonetic substance of these things'. Quoting from 'The Tempest' he tells us that 'sounds and sweet airs, that give delight and hurt not' will fit as a description of poetry. For the poet himself, finding the right expression by wrongfooting the language is one of the principal paths into poetry. 'A poem that comes out ahead will often have crept up from behind' and the result will be 'language in orbit'. Speaking to Dennis O Driscoll he tells us that it may start with recalled emotion or immediate anger or rapture, 'but once the personal boost has helped a poem to lift off, it runs on its own energy circuit.' And once a poem is written it is no longer the poet's business. The best poetry always embodies a transformation of the writer's excitement and is a guarantee of his or her engagement with the subject of each poem.

Heaney could not ignore the injustice, the violence and the savagery of his own place. Unjust Ulster hurt him into the poetry of protest and 'the hob-nailed boots from beyond the mountain' tramped across the lawns of civility.

Readers can trust Heaney when he says 'poetry isn't so daunting, you shouldn't be shy of it, you too, have a right of way into it and can enjoy it'. Remember the sun has never seen a shadow.

At the heart of his poetry is language facility. Words give the sense of touch, of smell, of texture, as he describes the loud slaps of the spade, the sour stink of turned earth and the strong gauze of sound. Heaney avoids obscurity as he describes with sensuous and vivid words a vanishing world of family and rural traditions. This is not a poet trying to keep culture aloof from the philistine masses. As described by Ciaran Berry (Poetry Ireland Review) this is a poet of childhood wonders and farmyard rituals celebrating the ordinary in the quotidian, an elegist, landscape-painter, master of the sonnet and maker of elaborate and daring metaphors.

He may be the poet of 'muddy-booted blackberry-picking' but we become aware of a 'steadily widening pool of reflection, question and recollection' (Elmer Andrews). Blake Morrison warns that Heaney's poetry is far less comforting and comfortable than supposed. It is tense, torn, divided, often layered with obscure allusions. Far from archaic it registers the tremors and turmoil of its age.

The eminent American scholar and poet Helen Vendler spoke of how Heaney's poetry expresses profound family affections, eloquent landscapes and vigorous social concerns. It tells of childhood, adolescence, adulthood, displacement, travels, sorrows and deaths. It looks with social engagement at what it means to be a contemporary citizen of Northern Ireland and the intolerable stresses put on the population by conflict, fear, betrayals and murders. To the autobiographical and political themes he adds the symbols of exhumed bog bodies, pilgrims on Lough Derg and parables of frontiers and misty islands. All expressed in daring language.

I have chosen a few of his thoughts at random:

'One clear stanza can take more weight/Than a whole wagon of elaborate prose'…Milosz

You learned that, from the human beginnings, poetic imagination had proffered a world of light and a world of dark, a shadow region – not so much an afterlife as an afterimage of life.

'The work that meant most to me was stuff born out of more stressful conditions…of knottier origin and tighter grain.

'You are confirmed by the visitation of the last poem and threatened by the elusiveness of the next one.

'I get this sudden joy from the sheer fact of the mountains to my right and the sea to my left, the flow of the farmland, the sweep of the road, the lift of the sky.

"What a poet can establish in the act of writing a poem is something a reader can get from the completed work, that is, a realisation that as persons and as peoples we can get farther into ourselves and farther out of ourselves than we might have expected; and this is one of the ways that poetry helps things forward". (Seamus Heaney 2001)

PART ONE

Seamus Heaney

CHAPTER

Christopher

1

The death of his little brother, Christopher, was one of the lasting sadnesses of Seamus Heaney's life. We have three accounts. The Mid Ulster Mail newspaper dated Saturday February 28th, 1953 reported that a three- and- a- half year old boy died as a result of a road accident 20 yards from his home at Mossbawn.[1]

More than fifty years later, Seamus Heaney said that he wasn't there on the evening it happened, 'but I do have a clear picture of it in my mind'.[2] Little Christopher had been taken hand-in-hand by his older brother, Hugh, to post a letter on the Belfast bus. Spotting his other brothers on the opposite side of the road, Christopher had rushed across straight into the path of an oncoming car. Hugh carried the bleeding, unconscious child down the short lane. Margaret, his mother, hearing the commotion as she hung washing on the line, laid the bleeding toddler in his cot in the kitchen. He died that evening in the Mid-Ulster Hospital.

At the time of the accident Seamus Heaney, the eldest of the family of nine, was a boarder at Saint Columb's College in Derry. He was two months short of his fourteenth birthday. A neighbour, Jim McKenna drove to the college to bring Seamus home. There can be little doubting the affection Seamus felt for his little brother. It was expressed in a poem written over fifty years later and published in 'District and Circle' (2006) titled[3] 'The Blackbird of Glanmore'.

'I want away/To the house of death, to my father/Under the low clay roof.'...'And I think of one gone to him,/A little stillness dancer —Haunter- son, lost brother —/Cavorting through the yard...' That stayed with Seamus all his life and came up more than fifty years later in the poem.

Elsewhere in his interviews with Dennis O'Driscoll Heaney refers to his sensitivity to the subject of the deaths of children. He relates how his reading of Frost's poem 'Out, Out' affected him. The poem describes the sudden death of a boy as a result of losing his arm in an accident with a buzz-saw.

Heaney was pursuing his second level education as a beneficiary of the 1947 Northern Ireland Education Act. Under the terms of this act a student who was successful in the eleven plus public examination could qualify to attend a second-level school and pursue their studies to university-entrance level. Seamus distinguished himself in the examination, was awarded a scholarship and earned a place as a boarder in St Columb's College in Derry. He went to the Derry school in September 1951. Christopher was killed in February 1953.

When he graduated from St Columb's, Seamus went on to Queens University in Belfast on a full scholarship and graduated with a first -class honours degree in English Language and Literature. Then, having completed his Diploma in Education, he was appointed lecturer in the English Department in Queens.

It was while he lectured in Queens that he published his first volume of poetry...'Death of a Naturalist' (DN), in 1966. It included one of the best loved of Seamus Heaney's poems, written in memory of his dead brother Christopher: 'Mid-Term-Break':

THE NIGHT OF OTHER DAYS

In February 1953 Seamus Heaney sat in the college sick bay and heard the bells knelling classes to a close. He had just been told that his little brother was dead. He was waiting for his neighbours to drive him home. They came at two o'clock.

His father met him in the porch. He was crying although he had always 'taken funerals in his stride'. Neighbours had gathered and were awkward in their sympathising, relying on the trusted formulas used on these occasions...'a hard blow' and 'sorry for your trouble'. 'Whispers informed strangers I was the eldest, / Away at school, as my mother held my hand/In hers and coughed out angry tearless sighs.'

Later that evening the ambulance brought the dead boy home.

Next morning Seamus went into the room where the corpse lay amid snowdrops and candles. The little boy who had cavorted in sheer delight at seeing his big brother return from boarding school only six weeks earlier '...lay in the four- foot box as in his his cot...A four-foot box, a foot for every year.'

'Mid-Term Break' was written early in 1963. Heaney was sharing a flat with two post-graduate students. He had finished a day's teaching in St. Thomas' school and was waiting for a meal which was being prepared by one of his flatmates (they shared duties in the flat). [7] It was close to the anniversary of Christopher's death and the poet sat in an armchair and wrote the poem.

The poem was first published in 'Kilkenny' magazine. It presents early intimations of mortality and shows the difficulties of a child trying to deal with grief and perceived injustice. The writing is remarkably mature and controlled. The joy of baby Daniel is in stark contrast to the pain, grief and anger in the home at Mossbawn. They would soon leave their farm at Mossbawn, the farm and landscape which has been lovingly described in so many of Seamus Heaney's poems. In his heart Seamus never left Mossbawn and he took it with him to his grave.

The voice in 'Mid-Term-Break' is that of the young Heaney himself. It contrasts with the final poem in the volume of poetry "District and Circle" published in 2006, where the voice is an anonymous and ominous rural speaker. "I said nothing at the time/ But I never liked yon bird." In both cases he is expressing his intimate feelings. He is putting his feelings into words, something that is central to every word that Heaney wrote.

In "Feeling Into Words" (2002),[4] Heaney wrote "finding a voice means that you can get your own feeling into your own words and that your words have the feel of you about them; a poetic voice is probably very intimately connected with the poet's natural voice, the voice that he hears as the ideal speaker of the lines he is making up...And your first steps as a writer will be to imitate, consciously or unconsciously, those sounds that flowed in, that in-fluence".

'The Blackbird' (2006) and 'Mid-Term-Break' (1966) occupy the same physical and emotional space and return us to the poet's past. The beauty of the language and the sensitivity of expression, in the words of Michael Parker, show... "how deeply sensitive autobiographical material can be transmuted into the finest public art." In Heaney's case into the finest lyrical poetry.

The Nobel Committee referred to Heaney's "works of lyrical beauty and ethical depth, which exalt everyday miracles and the living past". In transmitting his feelings into words, he masters the art of reporting his own emotional responses to the life around him in language that is authentic and totally accurate. And from the publication of his first book, DN,1966, it was clear that Heaney was a poet of immense power with a language facility to match.[7] The book was greeted with enthusiasm and admiration. Here was a painter of landscape whose words entered the sense of touch, sound and feeling...'Bubbles gargled delicately, bluebottles/ Wove a strong gauze of sound around the smell.' (DN). The poems are loud with the slap of the spade and sour with the stink of turned

THE NIGHT OF OTHER DAYS

earth. The language awakens the senses and unites self, world and word...'when the bath was filled we found a fur'.

His language is sometimes 'cultivatedly unmelodious' and thick in texture...'the squelch and slap of soggy peat', or 'a thick crust, coarse-grained as limestone rough-cast,/hardened gradually on top of the four crocks', ('Churning Day',DN). All of this made his poetry accessible and popular[9] as he recreated farm activities and celebrated vanishing family traditions and rural crafts. He has written rough lyrics of rustic life ('Digging') and sophisticated lyrics of delicate strength and beauty ('Follower') dealing with rural subjects and themes. In later poems he would turn inwards and write of self-scrutiny and classical parallels.

Although he went on to publish a dozen books of poetry, he regarded the publication of 'Death of a Naturalist' with special affection. The opening poem is 'Digging' and in this poem we meet his father Patrick. 'Digging', along with 'Mid Term Break' holds a very special place in the hearts of Seamus Heaney and of his readers.

Heaney fixes the time and place of the poem 'Digging' in the present because for him the reality of a poem lies within it. Past, present and future are seamlessly merged. An image that has been stored in his memory is worked on by his imagination and eventually transformed into an immediate actual occurrence. In the poem 'Digging' the poet writes of sitting at the window in Mossbawn, observing his father as he digs potatoes. But in reality, he is not looking down at his father as he digs and the Heaney family are not, at the time of writing, living in the poet's beloved Mossbawn...they had moved from Mossbawn in1954 the year after Christopher's death, understandably, given that Margaret constantly used the bus to go shopping, and this would have involved standing at the very bus-stop where her child had been knocked down and fatally injured.

HUGH MULROONEY

Heaney is writing from memory and memory is central to all of his writing. 'Memories that collapse space and time into a condensed, obdurate place in consciousness'. Poems in his first three books are mainly concerned with personal memories, memories of childhood and life in his home and neighbourhood. Later poems involve reflection on the wider memory-bank of community, past and present, and these poems lead the poet outward, from his family, from his home and from the farm at Mossbawn to the history, legend and tragedy of Ireland. In turn, memory and his search for meaning will lead him from the fields and bogs of Ireland to the bogs of Denmark and beyond. Writing in 'Feeling into Words' he said that memory was the faculty that supplied him with the first quickening of his own poetry...'I had a tentative unrealised need to make a congruence between memory and bogland and, for want of a better word, our natural consciousness". Drawing a comparison between the wide open spaces of the prairie lands of America and the more restricted scope of an Irish vista he wrote "We have no prairies/To slice a big sun at evening- /Everywhere the eye concedes to/ Encroaching horizon,/ / Is wooed into the Cyclops' eye/Of a tarn..." We may not have prairies in Ireland, Heaney notes, but 'we have bogs'... bogs that hold, and will reveal, their memories.

In his essay 'Learning from Eliot' Seamus tells us that in the early sixties he began to "take pleasure in the basement life of Eliot's ear and to teach myself 'to sit still' and let its underworkings work". Through the eye and the ear sensations will ease into the memory if a receptive stillness is there, and memory will, in turn, feed the imagination. When the time is ripe the anvil is struck and the fantail of creative sparks explodes.

"Footfalls echo in the memory/Down the passage which we did not take/Towards the door we never opened/. Into the rose garden."[11] And memory will summon the dead:

THE NIGHT OF OTHER DAYS

"Soft voices of the dead/ are whispering by the shore.."[12] Memories become realities in the hands of the poet.

One of the first recorded memories is that of his father. Patrick Heaney worked hard on his forty acres, digging, ploughing and providing for his large family. And he also worked as a cattle dealer and would have been a familiar figure at the village and town fair-days which are now a thing of the past. The first picture we get of Patrick Heaney is in the poem 'Digging' in 'Death of a Naturalist' published in 1966, (DN,66). In the poem, Heaney appears to be observing his father as he works, but it is in fact a memory of twenty years earlier.

'Under my window......my father digging.....the coarse boot nestled on the lug....By God, the old man could handle a spade.... just like his old man'. He goes on to tell how his grandfather cut more turf in a day than any other man on Toner's bog. The picture is painted in crisp spare words. The atmosphere is created with 'the cold smell of potato mould' and the 'squelch and slap of soggy peat'. But notice is given. Seamus will dig into soggy peat, but not with a spade.

In the poem 'Digging' a distance is being acknowledged. The writer is not a young country boy watching his father dig. The writer is a sophisticated scholar reflecting on his own displacement. He will not follow his father. But his father will not go away. Not now, not for the rest of his life. The distance is acknowledged but so is the cost and the guilt...'But to-day/It is my father who keeps stumbling/Behind me, and will not go away.' ('Follower', DN.)

Seamus Heaney considered "Digging" to be one of his most significant poems and it is fortunate that he has recorded his reasons for believing this to be so. In a lecture to The Royal Society of Literature, October 1974[13] he said "I now believe that the "Digging" poem had for me the force of an initiation; the confidence I mentioned arose from a sense that perhaps I could do this poetry thing too, and having experienced the excitement and release of it once, I was doomed to look for it again and again." In the words of Wordsworth he had opened a 'hiding place of my power' and he could now give a "A substance and a life to what I feel:/ I would enshrine the spirit of the past/For future restoration". He came to the realisation that the poem had been "laid down in me years before" and that the pen/spade analogy was the simple heart of the matter. He knew that 'digging' is a versatile metaphor for the creative endeavour and the search for truth. And he knew that he had found the gift of putting his feelings into words. Several messages are transmitted in this poem, some explicit, some less so. His pen rests snug as a gun. He will dig with it. He will dig down through the layers of memory and history, in the fertile soil of his imagination. Like his grandfather, he will uncover the rich deposits which lie in the bog. But he has no spade to follow them: 'Between my finger and my thumb/The squat pen rests./I'll dig with it.'

Before the publication of his books he wrote his early poems under a pen-name 'Incertus', trial pieces, which he 'hadn't the guts to put his name to them'. They were the work of a shy, uncertain and fretful young man. 'Oh yes I crept before I walked...I was in love with words themselves, but had no sense of a poem as a whole structure and no experience of how the successful achievement of a poem could be a stepping stone in your life'.

Later he expanded his thoughts on the nature of poetry: "poetry as divination, poetry as revelation of the self to the self, of restoration of the culture to itself; poems as elements of continuity, with the aura and authenticity of archaeological finds, where the buried shard has an importance that is not diminished by the importance of the buried city; poetry as a dig, a dig for finds that end up being plants." Seamus Heaney believed that 'Digging' was the first poem in which he succeeded in getting his feelings...or his feel into words. He felt that he had 'let down a shaft into real life'.

THE NIGHT OF OTHER DAYS

As he said, he dug it up rather than wrote it down and years later he recorded that its rhythms *and its noises still pleased him.*

He also seems to suggest that he was the passive instrument rather than the active creator…that the poem was already there when he began to write it. This is a reference to the nature of 'Creativity'. When Heaney lectured in the Colleges of Education in Belfast and in Dublin (Carysfort, 1976-1981) there was a lively debate on the question of 'creativity' and whether it could be fostered in primary schools. I recall several occasions when Seamus participated in discussions on the nature of creativity with my Philosophy of Education students in Carysfort. He warmly contributed to the sessions but never dominated. One of the theories, current at that time, suggested that creativity was the outcome of an initial tension within the mind of the artist where it became an unresolved problem, an idea which could not be expressed…'a lump in the throat'. When the artist relaxed and temporarily forgot about the problem it lowered into the sub-conscious where it roamed freely and without inhibition and established unlikely and unforeseen connections in the glorious chaos of the sub-conscious. And the result was creativity, a Eureka moment, rather like Archimedes in his bath or the great Irish thinker William Rowan Hamilton who 'found' his mathematical formula as he walked along Dublin's Royal Canal. The question of the nature of creativity and its significance will be discussed in a later chapter.

In Heaney's case this theory would suggest that feelings of grief, joy, guilt, tension and concern might be resolved when left free to roam the sub-conscious, where, having made unexpected connections, they would surface and be expressed in poetry.

The poet experiences initial stirrings somewhere in the 'dark hutch' of the sub-conscious; 'sensings' which seek a shape, a form, achieve an incarnation in words. He said that many of the lines just wafted themselves up out of a kind of poetic divine right. They

HUGH MULROONEY

felt given, strange and unexpected; 'I didn't quite know where it came from, but I knew immediately it was there to stay. It seemed as solid as an iron bar'.

In "Mid-Term Break" and "The Blackbird of Glanmore" he puts into words his feelings and his grief on the untimely death of his little brother Christopher. In "Digging" and a number of other poems he uses the power of imagery and language to introduce the reader to his father, and to the deep feelings of love, guilt and estrangement which characterised their relationship. The simplicity of language, the facility to express the deepest emotion in the directness of everyday words, the use of the most apt of descriptions seem to come so easily. So it is that having read just two of his earliest poems, the reader can anticipate the riches still to come.

CHAPTER

Patrick

2

In the first poem of his first book, 'Death of a Naturalist', Seamus Heaney wrote of his father Patrick and he located this poem, 'Digging' in Mossbawn, the townland where he spent the happiest years of his childhood. The following picture of his father is painted entirely in Heaney's own words, taken directly from his poetry, his prose writings and from his interviews with Dennis O'Driscoll. But first a look at the context and setting.

Seamus was born on April 13th 1939 in Mossbawn, a townland located within a triangle formed by the settlements of Toome, Castledawson and Bellaghy, where the poet now lies. He always described himself as a man from county Derry and never used the 'Londonderry' label. Seamus was the eldest of a family of nine children, two girls and seven boys. The family farm of about forty acres was made up of a core of fields which were contiguous, with the addition of a few scattered fields. The single-storey farmhouse was thatched and without internal water or electricity supply.

In December of 1995 Seamus Heaney addressed the assembled members of the Swedish Academy and the Nobel Foundation as he accepted the Nobel Prize for Literature. The medal was presented by King Carl XV1 Gustaf of Sweden. This is what the poet said of his old home in Mossbawn:

"In the nineteen-forties, when I was the eldest child of an ever-growing family in rural County Derry, we crowded together in the three rooms of a traditional thatched farmstead and lived a kind of den-life which was more or less emotionally and intellectually proofed against the outside world. It was an intimate, physical, creaturely existence ...' They took in everything that was going on, of course - rain in the trees, mice on the ceiling, a steam train rumbling along the railway line one field back from the house. Ahistorical, pre-sexual, in suspension between the archaic and the modern, 'we were as susceptible and impressionable as the drinking water that stood in a bucket in our scullery: every time a passing train made the earth shake, the surface of that water used to ripple delicately, concentrically, and in utter silence."[1]

The water in the bucket came from the pump in Heaney's yard and supplied their house and a number of neighbouring households and this pump assumed a symbolic life-long significance for the poet.

The farm was average size for a small family holding in rural Ireland and output varied. On the one hand it produced crops of potatoes, corn and vegetables while on the other supporting cows, a horse, hens, chickens, geese, turkeys and pigs. Although mainly self-supporting, it could rely on the travelling shop to supply tea, candles, soap, coal and various other items. In addition, the home was on a bus route which facilitated visits to shops in neighbouring towns. It might have been expected that Seamus, the eldest son, would eventually take over the small farm but his education pointed to a road less travelled.

Seamus attended the local primary school at Anahorish ('the place of pure water') and was a model pupil. The teachers there, through voluntary extra tuition, ensured his scholarship to St

THE NIGHT OF OTHER DAYS

Columbs school in Derry from where he graduated to a a first-class degree in English literature at Queens University Belfast (QUB). Although he probably could have continued his studies leading to an academic career he chose to pursue a diploma course in teaching at St Joseph's College of Education in Belfast. This involved teaching practice. His teaching practice was at St. Thomas's Secondary intermediate School in Ballymurphy in Belfast. The headmaster was Michael McLaverty, the short-story writer. Years later Seamus wrote an introduction to a volume of short stories by Michael McLaverty and it was McLaverty who introduced him to the work of Irish writers, south of the border in the Republic.

In 1963 he was appointed Lecturer in English at St Joseph's and he joined 'The Group' poetry workshop which was established by Philip Hobsbaum, Lecturer in English at QUB. In 1966 he succeeded Hobsbaum in Queen's and eventually chaired the meetings of The Group. So the son of a farmer in County Derry was now a university lecturer in Belfast...and he was writing poetry. Between 1966 and 1975 he published four volumes of poetry:

Death of a Naturalist 1966;(DN) Door Into the Dark 1969;(DD)

Wintering Out 1972;(WO) North ; 1975(N)

All were published by Faber and Faber, London.

Of his father he wrote: "I look down/Till his straining rump among the flowerbeds/Bends low, comes up twenty years away..." 'Digging' (DN). But now, twenty years later there is a distance between the writer and his father and it is a distance which is more than temporal. It is the distance between two different worlds, and it is the guilt-laden distance between two family members. The poet has never intended to follow in his forebear's footsteps either in the physical sense or in the sense of lifestyle. He writes 'But I've no spade to follow them./Between my finger and my thumb/The squat pen rests./I'll dig with it.' The poet will not dig potatoes or cut turf or be a party to the closing of a sale at a fair. He will dig with his pen.

In turning his back to farming and his father's way of life and in following the opportunity which has opened-up through his education he will be doing no more than hundreds of young Northern Irish people of his generation. The difference lies in his own conscience. He feels guilty, and this guilt, never openly aired to his parents, will remain with him for the rest of his life. "Already in the earliest work of the young poet, his father had become an elegiac presence, a focus for his own mourning of change." As a child he had looked up to his father as a man possessed of magical skill and strength ... the images and allusions 'are evidence of love and admiration, but are also the product of separation, a distance, born of time and education, which the young man half regrets." (Parker)

In 1991, twenty five years after 'Death of a Naturalist', Heaney published "Seeing Things"(ST) and in poem xxvii he wrote of his father, with admiration, guilt and regret: 'Even a solid man,/A pillar to himself and to his trade...Can sprout wings at the ankle and grow fleet/As the god of fair days, stone posts, roads and crossroads'.[2]

The image of his father Patrick, which recurs, is the image of a silent man wearing a soft felt hat and wellingtons and carrying a stick. Patrick was a yeoman farmer, who served as a member of the rural council and 'he embodied solidity'.[3] But although the portrayal is that of an admired father, a skilled farmer and cattle-jobber, he was a figure from a past world and the ashplant, his badge of office and authority, would finish up abandoned behind the door.

Heaney does not hide his admiration for his father's skill... but Patrick belonged to a world which was disappearing. The glory of Fair Days faded, agriculture was increasingly mechanised, and the authority symbolised by the ashplant was a thing of the past.

THE NIGHT OF OTHER DAYS

Heaney wrote in 1996, ten years after the death of his father, and described a lonely silent figure on Sandymount Strand, a man who is as distant from his old familiar world as he is from his son, and the poet is unable to reach across the silence.

The ashplant is a permanent feature in the life and in the images of Patrick Heaney. Along with the soft felt hat and the 'tubs' [5] of his wellingtons it represents his status, his authority and his expertise as a cattle jobber. Years after writing 'Digging' when Seamus was driving a friend, Louis Simpson, from Belfast to Coleraine he detoured to visit his childhood home in Mossbawn and there they met Patrick, quite by accident. Heaney describes the scene: his father, "unshorn and bewildered/in the tubs of his wellingtons, /smiling at me for help,/faced with this stranger I'd brought him" These lines are from 'Making Strange' ('Station Island', SI 1984). Patrick died in 1986.

Patrick was a cattle-jobber in addition to his farming work. In nineteen fifties Ireland, north and south, cattle were marketed on Fair Days. There was a fair day in Bellaghy on the first Monday of each month. In the early hours of the morning of a fair day, cattle were driven on foot from the hinterland into the town. Heaney recalls that the streets would be crammed with cows and heifers and bullocks, the whole place loud and stinking with the smells of the beasts and their dung." His father Patrick, cattle-dealer, would negotiate, either on his own behalf or that of a third party. He usually bought a few cattle for himself and would offer for sale cattle he had purchased at a previous fair. On occasion, he worked for commission in the purchase or sale of cattle for a third party. There was much theatre at fairs and Heaney was was familiar with the milieu of 'fair hills and cattle pens' and he knew men in the trade and enjoyed the banter and the bidding and bargaining, slapping hands, throwing up the hands, walking away, pretending you were at your limit,'it was terrific theatre and I didn't feel out of it; but, still, I didn't have an ambition to grow up and do it[7]."

HUGH MULROONEY

His calling as a cattle dealer conferred on Patrick a certain distinction, in Heaney's words 'a trans sectarian licence to roam' and Patrick considered himself to be a cut above men of no property. As Seamus said 'There was a strong streak of fatalism in my father... he would have regarded himself as more lord than labourer. There was a touch of the artist about him.'

Heaney goes on to say that his father might have viewed his eldest son Seamus as belonging to the woman-world of the home rather than the man-world of the road.

Seamus did not follow in his father's footsteps, either on the farm or on the road but one thing he took from his involvement in the activities of the cattle-fairs was the Scottish idiom of the people he met at fairs in various towns in Northern Ireland. He says that many of his poems are tuned to an Ulster register.

Fair days ceased in the nineteen sixties and were replaced by cattle-marts held in purpose-built units and organised as auctions. The days of the cattle-dealer were over and the ashplant was parked behind the door, its significance much diminished. Its earlier significance was aptly illustrated when Patrick Heaney had advised his sister, 'Look for a man with an ashplant on the boat'/ My father told his sister setting out/For London, 'and stay with him all night/And you'll be safe'.[6]

The picture we see of Seamus Heaney's father is that of a strong silent man who has carved out a place in a disappearing world. Patrick Heaney did not communicate well with his son and as the poet continued his advance through school the silence deepened and the gap opened wider, even more so when Seamus began to write. There was not much conversation or reading in the house in Mossbawn. We have a picture of Patrick stretched out on the big kitchen-sofa as he 'rehearsed the acres, roods and perches of arable and meadow land in a formal tone and with a certain enlargement of the spirit."[7] A cousin, on the father's side, came to the house on a regular basis and read to the children and Seamus

THE NIGHT OF OTHER DAYS

was eventually able to persuade his mother to place an order for 'The Champion', a higher class of comic altogether! (There was suspicion of comic books as being the thin end of the wedge which might lead to 'The News of the World'.) All in all there was little reading and less conversation in the thatched house. Years later, when 'Death of a Naturalist' was read in Mossbawn the greatest commendation at home was 'Lord knows Pat would fairly have enjoyed this.' Pat McGuckin was a cousin "who was said to burn his scone like King Alfred every time he lifted a book." [8]

The opening of the gap between father and son was marked in his primary school in Anahorish. One day in the school the principal teacher, Master Bernard Murphy, lined-up his pupils at the top of the classroom. "At the end of the holidays this man's going away to Derry, so this is for him, for winning the scholarship…We all wish him good luck." And the master crossed Seamus's palm with silver.[9] The young boy was going to boarding school in Derry and this was a step forward in his education; but it also marked the beginning of his exile from his home and from the world of his childhood.

There are three poems in particular which evoke the world of his father Patrick and the relationship between this world and the childhood world of the young poet: "Follower", "Ancestral Photograph" and 'Digging'.

Seamus Heaney always considered 'Digging' to be a significant achievement because it not only described in lyrical language the images of his toiling father and grandfather, it also gave exquisite expression to his own feelings.

There is the precision of the language as he describes the skill of his father….'a clean rasping sound/When the spade sinks into the gravelly ground…' or 'The coarse boot nestled on the lug, the shaft/Against the inside knee was levered firmly', There is the laying bare of emotion…of guilt as he indicates that he will not follow. And in the poem 'Follower' he focuses on his father again as he describes him working with a horse-plough....'His shoulders globed like a full sail strung/Between the shafts and the furrow ...an expert'. 'I wanted to grow up and plough' he says, but 'All I ever did was follow/In his broad shadow'. And to-day 'It is my father who keeps stumbling/Behind me, and will not go away'. The heroic figure of the past is contrasted with the bewildered old man of the present, and his lost world is being replaced by a new one in which there is no room for Patrick Heaney.

The photographs of the men who populated the old world are being taken to the attic, and so it is with Patrick. Seamus tells us how in his youth he accompanied his father to fairs, how he herded cattle into pens, how he watched his father triumph in bargaining. But now 'Father I've watched you do the same/And watched you sadden when the fairs were stopped...Closing this chapter of our chronicle/I take your uncle's portrait to the attic.' The images and the photographs were of the farmers, cattle-jobbers and turf-cutters and the three poems constitute an evocative record of their skill. But they also constitute "a poignant record of the changing relationship between father and son".[16]

A significant rupture in Heaney's relationship with his father occurred when he left Mossbawn to enrol as a boarder in St Columb's second-level school in Derry. Once he went there, there was a presumption that he was being educated and that meant being set a bit apart. It was accepted that Seamus would not be back on the farm.

The parting was traumatic. He describes a young boy "standing in the middle of a space that is separate and a little sorrowing" and he tells us that the 'sword of sorrow swung widely on the day I went as a boarder to St Columb's College.' On that day there was some acceptance that he was off to a different place.

He stood watching them walk down the central avenue and away from the school, brimming with grief. Unblaming, unavailing

THE NIGHT OF OTHER DAYS

grief. A space that was separate and, for sure, not a little sorrowing".[10]

Writing in 'Human Chain' in 2010 (almost sixty years later and after the death of both his parents) "Seeing them as a couple, I now see,/For the first time, all the more together/ For having had to turn and walk away...'

Having parted with their eldest son, Patrick and Margaret returned from the College to Mossbawn and to their way of life. A tragedy lay ahead. The death of Christopher would result in their leaving Mossbawn and already their old way of life was being swept away. Meanwhile Seamus continued with his studies. His parents moved to 'The Wood' and Seamus followed a path to university but for all of them the move out of Mossbawn and the death of Christopher was the first great wrench in the fabric of their lives. And Seamus never left Mossbawn. His poetry is rich in memories of his youth and childhood there. To accompany those memories were thoughts of betrayal, of guilt and of rejection and these were the result of years of inner conflict. In describing them he uses language of great sensuous richness and directness. His language 'carries in itself the touch, the feel, the apprehension of a solid world in which the poet makes his way but is aware that his own powers and interests are taking him out of.' His poetry describes the density of the darkness, the emotions of sadness, of nausea and of wonder...all in an almost physical language.[11]

In his portrayal of the passing of a way of life, and in his rejection of his participation in it, the poet tries to soften the difference between the life of a rural craftsman and that of a writer/poet, but with limited success. To illustrate the contrast he distinguishes between 'craft' and 'technique'.

Craft is something that can be learned or imitated, digging or cutting turf. Technique calls for a contribution of emotion or sentiment which comes directly from the heart and mind of the poet. Digging is a matter of craft and the use of a spade, but poetry, while it too can involve craft will require from the pen an increment of emotion which emanates directly from the very being of the poet. It may well be that the pen/spade analogy "was the simple heart of the matter" and that this analogy may suffice in relation to the poem 'Digging' and many of his early poems, but it is inadequate to accommodate the depth of feeling and the breadth of description which is characteristic of his poems overall and thus it is that, when Heaney later draws the distinction between craft and technique, it becomes clear that craft may be a necessary component of spadework but technique lies squarely within the ambit of the poet. (The subject 'of craft and technique' were dealt with in the poet's lecture to The Royal Society of Literature in October 1974).

The symbol which characterizes Patrick is not the spade but rather the ashplant. His role as cattle-jobber separated him from the ordinary farmer and Heaney uses the ashplant to represent this in a number of poems. 'Two Stick Drawings' is included in The Spirit Level (SL 1996) and the poem is a salute to two ashplants. The first ashplant is Claire O'Reilly's. She used her granny's stick to snare the highest blackberries along the railway line as the train tore past 'with the stoker yelling like a balked king from his iron chariot'.

The second stick drawing describes 'Jim of the hanging jaw' and how Patrick Heaney would take the selection of ashplants from their ledge of the back seat of the car, display them along the front mudguard for Jim and allow him his pick 'until he found the true extension of himself in one that made him jubilant'. Carrying his chosen stick 'He'd run and crow/Stooped forward, with his right elbow stuck out....'

In 1991, five years after his father's death, Seamus published "Seeing Things" and in this volume he included a poem "The Ash Plant". In this poem we have a picture of an elderly frail man looking out of the window of his bedroom, seeking a long-lost world of fairs and markets.

'He'll never rise again but he is ready...his wasting hand/ Gropes desperately and finds the phantom limb/Of an ash plant in his grasp, which steadies him.' [23]

Now, the poet tells us, his father can stand in and on his own ground. He has found his ashplant and with it he has re-established himself with himself. Heaney establishes this scene in his own imagination in memory of a father who is long dead but whose memory will not go away. The hero of yesterday, who then became the encumbrance of later years, has now become a ghost who can never be wholly exorcised. In the poet's childhood and youth Patrick Heaney had been a figure of strength, authority and stability and Seamus had admired him as such. Now, as Seamus turned away from a future in farming and from continuity with the past, he experienced feelings of great sadness. Although the world of his father was disappearing in any case, and would never have continued as before, his turning away from this world haunted Seamus for the rest of his life.

Part of the problem lay in the silences of both father and son. It has been suggested that many of the problems which we encounter in later life have originated in our inability to express the early problems, emotions and inhibitions, which we have suppressed and failed to ventilate.[14] Our impressions of Patrick are those of a man of few words and Seamus repeatedly refers to occasions when, in words or through a physical gesture, he could have expressed his love and admiration for his father but failed to do so.

This reservation in the expression of love between a parent and child, especially a father and son would have been the norm rather than the exception in the Ireland of the forties and the fifties. But it represented a very real difficulty for the poet and this is referred to in many of his writings. While it is understandable that a distance would have opened over time, the early difficulties

HUGH MULROONEY

in communication probably rested with the father. By the time of the poet's departure for boarding school a gap had opened-up between father and son and with time, further education, and the choice of a middle-class life, it was probably never amenable to closure.

Central to the relationship with his father is the inhibition in the expression of emotion and it may have applied on a wider scale than just that of the father/son relationship. In an early poem included in his first published volume he wrote 'Our juvenilia/ Has taught us both to wait,/ Not to publish feeling/And regret it all too late': ("Twice Shy" 1966). The context was an embankment walk with a girl, both of them shy and reserved, and resorting to 'nervous childish talk'.

The situation with his father was addressed more directly when he wrote: "Blessed be the attachment of dumb love/In that broad-backed, low-set man/ Who feared debt all his life…"

There are a number of incidents which record the difficulties which both men had in the expression of emotion such as, when the young boy watched from his seat on the fence at a fair, as his father marshalled cattle with his ashplant. Eye-contact is momentarily established and lost…'So that his eyes leave mine and I know/ The pain of loss before I know the term'[16]. Then there was the time when his father harnessed the horse to the new potato-sprayer. The young Seamus, to his disgust, was left at home because of the father's concern for his safety. In the event the horse shied at the river-bank and plunged the entire enterprise into the Moyola river. "Once upon a time my undrowned father/ Walked into our yard… That afternoon/I saw him face to face, …And there was nothing between us there/That might not still be happily ever after "(1991).

In 2010 Heaney published Human Chain, his last volume of poems. His father was dead twenty four years and indeed the poet's own death was a mere three years away. In the short poem 'Album

THE NIGHT OF OTHER DAYS

iv' we find in summary the grief of a man who has failed to tell his father of his love:

Were I to have embraced him anywhere/It would have been on the river bank/That summer before college. In this poem, as elsewhere, there is no doubting the love between father and son. In the poem 'the Call' included in The Spirit Level (SL, 1996) Seamus Heaney tells of a telephone call he made. It was answered by his mother Margaret and she left the poet on hold as she went to find her husband who was doing 'a bit of weeding'. "Next thing he spoke and I nearly said I loved him", wrote the poet. But he didn't and he lived to regret it.

The most affectionate portrait of his father is given in the poem 'The Harvest Bow', 1979. Here, in companionable silence, the father plaited the bow as he implicated the mellowed silence 'in wheat that does not rust…A throwaway love-knot of straw' which the son, already homesick before his departure for college, can read like braille, 'gleaning the unsaid off the palpable'. And so the silent man whacks the tips of weeds and bushes as he walks with his eldest son along the railway line. The father is 'Still tongue-tied in the straw tied by your hand'. Although the silence between them may be one of ease and companionship on the part of the father, his son is experiencing the agony of a loss and a longing which he is storing in his memory and which will find expression in his later writings. And he will pin the Bow to his deal dresser. Later, Seamus recalls an occasion when his father was visited by two second-world-war demobbed Protestant neighbours, George and Alan Evans. They presented Pat with a large rosary beads. "Did they make a Papish of you over there?" asked Pat. 'Oh, damn the fear' came the reply, 'I stole them for you Paddy off the pope's dresser when his back was turned'. "You could harness a donkey with them" came the reply "as their laughter sailed above my head…two big nervous birds…making trial runs over a territory."

HUGH MULROONEY

Patrick was on good terms with all of his neighbours and did not seem to have any difficulty in communicating with them, even at a time when differences of faith and religious beliefs were at the root of tensions which would soon tear apart the fabric of society in Northern Ireland.

The light-hearted encounter with the Evans brothers is untypical and from within the family circle Heaney recounts incidents which add further to our impressions of a silent authoritarian figure with whom there was little rapport. One such incident was at the wedding of Seamus to Marie Devlin, in 1965, when his father refused to wear a formal suit and refused to make a speech. [34]

However, there was one occasion when Patrick Heaney spoke with simplicity, with eloquence and with emotion. It was at the bedside of his dying wife, Margaret, in 1984. Heaney wrote 'In the last minutes he said more to her / Almost than in all their life together." The family stood around the deathbed as she lay propped up on her pillow. Patrick leaned down and said "You'll be in New Row on Monday night/and I'll come up for you…He called her good and girl. Then she was dead." (Clearances)

Patrick died in October 1986 and this was the final 'unroofing' of Heaney's world and "it affected me in ways that were hidden from me then and now."

He describes Patrick's meeting with his maker. On the day of final judgement let it be 'like the judgement of Hermes'. As he stands in the judgement place "With his stick in his hand and the broad hat/Still on his head…He will expect more than words in the ultimate court/He relied on through a life's speechlessness."[20] So let the stones pile up to build a cairn waist deep as the poet salutes his dead father with a classical reference to the trial of Hermes, who had been accused of the killing of Argos. The Gods threw stones and built a cairn around the one who leads the dead to the underworld and thus proclaimed the innocence of Hermes.

THE NIGHT OF OTHER DAYS

Patrick's death in October 1986 was followed by a number of significant developments in the life of the poet. He was to enjoy the freedom of a sabbatical year from Harvard. He completed the purchase of Glanmore Cottage his beloved retreat in County Wicklow, where he could write in peace and without phone interruptions. Here he could celebrate an immediate act of thanksgiving for the cottage as 'a bastion of sensation'. He was now free of teaching duties for a year. He owned his beloved cottage. His father was dead and Heaney was at peace with himself.

He describes a powerful surge through the system... as with the writing of 'Fosterling' ... "Me waiting until I was nearly fifty/ To credit marvels............So long for the air to brighten,/Time to be dazzled and the heart to lighten'.[39] There were a number of factors contributing to the feeling of freedom felt by the poet and undoubtedly the liberation from regret and guilt associated with his relationship with his deceased father was prominent among them.

"Go and tell your father", the mower says/(He said it to my father who told me)/I have it mowed as clean as a new sixpence". And so the young Patrick Heaney ran to the house to find that it was too late. His father was dead.[41] Perhaps this boyhood shock provides a partial explanation for the reticence of the adult Patrick Heaney. He had not experienced the relationship that can develop between father and growing son. As a young boy he had suddenly lost his father. Perhaps the roots of his later silence went deep. Perhaps they lay deep in the soil and silence of great pain. Perhaps he didn't express emotion because he could not.

CHAPTER

Margaret

3

Margaret Heaney presided over the household in Mossbawn. Speaking of her the poet said he could see that religion was a powerful compensation for her. There she was, doomed to biology, a regime without birth control, 'nothing but parturition and potato-peeling in saecula saeculorum'[1], and the way she faced it and, in the end, outfaced it was by prayer and sublimation... toiling on in the faith that a reward was being laid up in heaven... 'It was defiance as much as devotion'.

Seamus was the first-born of her nine children. He paints a picture of an attractive, resilient woman who retained her sense of dignity and her sense of humour all her life. It was a hard life and it had its share of great tragedy. Through it she remained a constant source of love, of security and of happiness. Much of what we know of her comes from a series of eight sonnets 'Clearances', included in his volume of poems 'The Haw Lantern' (HL,1987) published three years after her death.

In the first of these sonnets he acknowledges the wisdom of her advice. She told the young boy of how easily a hard block of

THE NIGHT OF OTHER DAYS

coal will split if the angle of the hammer is aligned with the grain of the block. 'She taught me to hit, taught me to loosen...taught me between the hammer and the block/to face the music.' In another sonnet she recalls that when her grandmother changed her religion and rejected Protestantism in favour of Catholicism she was subjected to the anger and hostility of a stone-throwing mob of villagers as she ran the gauntlet, on her dash to mass, crouched low in her pony-trap. The moral of these two parables was not lost on the young boy. He learned that there is an appropriate course of action to be followed in life and one's conscience dictates that course. This could sometimes lead to situations where difficult choices have to be made and difficult stances have to be maintained. Whether Seamus himself always remained constant in the face of difficult questions and difficult situations is the subject of some debate.

When talking about his family the poet constantly refers to earlier generations and he proudly mentions their expertise and their crafts as in the case of his grandparents on his mother Margaret's side. They lived in Castledawson and worked in the linen mills. Seamus' other grandparents were farmers. There is a suggestion of quiet nobility in all cases. A boyhood visit to his mother's people in Castledawson was a regimented affair with 'Sandwich and tea-scone...present and correct'. A code of behaviour operated there in 'Number 5, New Row, Land of the Dead...Don't tilt your chair. Don't reach. Don't point. Don't make noise when you stir.' But yet a warm welcome for a 'bewildered homing daughter', Seamus's mother Margaret, as the bespectacled grandfather ushers her into the celestial 'shining room'.[2]

Margaret Heaney was born in 1911 and lived all of her married life in houses that belonged to her husband's side of the family. Her sister-in-law, Mary Heaney lived with them in their first house at Mossbawn just down a small laneway off the main road linking Toome and Magherafelt. It was down this laneway that her unconscious son, Christopher, was carried after he had run from behind the bus, into the path of an oncoming car. The Heaney family moved out of Mossbawn to 'The Wood' some distance north of Bellaghy after the death of Christopher. They built a new two-storied house there and the old thatched house in Mossbawn was sold, remodelled and refurbished. Mary Heaney, Margaret's sister-in-law lived with them in Mossbawn and moved with them to The Wood. There was a very special bond between Seamus and his aunt Mary.

Margaret presided over a household which was secure, united and 'the family she created was very close knit, utterly together, like an egg contained within the shell. They had confidence in the way they lived, a lovely impeccable confidence in their own style'.[3] Margaret had a sense of humour which was sorely needed as the life she led was 'doomed to biology'.[4] (When David Hammond enquired about a frail young man who had recently married she replied that he was now 'under new management').[5] Through the years of her pregnancies she could still find her sense of humour... 'pregnancy is not a killing disease', she observed.

As a child Seamus listened with delight as his mother belted out a verse of Longfellow's and taught him Latin prefixes and suffixes which she had learned at school. Speaking of his love of words Seamus recalled how Margaret used to recite lists of affixes and suffixes, and Latin roots with their English meanings, rhymes that formed part of her schooling in the early part of the century. Eventually, as his education progressed, a space opened between the young man and his mother. She couldn't keep pace and this gave rise to awkwardness and guilt on his part. "You know all them things" she would say as he lapsed into bad grammar to cover his own guilt in the face of her inadequacy. He acknowledged the influence of his mother in his lecture to The Royal Society of Literature in 1974. 'I was getting my first sense of crafting words and for one reason or another, words as bearers of history and

THE NIGHT OF OTHER DAYS

mystery began to invite me. Maybe it began very early when my mother used to recite lists of affixes and suffixes…'.

We know that people spoke of her sense of humour and of her warm, animated and imaginative personality. And we know that religion played a big part in her life. The greatest manifestation of religion in the home was the nightly participation of the whole Heaney family in The Rosary.

The Rosary was a central form of prayer and devotion in The Catholic Church. Five (or fifteen) decades of Hail Marys are repeated, each decade preceded by an 'Our Father' and followed by a 'Glory Be'. The prayers are finger-counted on the Rosary Beads. The Rosary is followed by The Litany, a series of petitions recited, in this case by the mother, and responded to in a recurring formula, 'Pray for Us', by the family in unison. Margaret brought more than devotion to the nightly Rosary. She also prayed for the strength to bear up. 'As she recited the rosary, you could almost hear a defiance in the strength of her voice…..as if she knelt to give challenge to the conditions'.[4] Heaney said that the longer he lived the more he realised the siege she must have experienced in body and spirit for the first two decades of her marriage…a child arriving almost every year to begin with, then being cooped in a small house, the family crowding in and growing up around her, living in a farm kitchen, her body thickening- 'some reinforcement was required and I believe it came from prayer and religious understanding.'

There is little evidence that she had any time to herself. She steeped her swollen feet nightly in the enamel basin and once she sat briefly on the swing in the shed, while the children competed to achieve the highest arc. Her respite on the swing was brief and she hurried off to attend to her many unending chores. There is a brief glimpse of a kitchen scene where she sits on her armchair and nightly steeps her swollen feet while her husband stretches on the big kitchen sofa.

HUGH MULROONEY

In a number of poems in 'Door Into the Dark', published in 1969, Heaney addresses the question of the role and status of wives and mothers using the form of dramatic monologue. In the poem Mother she speaks of her utter exhaustion…'I am tired of the feeding of stock…I am tired of walking about with this plunger inside me'. She talks of the gulp of the plunger and of the 'gulp in my well'. She feels the heaviness of her pregnancy and longs for her identity as a person to be restored. She is tired of meeting the demands of those who 'play like a young calf gone wild on a rope'.

There is little evidence of appreciation for her dedicated work. In the poem 'The wife's Tale' she carries food out to where the men in the fields are busy with the threshing of corn. She brings thick slices 'that he likes' and pours tea into cups. He mocks the linen cloth she spreads on the grass…'I declare a woman could lay out a field', he says and then directs her to inspect the corn in bags hooked to the side of the thresher. He is proud of the good clean seed but ignores his wife. He lies on the ground with his band of helpers, able to mock his wife but not to appreciate her. She gathers the cups, folds the cloth and leaves the harvest field. 'I'd come and he had shown me/So I belonged no further to the work'.

There is no sign of affection or appreciation from her husband. Her sense of decorum is wasted 'on boys like us' but she is required to show her approval for his work and once she has done so she is effectively dismissed, all the while remaining a passive silent observer. This is the wife's tale.

Asked about his mother by Dennis O Driscoll, Seamus gave many small but telling details which help to form a rounded impression of her.[5] He described her as being volatile, humorous and nimble-minded. She was 'readier to be provoked' than her husband, Patrick. She had a capacity for endurance, but was also defiant. Perhaps above all she was religious and had confidence in the power of prayer. People talked of her sense of humour and of her warm animated imaginative personality. Patrick was a more

THE NIGHT OF OTHER DAYS

distant figure and had a gift for solemnity and distain but she was a song-loving, caring and motherly figure. She was no singer, but she always 'made a shot' at singing (songs like 'Boolavogue' and 'Who Fears to Speak of 98?'). In her singing she also liked to recall the barn-dances of her youth. When they moved to the new house in The Wood and when the children grew up she enjoyed great pride in her family and although she continued her practice and belief in religion it became a matter of wager rather than insurance. A healthy scepticism manifested itself as her life became easier. But there was always the nexus between pregnancy, suffering, religion and womanhood. This was the lot of Catholic women in Ireland at that time and there was little comfort forthcoming from a church which taught that it was the lot of a woman to obey and support her husband in this life and her reward awaited her in the next world. A woman's life often involved passive suffering, sublimation, prayer and the distant prospect of reward in heaven. But as Margaret grew older and wiser she remained her own woman, gaining in confidence, rejoicing in her family and acquiring an independent scepticism which just fell short of disaffection.

She held her own views on questions of the day and they were not always at one with her husband. Seamus describe the scene when a matter of discipline arose. Neither parent ever raised a hand against a child. When a serious breach was detected Patrick remained silent and eventually this proved effective. A stand-off would develop between the parents but it was a sympathetic one and it often showed their affection for one another...a case of a couple not looking into each other's eyes but rather training their gaze in the same direction.

On the bigger questions of the day, questions related to politics, religion, history, power, sectarianism and the place of Catholics in the society of Northern Ireland, the situation was blurred both in the domestic context and in the context of Northern Ireland as a whole. As he grew older Seamus had to face these questions but he would have sensed their presence even from an early age within the confines of home. Overall, he felt that his parents, like so many others, fought shy of the big questions which would soon galvanise the entire community in Ireland both north and south. Margaret would appear to have been the more aware. Seamus has written of her 'alertness to the sectarian strains' and her readiness to be provoked by the hidden operations of the system'.

A phrase or slogan that gained much currency in Northern Ireland in the late 1960's: 'whatever you say, say nothing' is often quoted as representing the stance of the minority Catholic population. Seamus Heaney vehemently rejected this as a description of his own position or that of his parents. According to him Margaret had a critical disaffected attitude while his father Patrick sailed through many of the aggravations as if he didn't notice. As for Heaney himself, all of the hidden questions and all of the manifest aggravations were to pre-occupy him for many, many years. Part of the differences in attitude arose from the fact that that Patrick considered himself to be a cut above 'men of no property' whereas Margaret identified more readily with the working class and the labouring class. She felt the inequalities more acutely.

Heaney explains the 'whatever you say say nothing' as an expression of anger rather than acquiescence, as a Catholic nod in answer to the Protestant wink, as an acknowledgement of the power structure which kept the allocation of jobs, housing and advancement strictly in the hands of the ruling Protestant Unionist class.

Being Catholic and belonging to the small-farmer class it followed that the Heaney household was Republican in its sympathies, but this was not overtly expressed and never caused any difficulty with close Protestant neighbours. Here again Margaret would have been more engaged but would have kept her opinions to herself. The larger questions that would pulverise Northern

THE NIGHT OF OTHER DAYS

Ireland in the future never impinged on the Heaney household in their daily effort to get on with life and living.

The relationship between Seamus and his mother is revealed in a number of his poems. In his volume Electric Light 2001 Heaney wrote: "All of us came in Doctor Kerlin's bag…The room I came from …and she's asleep/In sheets put on for the doctor…" And his mother would ask "And what do you think/ of the new wee baby the doctor brought for us all/ When I was asleep?" Eight new babies in all.

The closeness of their relationship was first wedged when Seamus was sent to boarding school at the age of twelve. The distance that opened between them was more than physical…a space that was separate and, for sure, not a little sorrowing. One result of being sent to St. Columb's in Derry was that an intellectual, cultural and linguistic rift now opened between mother and son.

Heaney's love for his mother is recorded in a series of eight sonnets titled 'Clearances' which are central to his volume 'The Haw Lantern' published in 1987 the year after Margaret's death. The volume is prefaced with 'in memoriam M.K.H., 1911-1984'.

Sonnet 3 'When all the others were away at Mass/I was all hers as we peeled potatoes'. They stood side by side as the potatoes fell into the bucket of clean water, breaking the silence between mother and eldest son. 'I remembered her head bent towards my head,/her breath in mine, our fluent dipping knives –/ Never closer the whole rest of our lives.' This he recalled as he stood at her deathbed.

Sonnet 5 They were folding sheets, just off the clothes-line, and taking part in a ritual dancing movement as they moved towards and away from one another, touching hands, breaking away and reaching towards one another again all the while folding the sheets which she had sewn 'from ripped-out flour sacks'. And

HUGH MULROONEY

so they would 'end up hand to hand/For a split second as if nothing had happened/For nothing had that had not always happened..'

Sonnet 6 Recalls mother and son together elbow to elbow towards the front of a crowded church for the Holy Week ceremonies. These ceremonies are among the most important in the liturgical year. The church would be in darkness as the celebrants chanted the blessings of the water and of the chrism at the back of the church. The congregation would intone 'As the hind longs for the streams, so my soul...' And the love and longing of mother and son would be echoed in prayers and chants...united in love which remained constant but unspoken. This unspoken intimacy reflected in 'the radiance of humble domestic chores, and in the joy of being united with her in fluent labour. Simple, humble domestic chores, peeling potatoes, folding sheets 'are transmitted into courtship rituals/acts of communion'...the unspoken love of son and mother; the hampered speech contrasting with the fluent movement; the delicate gesture as 'her head bent towards my head'; the voice of the Bible and the music of the liturgy all combining to chorus their love.

Of all the sonnets in 'Clearances' none are more moving than the final two, sonnets seven and eight. Margaret lay on her deathbed. Patrick leaned towards her propped-up head and said more to her 'almost than in all their life together. Denying the immanence of her death he tells her "You'll be in New Row on Monday night and I'll come up for you...". The family ranged around the bed hear him break a lifetime of silence and are happy when he called her good and girl.

Then she was dead. The family knew one thing by being there. 'The space we stood around had been emptied into us to keep', clearances had opened and a pure change had happened. It would never be the same again. Now there would be a space, silence, emptiness. She had held the family together all her life and now she was dead. And two memories flooded the poet's mind. '...

while the parish priest at her bedside went hammer and tongs at the prayers for the dying and some were responding and some were crying' he remembers her head bent towards his as they silently peeled potatoes into a bucket of clear water.

At her deathbed he also remembers the chestnut tree. When he was born his aunt Mary had planted a chestnut in a jam- jar. Transplanted to the hedge above the wallflowers, the tree grew and was associated with the growing child and so it became his tree. Then following the death of Christopher the family moved out of Mossbawn and relocated to 'The' Wood some miles away. The tree was cut down. Seamus now heard the cut, the crack, the sigh of the falling tree and he thought of walking round and round the empty space where his beloved tree had stood. The tree was gone and its heft and hush became a bright nowhere. Like his dead mother it was a soul ramifying and forever silent, 'beyond silence listened for'.

CHAPTER

Absence

4

Seamus Heaney was on tour promoting the joint publication of 'Station Island' and 'Sweeney Astray' (published in 1984) when he returned to be at his mother's deathbed. Her death led Seamus to ponder and confront questions in which, (as Michael Parker expressed it) [1] 'his love for her and his grief at her loss found shape and sound in the beautiful sequence of sonnets published in 'The Haw Lantern' 1987' where Heaney wrote that her absence would create a space 'utterly empty but utterly a source'. Speaking after the death of his father in 1986 he said 'The most important thing that has happened to me in the last ten years is being at two death beds'.[2] The deaths of Patrick and Margaret left a colossal emptiness which he struggled to fill with his poetry. Many of his finest lyrics in 'The Haw Lantern' 1987 and in 'Seeing Things' 1991 'spring directly from this well of grief, and are a reflex action/vatic reaction to it'. Helen Vendler says that the deaths of his parents caused a tear in the fabric of Heaney's verse, reflecting the way in which an unalterable emptiness had replaced the reality

THE NIGHT OF OTHER DAYS

that had been his since his birth, and that from then onwards her absence became more real than her presence.[3]

Seamus Heaney realised that the space left by the absence of the dead takes on a shape so powerful that it becomes a presence in itself. This empty space is also a silent space, the silence of emptiness itself. In life the poet and his mother lived to some extent in a world of their own creation...'wherever the world was we were somewhere else/Had been and would always be'[4] and in this world he wrote 'if self is a location then so is love'. Small wonder then that when Margaret died she left an emptiness, an empty space, an emptiness that emptied itself into the loved ones she left behind. This emptiness was a place of silence from whence came the voice of memory, of loneliness, loss and pain. It was also 'utterly a source', a place of origin of creative inspiration and it was the place where life confronted death and profound questions sought answers.

Heaney was fully aware of the fact that poetry is always at some level a confrontation with death...we live on the edge of eternity. He saw death as an infinite set of doors, an endless threshold and also the limit of representation. John Montagne wrote [5] 'When you write about the dead, you are expiating your connection with them, you're cleansing it. And that means they are also present. Even if they're not there as spirits, your own mother and your father...are actually inside you and you must come to terms with them'.

Heaney has written that death lies and the void deceives, 'we do not fall like autumn leaves to sleep in peace...we earn our deaths'[6]. He believed that whereas for the dying there may be a phenomenal instant when the spirit flares with pure exhilaration in anticipation of eternity, for those left behind there is just the old truth dawning: 'there is no next-time-round; there is a letting go which will not come again, or it will, once, and for all' (Human Chain 2010). What lies beyond death is unknown but what remains in this world must be endured by those who are left. And what remains is an empty space and a silence beyond the silence called for. But in that silent space creativity may be born. For the poet the space and the silence may eventually become a resource for sound, for creativity and for the expression of feeling through the medium of lyrical poetry.

To put his feelings into words the poet recalls the chestnut tree which his aunt Mary had planted in Mossbawn when he was born. The tree is now gone and in its place an empty space, a clearance. In the emptiness of the space there is silence, and in the silence of that clearance, 'utterly, utterly empty', he finds a resource for his voice, for the expression of his own feeling, for the expression of a poem. Osip Mandelstam likened the creation of this space to the work of bees, each individual bee 'constantly keeping their eye on the whole', co-operating in the formation of the combs, 'by means of which space virtually emerges out of itself'.[7] That empty space can be the source of an image, an idea, an emotion, which may germinate and seek expression.

A permanent problem lies in the fact that something of the intensity of emotion is lost in the process of putting feelings into words. The poet knows that in expressing his feelings he can be taken further away from the core of their truth. Like hand-held melting hailstones the real thing dissolves 'smarting into its absence'. His mother first taught him how to listen, to listen in the silence, beyond the music of what happens, as mother and son fold sheets or incline towards one another as the peeled potatoes drop silently into the clear fresh water. And in so doing he is also practising what he has learned from Eliot, the ability to be still and listen.[8] Words will emerge from this silence even if they are inadequate to fully express the poet's feelings.

In his volume 'The Haw Lantern' (HL,1987) Heaney looks towards the virtual world as he searches for the words, the images and the language appropriate to the emotion and the emptiness

THE NIGHT OF OTHER DAYS

which he feels. As expressed by John Carey[9] 'Ultimately this most sensuous of poets is engaged in a quest for silence, a bright nowhere beyond the stain of words' because poems, being words, recede from the truth. In recognition of this Heaney acknowledges the veracity of silence and the weakness of speech. He acknowledges the historical link between silence and his own ancestry because silence has always been associated with Northern Irish folk whether Protestant or Catholic. Heaney believed that his silent ancestry shaped his art. He sensed his place as belonging to a silent ancestry of inarticulate farming stock; he sensed the political and religious factors which lay behind the silence of Northern Ireland Catholics and he acknowledged the inherent reservation of Northern Ireland folk. And so as he wrote, in the wake of the deaths of his father and his mother, he acknowledged his world of silence, of empty space, of utter aloneness: 'I thought of walking round and round a space utterly empty/ Utterly a source, like the idea of sound; like an absence'. And as he wrote in Squarings[10] 'The emptier it stood, the more compelled the eye that scanned it'.

The connection between the emptiness of death and the fullness of life is established by memory. For Seamus Heaney death is flanked by life on the one hand and memory on the other; there is a continuum whereby life, death and memory merge into an uninterrupted flow. This continuum lies at the base of much of his poetry. Memory covers all of life not just for the individual but for the entire community. It is always personal but there is also cultural memory, a shared community memory which draws us back from the present through history to the very source of origin. In this way we discover where we are because we know where we have been.

Memory is the well from which all of his Mossbawn poetry is drawn. His first poetry was written from memory in his twenties when he was living in Belfast (1966-1972). Much later in 'Clearances' (1987), he remembers that while the priest, at the bedside, went hammer and tongs at the prayers for the dying, 'I remembered her head bent towards my head, her breath in mine'. Perhaps it is in the moments of dying and of death that life and memory converge. Memory can embrace and protect a life that is ending, can preserve that life in the present and project it into the future.

In the poem 'Two Lorries' (The Spirit Level 1996) he presents his mother through a double narrative. In both narratives 'It's raining on black coal and warm wet ashes'. Agnew, a Belfast coalman, has pulled into the yard at Mossbawn. In light-hearted banter he suggests that Margaret might come with him to the cinema in Magherafelt 'to see films, no less'. The mother admires the tasty ways of the leather-aproned coalman as he folds the empty coal-bags. She moves to her kitchen and she attends to the stove where the silk-black coal will burn to the silkiest white ashes. The bolted lorry 'gets revved and turned and heads for Magherafelt'.

In the second scene a different lorry groans up Broad Street on its way to blow up the bus station in Magherafelt. A huge explosion and the bus station is reduced to rubble and ashes. And Heaney has a vision of his dead mother, her shopping bags full of shovelled ashes, waiting to surprise him when he alights from the school bus, 'and death walked out past her like a dust-faced coalman, re-folding body-bags'.

In Heaney's poetry many dead are remembered and recorded; members of his family, neighbours, victims of chance, of accident, or of pre-meditated violence, and as they are encountered, they are named, spoken to and described. Many of his memories he inherited 'in that earth house in Mossbawn', what he describes as 'a stack of singular, cold-weights to load me hand and foot in the scale of things' (Squarings xl). Now, he wrote, memories can have for him a life of their own and 'like ivy shoots' that have been so long trained, they can keep their face, keep their distance and maintain their independent existence.

THE NIGHT OF OTHER DAYS

Childhood events are located in and around Mossbawn and memories of these inform his early poetry. Gradually memories fan outwards to embrace family, farm, neighbours and neighbourhood. Linkage is established with earth, water and the life of nature. Later, when he observed the wider social realities it led to perspectives on the religious, political and cultural spheres. He became aware of convictions, tensions and problems which resulted in fault-lines within and between communities. Many of these would eventually explode in hatred and violence and would shatter the deeply-flawed political and social system. By the age of thirty Heaney was already confronted with communal violence of an unprecedented nature and he looked for answers and remedies within himself and within the wider community. His search led him to 'the question of Ireland' and its sociology, history, anthropology and mythology. It pointed the way from personal intimate memory to the collective broad memory of the community with its inbuilt myths, beliefs and prejudices.

CHAPTER

Schooling

5

Seamus Heaney was appointed to the English Department in Queens University Belfast (QUB) when Philip Hobsbaum left in 1966. He also replaced Hobsbaum as convenor of 'The Group', a poetry workshop which Hobsbaum had set up three years previously. The intervening years were spent first as student teacher and then as lecturer in St Joseph's College of Education, Anderstown in Belfast. In St Thomas' school, where he completed his teaching practice, he met the principal, short-story writer Michael McLaverty[1], who lent him copies of the works of Patrick Kavanagh. Although he had completed four years study of English literature in Queen's University Belfast Heaney was totally unaware of the treasury of literature that had been produced south of the border including the works of W.B.Yeats. But he was learning fast.

He did not enjoy his year as student teacher and he was dismissive of the school staff ('gobshites') and students ('returned from the school to street-corners where they would measure the length of their spit' and be attracted towards violence). This verdict on St Thomas's school may appear somewhat harsh

42

THE NIGHT OF OTHER DAYS

when placed in context. Seamus himself was rescued from rural obscurity by the 1944 English Education act which came into force in Northern Ireland in 1947. Under this Act free secondary education was guaranteed to all pupils. They could advance from primary school to three different types of second-level school, Grammar School, Secondary School or Technical School. The type of school which lay open to pupils was decided on the result of a national examination taken by all at the end of primary school and known as 'The Eleven-Plus' examination. The results of this exam created three streams based on academic achievement. The top achievers went forward to Grammar School and the less successful went to Secondary Modern or Technical School. Thus at the age of eleven the future of a child was largely determined. The school at St Thomas's was an intermediate Secondary School and whereas it was possible for a student from the school to proceed to university it was, in practice, very difficult. An air of defeatism would have prevailed in a secondary intermediate school where pupils were almost programmed to drop out aged sixteen. They had little or no chance of educational advancement. Many were doomed by birth and by social status to remain at the bottom of the ladder. Some were attracted to violence and died in the Troubles.

The contrast with the scholarship boys who were educated at Seamus' old school, St Columb's in Derry, was stark. Many of the scholarship boys, rural and urban went on with Seamus Heaney to make their mark in the world...John Hume Nobel winner, Bishop Edward Daly, Phil Coulter, Seamus Deane and Eamon McCann to mention a few. But as Seamus remarked what happened to him in the first three decades of his life wasn't a matter of personal decision; it was typical and generational. Along with his cohort he was carried along on the conveyor belt of the times. Master Murphy had given free tuition to the young Seamus. He had earned a scholarship, gone to St. Columb's and graduated from there to study in QUB. The boys in St Thomas's weren't so lucky.

HUGH MULROONEY

Seamus completed his teaching diploma with the customary distinction, and his talent was now being recognised. 1966 was a decisive year for him. Their first child was born to Marie Devlin and Seamus Heaney. He was now Lecturer in his home university and participating in 'The Group' along with Michael Longley, Edna Longley, James Simmons, Stewart Parker, Joan Newman and Bernard MacLaverty. Through The Group he met and befriended poets John Hewitt and Derek Mahon, artists T.P.Flanagan and Colin Middleton, and singer and film-maker David Hammond. All of those illustrious figures are mentioned in Heaney's subsequent work.

'Death of a Naturalist' (DN) was published in 1966 and marked the beginning of a lifelong relationship with publishers Faber and Faber. The outstanding merit of the volume was immediately recognised and the reputation of the young poet was firmly established. He was also making his name as a talented and much-loved Lecturer, Speaker and Broadcaster. A second volume 'Door Into The Dark', (DD) followed in 1969 and this, in turn, was followed by 'Wintering Out', (WO) in 1972.

But by 1972 life in Northern Ireland had 'changed, changed utterly'. Northern Ireland was entering a cycle of violence and terror which would pulverise the entire community and lead to thousands of dead and tens of thousands of injured traumatised victims.

In 1967 he visited Trinity College Dublin, met Patrick Kavanagh and extended his circle of friends and acquaintances to include Frank Ormsby, Paul Muldoon, Medbh McGuckian and Ciaran Carson.[3] His first visit to the United States in 1969 was followed by a year-long stint as guest-lecturer in Berkeley, University of California 1970-1971. His comments on the atmosphere in the staff common-room at QUB on his return are less than complimentary. In Berkeley the atmosphere was free and open in contrast to Queen's where the British-Ulster element and the Catholic element maintained an at-arms-length distance and where Heaney said that he 'narrowed and tightened a bit'

THE NIGHT OF OTHER DAYS

in the face of a provincial British academic style 'that was halfway between briskness and prissiness'. Tom Flanagans' verdict seemed to say it all when he visited the QUB common-room: 'Jeez, Seamus! The sooner you get out of here the better'. And he did, with his wife and young family, in 1972.[4]

This, then, was the context in which Seamus Heaney published his first three volumes of poetry. But the reading of these volumes does not give an account either of the young poet or of his years in Belfast. There is little reference to his university education, to his teaching work in school and college, to the poetry sessions with 'The Group' or to the friends and colleagues with whom he collaborated in his role as educator, broadcaster and spokesman. In fact, very little of his personal or professional life is gleaned from his poetry. Fortunately, there is a comprehensive account, in his own words, in the wonderful book 'Stepping Stones'. This book published in 2008 records written- interviews with the poet Dennis O'Driscoll over the seven-year period September 2001 to 2008. It begins with Mossbawn. Michael Parker says that 'The locations of his childhood prove to be almost as important to the later development of the poet as the human landscape. At the centre of his world was the thatched farmhouse at Mossbawn, the family home until 1953, a place which he has transformed into a country of the mind'.[6]

From Heaney's own words we have a picture of a long, low one-storey thatched white-washed house, separated from the Toome Road by a small garden which contained the clothes-line. There were beech trees on either side of the lane. It continued past the house, between hedges and through the fields, skirting the marshy wet mossland and through a land of rabbits, wrens, goldfinches and badgers. This was a land of swamp, of fern and of mystery men. Two families lived at the end of this remote lane and so did Tom Tipping. Children often saw the smoke rising from the chimney of Tom Tippings' house as they made their

45

way to the school at Anahorish but they never saw him and he remained the mystery man. The people from the houses at the end of the lane came from their remote world to draw water from the pump in Heaney's yard. They belonged to the Moss and it was forbidden ground, but the pump outside the backdoor was the centre of the world for the young boy and indeed for families in the neighbourhood.

Across the fields to the back of the house there were three landmarks in the child's world, the flax-dam, the railway line and the river Moyola. All of these places were within the bounds of the small forty acre farm at Mossbawn.[7]

"I come from scraggy farm and moss,/Old patchworks that the pitch and toss/ Of history have left dishevelled...' he wrote to his niece Daisey Garnett 'A Peacock's Feather' in 1987, (HL)[8]. 'You are deserting the ground for the grid' he told Dennis O Driscoll as he described how, at his beloved Mossbawn, the beech trees were cut down, the hedges between the fields taken out, the rail-spur closed and removed. This, he said, was happening not just in Mossbawn but all over the country as the old sense of tillage and season and foliage disappeared. 'Once trees and hedges and ditches and thatch get stripped you're in a very different world'. Although he later went to 'The Wood' for school holidays and on visits during his early years in Belfast, the move from Mossbawn to 'The Wood' 'must have constituted another physical and symbolic break with innocence.

When questioned about poems sited in Mossbawn, Heaney told of how memory always led him back to the home of his birth and the place of happy childhood.[9] He identified 'The Other Side' in 'Wintering Out' (WO,1972) and 'Digging' as poems actually grounded in The Wood. The first poem refers to Johnny Junkin, one of three protestant neighbours whose farms marched (bordered) the farm at 'The Wood'. The poem 'Digging' (DN 1966), was written upstairs in the new house built at The Wood

THE NIGHT OF OTHER DAYS

where Heaneys had turbary rights (the right to dig or cut turf on common ground or on another's ground) in Toner's Bog. This is the bog where Seamus's grandfather (in fact his great uncle Hughie) cut more turf in a day than any other man and great-uncle Hughie is 'god of the wagon' in Kinship, (N,1975).

The days spent with Hughie on Toner's bog were among the happiest days of Heaney's life. He would have been involved in all of the steps involved in saving the turf, which was cut from the turf-bank, dried and footed in the bog and built into a stack beside the dwelling-house to provide fuel for the year. But even though those two poems were set in 'The Wood', the reader is firmly sited at Mossbawn. In 'Seeing Things' (ST,1991), the setting for the poem 'The Ash Plant' is in the upstairs bedroom of the house at 'The Wood'. But the house there is dismissively described as 'one of those 1950s take-me-or-leave-me dwelling houses, facing the road, bare faced, built on a bare field… 'The age of Formica triumphing in farmland Tarmac and kerbstones.' The fact that the family left Mossbawn for 'The Wood', when Seamus was away at boarding school, did not confer any rights to the place in Heaney's poetry because it never gained a place in his world and never replaced Mossbawn as the centre of his affection.

Seamus Heaney placed Mossbawn at the centre of his early poetic world. In his poetry and prose he has described in detail the house, the farm and the general geographical location, and he populates this world with members of the household, with local residents, with neighbours and a variety of folks, mainly craftsmen, visiting the locality. From his poems there is a fairly full picture of his mother, Margaret, his father Patrick, and the relationships between the three. In his poetry notebook Heaney wrote, in a quotation from the French writer Gaston Bachelard, "what is the source of our first suffering? It lies in the fact that we hesitated to speak. It was born in the moment when we accumulated silent things within us."

CHAPTER

Afterlife

6

The poems in his first three books are primarily descriptive of a sheltered childhood, spent in the security of a happy family on a small farm, where he rejoiced in the natural world of everyday activities. He recalls life as it happens. But to recall the past is not a matter of re-constituting it. To recall the past is to create it and to listen to the music of what is happening not just then but now. So, as he merges present and past, his thoughts inevitably turn to the future and, ultimately, to questions of death, the afterlife and eternity. This happened at the deathbed of his mother. As she lay dying he lived the world of their love peeling potatoes into a bucket of fresh water and as the priest belted out prayers for the dying he remembered the fallen tree and the emptiness it left behind. Then she was dead and an emptiness emptied into those who stood around. Where had she gone? All his life as Heaney thought on the substance and reality of death he faced some of the most fundamental questions in human experience. A number of ideas and concepts came to his mind. He found himself ruminating on

THE NIGHT OF OTHER DAYS

questions related to space, to emptiness, to silence, to finality and separation, and possibly to consideration of a new reality.

Much of what we know of his thoughts on Death are gathered from two works: His own volume 'Finders Keepers' and that wonderful work 'Stepping Stones' by Dennis O'Driscoll. Along with his poetry these are the sources for this chapter.

His imagination, and indeed a growing conviction, lead him to visualize beyond death a threshold and an infinite set of doors leading nowhere and to nothing (or perhaps, for those who can believe in religious doctrines, to infinity). The doorway to a megalithic tomb 'With its slabbed passage that keeps opening forward/To face another corbelled stone-faced door/That opens on a third. There is no last door... just the arrow 'travelling towards the vacant centre.' These lines are from 'In Memoriam: Robert Fitzgerald' in The Haw Lantern 1987.

At the moment of death time and eternity are interfaced. This he considered in another context, when he addressed the difficult subject of Incarnation and its meaning, (on this occasion in relation to Milosz's Christian humanism); he wrote '...the eternal has intersected with time, and through that intersection human beings, though creatures of time, have access to a reality out of time'.[1]

In the finality of death we reach the limit of the representation of life. There is no second time round and the silence imposed by death is eternal. This we think we know, but when it comes to giving voice to what we think we know, all a poet can do is to pronounce an elegy, 'in words which cannot convey the true matter of what they signify'. The poet is aware of the inadequacy of words and knows that in the very effort to express his emotions, to describe what he feels, to confront a mystery, his choice of words is diluting the strength and impact of the emotion he is trying to describe.

Heaney was aware of this and in particular he was aware of the limits of poetry. He is a poet whose consciousness of those things has become his chief strength. His poetry is continually aware that it does not live in its own area of discourse, but only visits it. His poetry is a pilgrimage to its own subject, like the journey of the pilgrims in 'Station Island'. (SI,1984).

In a poem titled 'A Dog Was Crying in Wicklow Also', (SL,1996), there is an account of how, when humans learned about Death, they sent a dog to Chukwu[3] with the message that they wished Death to be temporary in nature, like a night spent in the wood. However, the dog delayed to bark at another dog on the far bank of the river, thus allowing the toad to reach Chukwu first. "Human beings want death to last forever", the toad told Chukwu and thus it has transpired. As a result, "The dog crying out all night behind the corpse house." Death is not for a night. It is forever, 'A letting go which will not come again/ Or it will once. And for all'. (HC, 2010). And, although we all die the same death, each one dies differently. This is what Heaney tells us in his essay 'Joy or Night'. Death is not the end. It is in the centre. It is flanked by life on the one hand and by memory on the other, on a continuum which is only vaguely comprehended.

As the poet advanced in life his poems mirrored a steadily widening pool of reflection, question and recollection[4]. Asked by Dennis O Driscoll whether his own death held any fear he replied, "Certainly not in the way I'd have feared it sixty years ago, fearful of dying in the state of mortal sin and suffering the consequences for all eternity. It's more grief than fear, grief at having to leave 'what thou lovest well' and 'whom thou lovest well'"[5].

In the event we now know that Heaney's final message to those he loved was 'nolli temere'...'do not be afraid'. And then he was dead.

In 'Joy or Night: Last things in the Poetry of W.B.Yeats and Philip Larkin', (Finders Keepers 2002), he considered the

THE NIGHT OF OTHER DAYS

reactions of those two great figures to questions of life, death and the hereafter and their different approaches to the overall purpose of life itself. Larkin lived his final years 'as if he stuck his pale face out /on a skewer from behind the graveyard wall'. In contrast, W.B. 'was always passionately beating on the wall of the physical world in order to provoke an answer from the other side', while his poetic eye was 'overwhelmed by the visual evidence of infinity and solitude'. Perhaps, W.B. says, there is an overall purpose to life. Perhaps, through poetry, an energy and an order can be created which promotes 'the idea that there exists a much greater, circumambient energy and order within which we have our being'.[6] Heaney finds in Yeats a sense of 'the spirit's vulnerability, the mind's awe at the infinite spaces and the visual evidence of infinity and solitude'. In Larkin he finds a different interpretation of the facts of the body's dissolution and the mind's disappearance after death. Larkin talks of the 'inexorability of his own physical extinction'. As expressed by Heaney, 'When Larkin lifts his eyes from nature, what appears is a great absence. Neither justice nor injustice is to be sought in the skies; space offers neither illumination nor terminus. Out there, no encounter is possible. Out there is not our business.' This contrasts with Yeat's preoccupation with The Ghost upon the Road, the soul's destiny in the afterlife and the consequences of the individual's actions in time. It is as a result of such speculations that in his imagination Yeats is enabled 'to hold in a single thought reality and justice', what is and what might be.

Not surprisingly Heaney refers and defers to Yeats when he writes 'The goal of life on earth, and of poetry as a vital factor in the achievement of that goal, is what Yeats called, in 'Under Ben Bulben', the profane perfection of mankind'. For Heaney, for Yeats, and for others, poetry is always on the side of life and 'it opts for the conditions of afterlife and rebels at limits'. As an attempt at expressing meaning for what occurs at the moment of death, they see that the spirit 'is carried beyond feeling into the aboriginal ice'. But they also see a continuum, a connection, the feeling of an ongoing process which will occupy the minds of those left behind. And, very particularly, these mysteries will occupy the mind of a poet.

"Where does the spirit live? Inside or outside/Things remembered, made things, things unmade? What came first, the seabird's cry or the soul/Imagined in the dawn cold when it cried? /Where does it roost at last?" asks Heaney, (set questions for the ghost of W.B.), 'Seeing Things', (ST, 1991 xxii).

In his lecture 'Joy or Night' Heaney considers these great questions and he tells us that in order to achieve its vision of reality in poetry the creative writer must, through his perception and expression, transform reality and the circumstances of its time and place[7]. In Yeat's poem 'The Man and the Echo', human consciousness 'is up against the cliff-face of mystery, confronted with the limitations of human existence itself'. So it is at the deathbed. For Seamus Heaney at the deathbed of his mother 'a pure change happened', the space they stood around had been emptied into them to keep, 'it penetrated Clearances that suddenly stood open'. In some mysterious sense death is not the end. We know that Heaney believed that death is flanked by life on the one hand and by memory on the other and when death comes, one kind of life continues in the memory and in the imagination of those left behind. And as for the dead "the space we stood around had been emptied into us to keep...a space utterly empty, utterly a source...a bright nowhere...a soul ramifying and forever silent, beyond silence listened for".

Space, emptiness, absence, silence and source, all occupy a central place in his memory and imagination and play a vital role in the creative work of Seamus Heaney.

In the early 1980s Heaney read a book on sacred and profane space by Mircea Eliade. He linked this work with his own space

THE NIGHT OF OTHER DAYS

'utterly empty and utterly a source'. Much space was desacralized in Heaney's lifetime. Pilgrims ceased to walk around the holy well; in churches people ceased to circle the Stations of the Cross; altar rails separating the sanctuary from the rest of the church were removed; in ordinary homes grates were removed and hearths blocked up and out in the countryside fairy rings became mere hill forts. Religion and myth seemed to be losing their grip.

The death of his mother Margaret and of his father Patrick led to the question of religion. Both parents lived the Christian life, knew and believed in the consolation of religion. They died in anticipation of an eternal reward. Not so their son Seamus. He gradually came to disbelieve the dogma of a Christian afterlife. So how would he remember his mother? Just as a corpse? With the dog crying all night? Or in some way as a life continuing beyond the grave? Enjoying the reward offered by her religious belief? Or part of a great nothingness? One wonders to what extent would Heaney's own religious faith, or lack of it, help him in his quest for answers?

When Seamus was young he tells us that he 'dwelt entirely in the womb of religion. Dominated by Catholic conceptions, formulations, pedagogies, prayers and practices'[8] 'Salvation, damnation, heaven above and hell below, grace and guilt, all were for real...you'd hardly got out of the cot before you were envisaging the deathbed.' He was oversupplied with religion. But he eventually grew from catechised youth into secular sceptic adult. By then, as he said of Ted Hughes, the scope of his own imagining had accommodated the idea of the divine. And in the storehouse of his imagining and of his memory his mother lived on, not as a corpse, but as a soul ramifying in a bright nowhere. Central to those memories of her was the question of her religious belief. Heaney talked of the importance of religious belief to her especially in the decades when she bore nine children, a time when religion offered some comfort and hope to a bright independent woman trapped by biology and finding little comfort in the teaching of the Catholic church... 'Be faithful to your husband and eschew any thoughts of improving your station'.

A protestant neighbour was 'dandering by' one night and remained silent outside the door until the rosary was finished 'A right-looking night', he might say, 'I was dandering by and says I, I might as well call.' And Seamus stands behind him in the moan of prayers and shyly wonders if he should open a conversation on grass-seed (The Other Side, WO 1972). Prayer, life, reality, belief and mystery, all in context outside the door of a small house on a right-looking night.

For the young Seamus, the religious influence of school and education replaced that of the home in Mossbawn and the impact was more pronounced. First at primary school he was introduced to the Catechism. This presented Catholic dogma in question and answer form. The answers were learned and delivered by rote: 'Who made the world?...God made the world'. In secondary school 'the formation became more systematic'. There was an annual religious knowledge examination for the five years and during those years the students lived the liturgical year in a very intensive way, a Latin mass every morning; aware, from the missal of the feast day and also the order of the feast; going to confession and communion.

Heaney made several pilgrimages to Lough Derg, the penitential island in Donegal. He also went as a pilgrim to Lourdes. He wrote of his first encounter with the poems of Hopkins, the claustrophobia and scrupulosity and religious ordering of the mind, the cold-water shaves and the single iron beds, the soutanes and the self-denial. 'That was the world I was living in when I first read his poems".(SS.38)

Included in 'North', 1976, was the poem 'Freedman' which seemed to summarise the poets religious and political perceptions at that time: 'I was under the thumb too, like all my class./

THE NIGHT OF OTHER DAYS

Subjugated yearly under arches/Manumitted- released from slavery...And again 'I would kneel to be impressed by ashes...I was under that thumb too.' Then, he tells us, poetry rescued him from political and religious subjugation. Interestingly this poem was not included in the 1998 selection of poems 1996-1998, titled 'Opened Ground'.

Years later he wrote (DC, 2006) 'Like everybody else, I bowed my head/during the consecration of bread and wine'. Words like 'thanksgiving', 'host', had an undying tremor and draw, he wrote, 'like well-water from far down'. In 1984 he wrote, (SI ix) of his hatred at the ease with which he conformed, 'hate everything/ That made me biddable and unforthcoming'. As years passed he gradually lost this faith... 'the loss occurred off-stage', he said.

When he went on to the 'Protestant' university at Queen's University Belfast there was little doubting the sectarian nature of the institution, although it would be a mistake to think that he would have fared any better in the south of Ireland where the ethos of the universities was clearly demarcated along sectarian/ religious lines. For example under a decree of the Archbishop of Dublin, Catholics entered Trinity College Dublin under pain of mortal sin, unless with the express permission of Archbishop, John Charles McQuaid. Those of us who defied this ruling can attest to its consequences.[9] As late as 1969 University College Dublin (UCD) refused to recognise a degree from London University as satisfying the entry requirements to their 'Higher Diploma in Education' course. Education at all levels was clerically controlled and the schools, colleges and universities were unapologetically sectarian in the south.

Michael Parker has written, "Clearly Catholicism permeates both his poetic consciousness, with its weighty emphasis on ritual supplication, on awe, grace, guilt, humility, responsibility, discipline, and its burdened and burdening vocabulary...The highly-charged language in which the Church's teachings were couched permeate the poets' idiolect. His religious metaphors and allusions are not to be dismissed simply as the products of nostalgia, the detritus of a belief long since abandoned; rather they incarnate a potency of feeling remembered and renewed'.[10]

It was inevitable that Heaney's attitude to Catholicism and Christianity was complex and ambivalent and eventually he lost his belief in them especially as they related to life, death and the afterlife. Written in 1991 'Seeing Things', (ST) : "And after the commanded journey, what?/Nothing magnificent, nothing unknown./A gazing out from far away, alone//And it is not particular at all,/Just old truth dawning: there is no next-timeround/Unroofed scope." Indeed, it was asserted as early as the publication of his third volume, 'Wintering Out' in 1972, that he found Christianity 'at best irrelevant and at worst a force for harm in Ulster'.[11] And in the Ulster of 1972 questions of life and death were immediate and relevant.

Many references to Church rituals and beliefs are found throughout his writings. In 'The Last Mummer': "The Moon's host elevated/in a monstrance of holly trees"; "I could risk blasphemy": 'The Tolland Man'; "She waded in under the sign of the cross...Even Christ's palms unhealed, smart and cannot fish there": 'Limbo';... and there are many more references in this and other volumes. Maybe it is accurate to say that Seamus Heaney was a Poet who was a Catholic rather than a Catholic Poet, and maybe like Columcille he kept the rich earth of Mossbawn and his Catholic beliefs in his footware all his life. It was a case of 'once a Catholic, always a Catholic'. He held the view that if you desert this system, you're deserting the best there is, and there's no point "in exchanging one great coherence for some other ad hoc arrangement." The Catholic Church provided a totally structured reading of the mortal condition and he himself never quite deconstructed it. The myths of the classical world and Dante's Commedia (where my Irish Catholic subculture received high cultural ratification) and the myths of other cultures matched and mixed and provided a cosmology that corresponded well enough to the original: 'you learned that, from the human beginnings, poetic imagination had proferred a world of light and a world of dark, a shadow region – not so much an afterlife as an afterimage of life."

He had no reservations about the importance of Catholic obsequies when life comes to a close. This is the right time for ceremonies. 'At that stage you want a stand taken against nothingness and a word spoken...a word that runs through interstellar fields, through the revolving galaxies, and calls out, protests, screams', (Heaney quotes Milosz's poem 'Meaning').

Religion in the personal and domestic context were of importance in Heaney's early life and education. But in the Northern Ireland of the time structured religion was a destabilising factor in the spheres of social and political life and it became difficult to disentangle the different strands. A later chapter will illustrate this. It will be argued that the very identity of a person in Northern Ireland was equated with their religion which in the case of Catholicism became linked with notions of submission, control, repression, subjugation. In the political field, when secular leadership was absent and Church leadership was called for, the Catholic Church was found wanting and perhaps open to the charge of collaboration with a bigoted and intolerant social order. This was the conclusion reached by people like John Hume, who felt that leaders were very unlikely to emerge from the ranks of a subjugated, silent and repressed Catholic minority. (Hume worked all his life in the service of peace and his fellow men. His contribution was overshadowed by men of violence but he remains one of the greatest heroes in the history of Northern Ireland).

Because Catholics were a minority in Heaney's Northern Ireland, and because Seamus was often, somewhat unwillingly, cast in the role of spokesman for his co-religionists, he has been accused of ambivalence in his comments on a situation where the political, the religious and the violent had become hopelessly intertwined. The situation in the early sixties was that of a community divided along religious, social, political and sectarian lines, a community where a bigoted Protestant ruling-class, committed to union within the United Kingdom of England, Scotland, Wales and Northern Ireland, rode rough-shod over a Catholic minority. Some concluded that Catholic authorities 'have connived in a conspiracy of evasion and compliance' which facilitated co-existence but left Protestant bigotry intact.[12]

It will be found in a later chapter that in his Volume 'North' (N, 1975) Heaney allowed himself to speak of the situation in a number of poems. 'Singing School' and 'Ministry of Fear', 'I was under the thumb too like all my caste... he wrote in 'Freedman'... until poetry arrived in that city, and poetry wiped my brow and sped me...' He had lost his faith in his Church not because it failed him personally, as a structured core of beliefs, but socially in its failure to offer any help or leadership in solving 'the dilemma of present predicaments'.

By the 1960s the old mantras no longer offered comfort. The pope in Rome was no longer 'a happy man this night' when Celtic won a football match. Soon the sound of explosions and gunfire would contrast with the silence of the moderate Catholic voice and young men would turn from their church to join the ranks of the men of violence. 'O land of password, handgrip, wink and nod,/ Of open minds as open as a trap'. And all around The Ministry of Fear. A later chapter will examine the basis for this fear and its consequences.

CHAPTER

Space

7

The final book of Seamus Heaney's poetry, 'Human Chain' (HC), was published in 2010. He was seventy one. He died three years later. Memory is the source of inspiration for almost all of the work, poems take the reader from his early boyhood and on through some of the significant days of his life. By this time Ireland was largely at peace and Heaney's poetry had achieved world-wide recognition. We can now read his entire corpus with the benefit of his own commentary and wisdom.

"I re-enter the swim, riding or quelling/The very currents memory is composed of,/Everything accumulated ever/ as I took squarings from the tops of bridges/or the banks of self at evening."[1] In the 1991 volume (ST), when he was in his early fifties, he wrote "Heather and kesh and turf-stacks reappear.....Fields of the nearly blessed/Where gaunt ones in their shirtsleeves stooped and dug/ or stood alone at dusk surveying bog-banks' By then memories of the days of his childhood and youth had been enriched by years of reflection and creative speculation. Past and present, reality and myth, recollection and speculation, all woven together in imagination and memory to produce a thing of beauty.

Memory linked Heaney's local parochial world with the universal. He moved from Toner's Bog to the bogs of Denmark and from contemporary Ireland to the mystic lands of pre-history. In the poem 'Bogland', the final poem in his second volume (DD,1969), he recalled a tentative unrealized need to make a congruence between memory and bogland and, for want of a better word, our national consciousness.' He returned again and again to bogland and found in bogs a rich deposit of inspiration and this inspiration is closely linked with a vast, silent, empty space in the word-hoard of his memory and imagination.

The centrality of space, of emptiness, silence and nothingness in Heaney's writings has been widely noted and commented upon. From this space the memory scans 'the offing' and "Strange how things in the offing, once they're sensed,/convert to things foreknown;/And how what's come upon is manifest/Only in light of what has been gone through"[2]. This creative space is inner and discreet. It belongs within the poet himself.

Heaney knew and experienced spaces way beyond himself, immense, vast and infinite spaces. Driving to Wicklow, with mountains to the right and the sea to the left the poet gets this sudden joy, "There's a double sensation of here-and-nowness in the familiar place and far-and-awayness in something immense". When he speaks of this infinite space he speaks of silence and he says that although the spaces may be silent yet they are continuously alive and fluent in their own wordless language. The poet feels drawn towards them and his poetry is a ratification of that impulse. "You can lose your belief in the afterlife…the infinite spaces may be silent but the human response is…if you stand out in the country under a starry sky, you can still feel a primitive awe at the muteness of the vault".

THE NIGHT OF OTHER DAYS

Reflections on the majesty and infinity of space led Heaney to speculation on questions of existence and the nature of 'being', and this in turn, led to speculation on how 'being' (existence) is grounded in another kind of nothingness, that of non-being.[3] Nothingness here 'can be defined as self-obliteration or annihilation as experienced through encounters with the void or abyss...or the discovered meaningless of existence per se'. The suggestion is that Heaney, especially from 1980 onwards, investigated this question with increasing interest. He considered the thinking of Yeats, Larkin and others in relation to life, death and what lies, or does not lie, beyond death. He gradually relinquished his Christian beliefs and this seems to have advanced to the point where he may have given a place in his philosophy to notions of nothingness.

In the poem 'The Plantation' (DD 1969) he can lose himself in the darkness of the wood, can come face-to-face with his own powerlessness. 'Though you walked a straight line/It might be a circle you travelled'. Any point in that wood was a centre. Traces of other people were everywhere 'in the hush and mush of its thread-mill' 'Someone had always been there/Though always you were alone.' And so he learns to lose and to find himself, to be both 'pilot and stray', to experience both a sense of being and non-being.

'The Peninsula' (DD 1969) advises that 'when you have nothing more to say just drive for a day all round the peninsula'. As you pass through the land without marks, in silence, note the visible and invisible, the known and the unknown and experience the mystery in silence. Then on return, after nightfall, recall the silhouetted log, 'islands riding themselves out into the fog', sea, field and hill swallowed into darkness 'things founded clean on their own shapes, water and ground in their extremity'. Shapes which are emptied into the clarity of their own outline, in memory, and against the background of oncoming night.

Another poem 'The Given Note' (DD 1969), tells of the spirit music brought from nowhere 'out of wind off mid-Atlantic'. The man had gone, alone, to far-off Blasket and in a dry-stone hut 'He got this air out of the night' and now as it comes off the bow it 'Rephrases itself into the air', reabsorbed into the nothingness from whence it came.

And there is the space underneath our feet. 'We have no prairies/To slice a big sun at evening' he writes in 'Bogland' (DD). Everywhere 'the eye is wooed into the cyclops' eye of a tarn'. Ours is a country of bogs where the ground opens underfoot and where each layer exposes previous encampment and where the wet centre is bottomless. As in 'The Plantation', here in the bogland there is silent witness to previous life, while its' bottomless centre connects to the vast Atlantic and its music of the night.

'And sometime make the time to drive out west/Into County Clare, along the Flaggy Shore….' he wrote in the 'Spirit Level' (SL 1996). With the wild ocean on one side and the slate-grey lake with its game of swans on the other, drive on. Useless to think you can park and capture the scene. Drive on because you are neither here nor there, drive through in silence. 'A hurry through which known and strange things pass/As big soft buffetings come at the car sideways/And catch the heart off guard and blow it open'. Heaney's world may be centred in Mossbawn and his interest is often centred on Ireland but he is a poet of the universe and the universal.

PART TWO

Death of a Naturalist....1966 *(DN)*

Door Into The Dark……..1969 *(DD)*

Wintering Out……………..1972 *(WO)*

CHAPTER

Water

8

The first three books plus the fourth 'North' (N. 1975) are often treated as one work or movement. In this chapter 'North' is not included and the third book (WO) is treated separately.

The poetry of his first two volumes (DN) and (DD) takes the reader from the bus-stop on the main road, where Christopher was killed, to the homestead in Mossbawn,[1] along a path or loaning with beech trees on either side. The house comes into view, a thatched, one-storey building with a lean-to stable at one end. There is no electricity, and water is brought in from the pump outside the door.

The horse spent his nights in the lean-to stable but now the stable is empty. Seamus's bedroom is located between the horse's lean-to stable and the kitchen. He can hear the horse at night. 'Dull pounding through hay,/The uneasy whinny...Muscle and hoof/ Bundled under the roof'. Those were the days when the 'night-mare' had a richer and more benign connotation. Now 'His hot reek is lost'. He cleared in a hurry 'clad only in shods/Leaving this stable unmade'[2]. Before mechanisation, the horse was of vital importance on a farm and provided the power for all farming operations. The disappearance of the horse was possibly the most significant indication of a permanent world change in agricultural practice. Seamus hears the sounds of the horse from one side of his bedroom and from the other side the sound of voices in the kitchen, usually those of his father Patrick, his mother Margaret, and perhaps his aunt Mary. Not that there is much conversation. His mother steeping her swollen feet and his father reading details of land on the market as he lies on the great sofa and reads with some expansion of spirit. Aunt Mary, perhaps in her wheelchair, mainly silent and at peace with her world. The other voice in the background may be that of the radio bringing the shipping forecast or news from abroad. The radio-reception is not always clear because the aerial is attached to a branch of a tree and is threaded through the window into the kitchen.

One piece of furniture, the cot, has a permanent place in the kitchen and for all of Seamus' youth it cradled the newest arrival to the household. His own children would, in time, sleep in this very cot. The cot has a base of loose slats which Seamus himself, as a baby, removed and then lowered himself onto the kitchen floor. This was his first manoeuvre on the frontier of discovery....'And is the same cot I myself slept in/ When the whole world was a farm that eked and crowed.'[3]

It is worth hearing what Heaney says about his adventure with the cot. He was two or three at the time. 'It was like a knowledge coming home to you. I was holding on to the rail of the cot but it could have been the deck-rail of the world. I was in two places at once'. One was a small square of kitchen floor and the other was 'a big knowledgeable space I had stepped into deep inside myself, a space I can still enter through the memory. Nowadays I would say it was to poetic discovery'.

As in all of his evocations of childhood this account is as vivid and detailed as if actually visible and these eidetic evocations

THE NIGHT OF OTHER DAYS

of childhood are found in all of his books. Everything he has written about childhood 'reinforces the sense of intimate domestic warmness and affection'.[4]

His aunt Mary Heaney held Seamus in very special affection. Mary lived with the family in Mossbawn and moved with them to The Wood when, after Christopher's death, Mossbawn was sold.

Mary's domain was the yard, the dairy, such as it was, and a small vegetable patch where she grew sweet peas. The domestic economy was managed by Margaret. One of Heaney's earliest memories was being lost as a small boy in Mary's patch. Mary was active and cycled to mass in Bellaghy every Sunday until she was invalided with arthritis. The young boy's first train trip was with Mary and her sister Sarah. They took him on holiday to Port Stewart.

Although Margaret and Mary presided over different domains there were chores which demanded a communal effort and one such was churning or butter-making.

Milk was collected over a period and stored in four large crocks in the pantry. Over time cream came to the top and hardened. When the time was ripe the contents of the crocks were emptied into the large churn in the middle of the kitchen floor. The churn, a large waisted wooden barrel, was then fitted with a lid. Through the hole in the lid the dash plunged to the bottom of the churn. For hours on end the dash was moved to the sound of the slush and slap of the contents. This was an uneasy time and a large folklore grew around the process of churning and the risks involved. Bad or tainted butter would result from a faulty process. The crocks, churn and all implements used were scrupulously scalded, scrubbed and sterilised. Each step in the process had to be finely judged.[6]

'A thick crust, coarse-grained as limestone roughly-cast,/hardened gradually on the top of the four crocks......Out came the four crocks, spilled their heavy lip/of cream, their white insides, into the sterile churn'. Now the dash, or staff, was plunged in and the lid fitted. 'My mother took first turn, set up rhythms/that slugged and thumped for hours. Arms ached./Hands blistered. Cheeks and clothes were spattered....' After hours of relentless toil a birchwood bowl was sterilised along with the little handheld corrugated butter-spades. The rich yellow curd was fished out of the churn and into a strainer to be transferred to the birchwood bowl. The kitchen echoed to 'the plash and gurgle of the sour-breathed milk,/ the pat and slap of small spades on wet lumps'. The result was butter, hard-earned and produced by a communal effort.

Our best description of the relationship between aunt Mary and Seamus is gained from the poem he dedicated to her in North (1975) 'Mossbawn Sunlight'.

'There was a sunlit absence./The helmeted pump in the yard/ heated its iron,/water honeyed /in the slung bucket......' Mary stood in a flowery apron by the window while the reddening stove 'sent out its plaque of heat' as she dusted the board with a goose's wing. Then she sat with whitened nails and measling shins....

'here is a space/again, the scone rising/to the tick of two clocks./

And here is love/like a tinsmith's scoop/sunk past its gleam/ in the meal-bin.'

Responding to Dennis O'Driscoll Heaney said 'There was something in our relationship, whatever it was, that stood still'. He recalled that she was eventually stricken with arthritis and confined to a wheelchair. Daily she was cared for by Margaret and each night carried upstairs in her wheelchair by her nephews until they all left home and Mary was confined to downstairs. Is she 'this woman who sat for years/in a wheelchair, looking straight ahead/ Out the window'? She certainly fits the description...'She never lamented once and she never/Carried a spare ounce of emotional

THE NIGHT OF OTHER DAYS

weight'…and she could see 'deeper into the country than you expected'. (Seeing Things 1991).

In the 1970's, before Mary had to go into special care, Seamus often visited his old home (now 'The Wood') and having greeted his parents and siblings he would go and sit, mainly in silence, with Mary… Just a deep, unpathetic stillness and wordlessness. Something in Seamus reverted to the child in Mossbawn… Something in her just remained constant, 'like the past gazing at you calmly, without blame'… all I'm saying is that I loved her dearly'.[5] Mary died in her late seventies.

Seamus Heaney gives brief mention to members of his extended family. His aunt Sally was very generous and he held her in high regard, describing her as very thorough, very kind, very refined. She had a good library and, in her house, the young boy got a feel for books. She gave him a big glass-doored bookcase for his twenty first birthday and five hundred pounds for a deposit on their first house. He felt very close to her. He describes her as a great woman, an emotional as well as a material provider.

Grandmother McCann, (Margaret's mother), is the old woman in 'Electric Light', (EL, 2001). She lived in New Row in Castledawson and that address was the one named by Patrick at the deathbed of his wife Margaret. She was born and raised in that house. And it was granny McCann who looked after Seamus when he stayed with her one night as a very young and fretful boy.

'She sat with her fur-lined felt slippers unzipped' and was helpless in the face of the little boy who cried himself to sleep the night he was left to stay. The radio was switched off. Earlier he had climbed onto the bow-backed chair to reach the switch and 'they had watched me as /As I roamed at will the stations of the world'. Now the silence of the blackout. Just the sound of 'Knitting needles ticking, wind in the flue' and the sight of her ancient mangled thumb, 'puckered pearl, rucked quartz' now among beads and vertebrae in the Derry ground.

HUGH MULROONEY

Of his siblings the only one mentioned is his brother Hugh. Hugh had witnessed the accident which killed his brother Christopher. He is the subject of 'Keeping Going' (The Spirit Level, SL 1996). 'The piper coming from far away is you/With a whitewash brush for a sporran/Wobbling round you, a kitchen chair/upside down on your shoulder,...'. This picture of the extrovert fun-loving child leading the younger siblings in a merry parade is in stark contrast with the assassination scene he witnessed, years later, when a car slowed down and stopped in The Diamond, in Magherafelt. A young man 'then fell past the tarred strip,/Feeding the gutter with his copious blood,...Grey matter like gruel flecked with blood/In spatters on the whitewash.'

Hugh still drives his tractor onto The Diamond, waves at people, keeps old roads open by driving on the new ones. 'You called the piper's sporrans whitewash brushes/and then dressed up and marched us through the kitchen,/But you cannot make the dead walk or right wrong'. Hugh keeps on going.

Parker has written "The locations of his childhood prove to be almost as important to the later development of the poet as the human landscape". At the centre of his world was the thatched farmhouse at Mossbawn, the family home until 1953, when they left for 'The Wood'. Heaney never left Mossbawn and it remained his place, a place which he has transformed 'into a country of the mind'." And at the centre of the Mossbawn world was the pump... Omphalos![6]

Omphalos, a Greek word meaning the navel, and hence the stone that marked the centre of the world. Heaney would repeat the word 'until its blunt and falling music becomes the music of somebody pumping water at the pump outside our back door'. Set on a concrete plinth the pump stands, a slender, iron idol, snouted, helmeted, dressed down with a sweeping handle...marking the centre of another world. It supplied five households.

THE NIGHT OF OTHER DAYS

His mother, Margaret would have held a less romantic view of the pump as she talked of the plunger within her and as she laboured bucket after bucket to satisfy the thirsty horse. To her it was a symbol of the enslavement of herself and of womankind. 'At each gulp of the plunger...I am tired of walking about with this plunger/Inside me...'[7].

The poet recalls the sinking of the well-shaft, boring down through the rich black clay to a seam of sand and through to the seam of gravel and aquifer. 'That pump marked an original descent into earth... made its foundation the foundation of the omphalos itself...' and often the water from a spring ran free and clear.

The pump was a visible monument to the presence of water. It was also a status symbol in rural Ireland, north and south in the 1940s. Indeed the pinnacle status was reached in the words of an old Irish saying... 'to have a priest in the house and a pump in the yard'.

It also enjoyed an erotic symbolism. In the poem 'Rite of Spring' (DD 1969), Heaney describes the way in which the frozen pump was 'defrosted' by wrapping straw around the mouth and handle. The straw was then set alight and 'we lifted her latch,/Her entrance was wet, and she came.' The water in a running stream also spoke of sexuality. 'Undine' (DD 1969), allows us to hear the response of the blocked water as the stream bed is cleared. 'I ran quick for him...He halted, saw me finally disrobed,...he dug a spade deep in my flank/And took me to him. I swallowed his trench...'.

The pump was in a prominent position outside the backdoor. Wells were less visible, but of great significance as expressed in the poem 'Personal Helicon' the final poem in DN 1966.

It begins: 'As a child, they could not keep me from wells/And old pumps with buckets and windlasses.' Some wells, he says, were so deep you could not see any reflection. Others, when cleared of soft mulch, mirrored a white face over the bottom, with echoes of

Narcissus. Once a rat 'slapped across my reflection' at the bottom of a well. Others had echoes, gave back your own call, and many were very, very, dark deep and dangerous.

The Helicon mentioned in the poem is a sacred mountain in Boeotia. Two fountains flow from its springs. Those who drank the water were inspired with the gift of poetry. This was the significance of the ancient wells in mythology.

In Ireland, as Heaney knew so well, wells were of significance in myth, religion and history. The Fianna and Fionn MacCumhaill drank from sacred wells and Saint Bridget bathed her feet in a well.

The poet, Patrick Kavanagh, wrote of a blessed well near his home in Monaghan. The local priests didn't like the well and they discouraged pilgrimages to it. This did nothing to dispel faith in its curative properties, or to shake the belief that Saint Bridget had bathed her feet in it. Heaney would have read Kavanagh's account and he was also familiar with the legend of Sinand and Connla's Well which he had learned at school. According to ancient Irish legend this well was located in Tir Na nOg, the Land of Youth, at the bottom of the ocean. Connla's Well was the location of the Hazels of Wisdom and Inspiration...the Hazels of the Science of Poetry.[10]

To the present day there are many 'blessed wells' in Ireland, many garlanded with ribbons and flowers, and held in high esteem. Not just in Ireland but in places of pilgrimage across Europe. Estyn Evans reckoned that there were as many as 3000 'holy wells' in Ireland in the 1940s. He says that the attributes of purification, healing and fertility are natural concomitants of the magic welling of spring water.[11]

The wells of Heaney's childhood become the springs of inspiration for his muse. They reveal the poet to himself, 'restoring in language what has been lost in reality.'[12] A well is a point of entry to the buried life of feelings and to the promise of putting feelings into words.

THE NIGHT OF OTHER DAYS

Looking down into wells takes him to the heart of a mystery, affords glances back at earlier experiences of childhood and forward to a future of poetic maturity.[13] Wells provide links with antiquity, the pagan past, the Catholic present and the poetic future. 'The Dark' of the poem is the dark at the bottom of the well, but it is also the dark of artistic creation, the dark of the Irish landscape, of its tragedy, its legend, its history, myth and mystery.

At the bottom of the well lies a potential vision of hope but there is also the threat of danger. It is a place of clear reflection but a place where rats can scurry across long roots in slime. A place of hope, potential and danger. And a place of creativity.

Heaney spoke of the parallel of poetry writing and the turning of a windlass at a well.[14] At first the bucket is wound down halfway and wound back up full of air, 'until one day the chain draws unexpectedly tight and you have dipped into waters that will continue to entice you back. You'll have broken the skin on the pool of yourself. 'Your praties will be fit for digging'.[15]

Years later Heaney wrote a poem in which he mentioned 'Keenan's Well'. He read the poem to his beloved neighbour, Rosie Keenan. When he finished his reading she responded with the words 'I can see the sky at the bottom of it now.' Rosie Keenan was blind.

The Mycenae Lookout in his Reverie of Water 'And then this ladder of our own that ran/deep into a well-shaft being sunk/ in broad daylight, men puddling at the source/through tawny mud, then coming back up/deeper in themselves for having been there,...finders, keepers, seers of fresh water/in the bountiful round mouths of iron pumps/ and gushing taps.' (The Spirit Level, SL 1996).

Water runs free in streams and rivers. Across the fields from the house at Mossbawn was the river Moyola. In his volume 'Seeing Things'. 1991 he included a series of poems titled 'Crossings' and poem xxxii says 'Running water never disappointed./Crossing water always furthered something./Stepping stones were stations of the soul.' At one location there were stepping stones across the Moyola. As a child he liked to step from one stone to the next until he reached mid-stream. Here he experienced sensations like those he experienced when he lowered himself from his cot onto the cold kitchen floor. As he stood on the mid-stream stepping-stone he felt giddy and rooted at the same time. He felt at once the sense of being isolated and alone but conscious of the rush of water at his feet and the 'big stately movement of the clouds in the sky above his head'.[16] He gave to those stepping stones a meaning and significance far greater than their size. To him they represented progress, boundaries, possibilities, reconciliations, poems, 'something to write home about'. All his life as a poet he saw each poem as a stepping stone, perhaps echoing Keats who saw each poem as 'a regular stepping of the Imagination towards a Truth'. In 'Feeling Into Words' Heaney tells us of how the successful achievement of a poem could be a stepping stone in your life. And each poem is simply a step towards the next. You are confirmed by the visitation of the last poem and threatened by the elusiveness of the next one, Heaney wrote.

When he stood on the stone in mid-stream he thought of the Roman god Terminus, the god of boundaries. The Romans kept an image of Terminus in the Temple of Jupiter on Capitol Hill. There was no roof on this temple. The image was open to the boundless space of the sky, the whole unlimited height and width and depth of the Heavens themselves. The humble river Moyola was also a boundary and the stepping stones which forded the river offered the potential to further something, 'Stepping stones were stations of the soul'.[17] Standing in mid-stream offered a perspective on the boundless and the possible. The rushing water underfoot; the boundless firmament overhead; the choice of river banks; the stability and security of remaining still; the possibilities of movement. Human beings possess the double capacity to be

THE NIGHT OF OTHER DAYS

attracted to the security of what is intimately known and the challenges of what is beyond and unknown. This double capacity, Heaney says, is a source of poetry.

In 1987 he published a volume 'The Haw Lantern' (HL) and included the poem 'Terminus'. He describes the extent to which he became conscious of the boundaries all round him. The banks of the Moyola marked the boundary between their land and that of their Protestant neighbour. At the river the two farms 'marched' or bordered. Away in the distance on one side was the town of Castledawson. This was a *neat*, planned, Protestant settlement with terraced slated houses and a way of life ordered by the factory siren. Here lived his mother's people. Away on the other side was Bellaghy and the Heaney farm, at 'The Wood'. This was a Catholic, Gaelic area, with scattered thatched houses and a rural way of life. The home at Mossbawn was located between a road and a railway line where they could hear the shunting engine and the trotting horse. 'I was the marsh drain and the marsh drain's banks/Suffering the limit of each claim.//Two buckets were easier carried than one./I grew up in between'. Baronies and parishes, counties and dioceses, histories and cultures met and marched everywhere he looked.

When he stood on the middle stepping stone he tells us he felt like the last earl. This is a reference to the last of the great Gaelic leaders of Ulster, Hugh O Neill, Earl of Tyrone. It was September in the year 1599. Elizabeth was nearing the end of her reign on the English throne. She had sent her favourite courtier, the Earl of Essex, to subdue the Irish. The Irish resistance was led from Ulster by the Gaelic Leader, Hugh O Neill. He had spent some time at the royal court. Now he represented a major threat to English power and now was the time of reckoning. O Neill had enticed Essex north and the two armies were separated by the river Glyde in county Louth. O Neill rode his horse to midstream and parleyed with Essex. For the moment 'the balance trembled and held, the water ran and the sky moved silently above them'.[18] Was a compromise possible? The answer was 'no', even if for a brief moment it might appear otherwise. Both men were locked into a political reality and the great power game was to cost both of them their lives. Hope and history did not meet that day and it opened the first chapter of the great tragedy of Ulster and Northern Ireland.

The significance of the river Moyolla might appear to be small. It was the boundary between Heaney's farm and that of a Protestant neighbour. That neighbour, Johnny Junkin, whose land marched the Heaney farm, expressed his view, as recorded in the poem 'The Other Side' (W.O.1972). He considered Heaney's land to be 'as poor as Lazarus' and dismissed their religious practices as 'hardly rule by the Book at all'. As will become clear in a later chapter he was expressing a conviction which poisoned relations across Northern Ireland for centuries. Yet this man whose brain 'was a whitewashed kitchen hung with texts, swept tidy as the body o' the kirk' would stand quietly outside Heaney's door until the rosary dragged mournfully to a close, before knocking and paying a visit. Even when neighbours are on the friendliest of terms the boundaries are intact and the lines of sectarian antagonism and affiliation still follow the boundaries of the land.

The young Heaney delivered a can of milk every evening to the next house down the road. Every time he walked the short distance, just as every time he walked to and from school, he was conscious of boundaries and divisions. As he walked he crossed from one townland to another. His home was in one parish and his school in another. Every time he crossed a little rivulet he changed location. The catechism he learned in school was that of the diocese of Derry but his confirmation took place in the archdiocese of Armagh. His paternal grandparents belonged to the Gaelic community of Bellaghy, while his maternal grandparents lived in the British town of Castledawson. The boundaries, divisions and differences were geographical, physical, cultural, social, historical and political. Some of the physical boundaries were crossed with ease. But many of them were crossed only with great pain, and the existence and maintenance of borders and divisions has caused untold grief, destruction and death across the four green fields of Ireland.

CHAPTER

Mossbawn

9

Asked if the loss of Mossbawn was the loss of a cornerstone of his poetic imagination Heaney replied 'definitely'.[1] Heaneys moved from Mossbawn to the farm at 'The Wood' after the tragic death of four-year-old Christopher. Seamus was fourteen and away at school in Derry and, although he never really left Mossbawn, the move to 'The Wood' constituted another physical and symbolic break with youth and innocence.[2] He refers to 'those in-between years' and suggests that their out-of-placeness mattered as much for the life of his poetry as the in-placeness of his childhood. Even in Mossbawn he was beginning to feel out-of-place and the gap was ever-widening between himself and his immediate social environment. For the rest of his life he would continue to walk the sandy loaning from the main road down past the thatched house and on between hedges through fields and a small bog, past the house of reclusive Tom Tipping, past the railway line and river until he reached the small schoolhouse. But only in his poetic imagination. The move to 'The Wood' and to the comfort of a big two-storey house meant deserting the ground for the grid

THE NIGHT OF OTHER DAYS

and also coincided with the passing of a whole way of life. At the old homestead in Mossbawn the beech trees were cut down; the hedges between fields were taken out; the rail line was dismantled and removed; the thatched roof was replaced. All over the country the old sense of tillage and season and foliage was disappearing. He knew that once trees and hedges and ditches and thatch got stripped he was in a different world. Fortunately he has left a lasting record of that disappearing world and of a way of life that is gone, as in 'The Seed Cutters' (N.1975), a poem dedicated to Mary Heaney.

The cutters kneel in a half-circle as they work. 'O calendar customs! Under the broom/Yellowing over them, compose the frieze/With all of us there, our anonymities'. The seed-cutters represent the poet's recognition of a way of life now gone, the immemorial nature of the work done on the family farm and the crafts which he is intent on remembering and perpetuating in language.[3] Even the word 'broom' is significant. Broom, gorse or 'whin' refers to a tough plant which even survives fire and represents 'the emblematic inheritor of values attached to the history of a specific landscape'. Because the figures are anonymous the voice of the poet will anonymous too. He makes himself an anthropologist of his native culture and testifies, in each poem, to his profound attachment to the practice he describes while not concealing his own detachment from rural life.[4] In Vendler's words 'He erects a monument to anonymous labourers who will be forgotten, whose tools will be in museums. He describes a life he does not and could not want to follow but recognises it as forever part of his inner landscape'.

In the early volumes of his poetry he commemorates the crafts and trades which were dying out. He describes the work of thatchers, blacksmiths, water-diviners, threshers, turf-cutters, ploughmen with horses, churners, hewers of wood and drawers of water and in the process shows his sensuous and evocative power in rendering the places, objects and activities of his childhood (Elmer Anderson). In describing them so beautifully Heaney demonstrates not only his own craft, but his poetic technique, and his ability to celebrate and dignify the local or parochial.

The first two books, (DN and DD) are based on his childhood and youth in rural Derry. The language reconstitutes the physical world and like a block of ice on a hot stove the words dissolve into images which melt and merge. We seem to be told nothing but we see and hear everything.[5] Words enter almost the sense of touch 'Vowels ploughed into other, opened ground,/Each verse returning like the plough turned round' (Glanmore Sonnets, FW 1979). His words bind individuals to his own people and to their history. In many of his poems the words do not imitate the action, they are the action and they fasten lines to the page and to the ear as when the bird sings very close to the music of what happens…'in language that can still knock language sideways' (in memory of Ted Hughes, EL 2001).

In his early poems he concerned himself with the 'parochial' because like Kavanagh he came to believe that the local and the ordinary were ultimately concerned with fundamentals and the universal. Professor Christopher Hicks described Seamus Heaney as 'the poet of muddy-booted blackberry-picking' while noting the subtlety and delicacy of his language, his use of myth, and the closeness with which he observed life. Elmer Andrews points out that it is a mistake to see Heaney as rural sturdy and domestic, with his feet planted in Irish mud. He is instead an ornamentalist, a word collector, a connoisseur of fine language and he has no hesitation in giving to humble everyday parochial farm activities the dignity they deserve.

In October 1974, Seamus Heaney delivered a lecture to The Royal Society of Literature which is reprinted as 'Feeling into Words' in Finders Keepers[6] (FK, 2002). He talked about the Water Diviner as a figure who connects man with nature and the

THE NIGHT OF OTHER DAYS

universe. Heaney also nominates him as a figure who represents pure technique. The diviner resembles the poet in his function of making contact with what lies hidden, and 'in his ability to make palpable what was sensed or raised.' 'Technique is what allows that first stirring of the mind round a word or an image or a memory to grow towards articulation...Technique ensures that the first gleam attains its proper effulgence.' Robert Frost said that a poem begins as a lump in the throat which finds the thought and the thought then finds the words. Each poem is a stepping stone and the confirmation required before proceeding to the next poem. As in the case of the diviner the poet is in search of what is hidden. The diviner searches for the pluck of water. Holding a forked hazel in his hand he circles an area and when the hazel jerks the pluck of hidden water comes 'sharp as a sting'. Water broadcasts its stations through the arm of the diviner. To an extent the diviner is passive. He is the conduit through which the water broadcasts its secret stations. The poet and the diviner are both searching for what is hidden but they possess a gift which is theirs alone. Bystanders can circle with the hazel stick but only when the diviner grips their wrists will the hazel stir.

The poems 'Helicon', 'Digging' and 'The Diviner' take the poet to the heart of the mystery. The moment of putting words on 'a lump in the throat' is the moment 'when your mind seems to implode and words and images rush of their own accord into the vortex'. Such a moment occurred one night after Seamus went to bed. The following morning it was as if the words wrote themselves: 'We have no prairies/To slice a big sun at evening-'... the first words of the poem 'Bogland'' and the last words in 'Door Into The Dark'. The hazel in the poet's sub-conscious had stirred and the pluck of creativity was as sharp as a sting.

The Diviner is just one of the many people featured in Heaney's poetry, both early and late. One of the earliest and most menacing is 'Docker'.[7] 'There, in the corner, staring at his drink'

HUGH MULROONEY

he cuts a menacing figure with plated forehead and sledgehead jaw. He is a foreman and it follows, in the Northern Ireland of 1966, that he is Protestant in religion and Unionist in politics. The only round collar he tolerates is the white collar on his pint of Guinness porter. He is in a position of authority and accustomed to silence and an armchair. 'That fist would drop a hammer on a Catholic... Tonight the wife and children will be quiet/At slammed door and smoker's cough in the hall'. There is a sense of foreboding in this poem and a hint of dark undercurrents. There may be dark days ahead. The Docker is a menacing figure in the city of Belfast. Perhaps he represents a future full of menace and fear. Time will tell. This is the voice of a Northern Irish Catholic voicing the poet's first attempt to face a Northern Ireland problem. Here the poet expresses a depth of feeling which is imaginatively spoken with a kind of tragic economy. The Docker is in sharp contrast to the kindly, friendly characters of Mossbawn, most of whom now belong to a bye-gone age.

One such character in 'Wintering Out' (WO 1972) is 'Servant Boy'.

'He is wintering out/the back-end of a bad year...a jobber among shadows'. His name was Ned Thompson. The house he lived in had a clay floor and clay walls. A throw-back to the Hiring Fairs, which survived in some places in Northern Ireland until the early years of the twentieth century, he came to Heaney's once or twice a week. He was at home in their kitchen and from him Seamus learned a great deal about Ned's different masters and the way the hired servant was treated. Along with 'The Last Mummer' the servant boy represents a minority who resent their station in life, are seething with anger at their inferior status but will soon walk tall behind banners declaring their claims. For now the servant boy will serve the 'little barons'. He will bear fodder for the animals and carry warm eggs into the kitchen. His response to his situation will be to work hard and keep patience and counsel, for now. And

THE NIGHT OF OTHER DAYS

so too with the last mummer who beats at the gate and throws a stone onto the roof of 'the little barons'. Both are aware of the need to break out of the consensus that Ulster is 'a good wee place'. While they acknowledged the lostness and unhappiness of their place and home[8], Heaney bedded them in the locale and setting of Mossbawn, and they are included in the population of local folk who lived, worked and visited.

In 2006 Heaney published 'District and Circle' (DAC) and in it he included 'The Lagan Road', one of three pieces of 'found prose'. The Lagan Road is the location of many childhood memories and the home of many childhood friends and characters. Ginger-haired Philomena McNicholl brought him down this road hand-in-hand on his first day at school. 'Ginger hair, freckled face, green gymfrock – a fey if ever there was one'. From a distance of a quarter of a mile they heard the children at play and the little boy, on reaching the Nissen huts which had replaced the original school, felt lost and homesick, rather like Saint Colmcille, banished to the lonely Isle of Iona; rather like the day his parents walked down the avenue of St. Columbs College and he was left alone... 'Towards Ireland a grey eye/ Will look back but not see/ever again/ The men of Ireland or her women' (Fil suil nglais HC, 2010,).

This was the road where he would encounter the tinkers, a peripatetic family group, hawking their wares and their craftsmanship around Ireland, tin-smiths, white-smiths, pony keepers, 'begging with all the stamina of a cantor. We called them gypsies but they were properly another race'. And away beyond the birches and hedges and across the marsh they would see smoke rising from a hidden chimney. Mystery man, Tom Tipping lived there. They never saw him but sometimes would hear unexpected scuttlings in the hedge. Annie Devlin would come down this road to fill a bucket of water at Heaney's pump. And here in his house of one room with its one chimney and its settle bed was Harry Boyle's barber shop, where Seamus would be lifted onto the upper deck of a chair and the dog would sleep through the drift of falling hair circling his nose.

Rosie Keenan was a much-loved neighbour. She was 'the one who first made time and space in our lives for art'. Rosie was blind and spent many hours at the piano. Being with her 'was intimate and helpful, like a cure You didn't notice happening'...Her hands were active and her eyes were full/of open darkness and a watery shine...she was a sweet-voiced withdrawn musician and when Seamus read his poem to her she said she saw the sky at the bottom of 'Keenan's Well'.

In 'The Spirit Level' (SL 1996), Heaney introduced two characters. Claire O Reilly used her granny's crook-necked stick to snare the ripest blackberries, fearless on the railway line as the train tore past with the stoker yelling 'like a balked king from his iron chariot'.

And then there was Jim of the hanging jaw. Jim would circle Patrick Heaney's car inspecting the many ashplants, blackthorns and drover's canes which were piled on the back seat, 'hands held up to both sides of his face, peering and groaning'. Sometimes the sticks were ranged against the front bumper to facilitate closer inspection. Having selected his favourite 'He'd run and crow, stooped forward, with his right elbow stuck out, and the stick held horizontal to the ground, angled across in front of him'.

'The Summer of Lost Rachel', (HL,1987), recalls a wet summer and a road accident. Her white face gashed, she was laid out in white and 'every merciful register inside us yearned to turn the film back', to straighten the twisted spokes, to clean away the awful skid-marks. But no: 'Let the downpours flood/Our memory's riverbed' and let the life you might have led waver and tug like the soft-plumed waterweed.

The community of Mossbawn was mixed. The farm lands at 'The Wood' and at Mossbawn marched (bordered) protestant farms owned by Johnny Junkin (of 'The Other Side', who referred

THE NIGHT OF OTHER DAYS

to the Heaney land as 'poor as Lazarus'), The McIntyres and The Sands. Heaney's house was happily open to all neighbours and until their last Protestant neighbour, Billy Steele, died visiting continued without prejudice.

There were various factors at work. Patrick's work as cattle jobber gave him a 'trans sectarian licence to roam'; there was the natural grace in the Heaney and McCann connections; and old friendships between neighbouring families for generations. Some people, orange-order bigots and B-Specials for example, were beyond the pale and would be avoided not only during the July triumphalist marching season, but all year round. But, as Heaney expressed it, if you were friends with people you conceded their rights to their affiliations. So the young Heaneys would go to the end of their lane to wave at Alan and George Evans as they marched past under their Unionist Banner. However, within the household, the family were unable to face the realities of sectarianism. 'For you and yours and mine fought shy/ spoke an old language of conspiritors/and could not crack the whip or seize the day'[9]

There was mutual respect, and the Junkins, the Steeles, the McIntyres and the Mulhollands 'had more than enough inner freedom and confidence to retain friendships and dignity in the face of the overall tension and hurt felt by everybody'.

It is easy to appreciate the humour in the presentation of a rosary beads to Patrick Heaney by two Protestant neighbours who had returned from the war and the defence of The British Empire! And there is the whimsical view of the Lagans Road where the poet lying on the bracken hillside observes Edward Thomas in his khaki tunic, 'Demobbed, 'not much changed', sandy moustached and freckled/ From being, they said, with Monty in the desert'.

A contrasting figure is that of a neighbour, Mr Dickson. He saw the last cavalry charge of the war and got the first gas. He walks with a limp. His real fear is gangrene. He awakes 'with his hand to the scar' and to the 'scatter of maggots, busy in the trench of his wound'.[10]

Those early poems, in particular those of the first two volumes, are concerned with the relationship between the poet and his first community. There are many affectionate family memories 'registering warmth, tenderly respectful recall'.[11] Here is Anahorish, his place of clear water, the warmth and security of the family kitchen and the after-image of lamps swung through the yards on winter evenings. But there is also a note of distress, regret and guilt, as he describes a dying world which is being overwhelmed by automation, progress and change. That world is now gone but Heaney has left a lasting record of its workings, its workers and their labours.

He has recorded the work of three visiting craftsmen, the water diviner, described earlier, the plasterer and the thatcher. The plasterer, on his ladder, skimmed the gable of the house and wrote the name 'Heaney' with his trowel point, 'letter by strange letter' to the delight of the little boy.[12] The hand that held the trowel of the brick-layer was stained damson. 'Damson as omen… Is weeping with the held-at-arm's-length dead/From everywhere and nowhere, here and now'. Unhealed ghosts with their tongues out for a lick of blood are crowding up his ladder. But the stain on his knuckles is the stain of damson jam and he will send them home to taste from the simmering pot.[13]

The thatcher was a respected figure. He arrived on his bicycle with a light ladder and a bag of knives. He inspected and tested sheaves of lashed wheat-straw and bundles of hazel and willow rods. Then, at what seemed a leisurely pace, he fixed the ladder, honed his blades, climbed onto the roof and spent days shaving, snipping and pinning down and 'left them gaping at his Midas touch'.[14]

The blacksmith, Barney Devlin, hammered twelve blows on the anvil to ring in the millennium. His nephew heard it in

THE NIGHT OF OTHER DAYS

Edmonton, Alberta. The cellular phone had been held high as a horse's ear and the ringing notes had spanned the Atlantic. All this reminded the poet of an ancient Gaelic poem which he translated from Irish...'Shaped from the anvil and sharp from the file, the ring of it, sweet as a bell'.[16] The forge is used as an analogy for creativity and poetry and is also the title for Heaney's second volume 'Door Into The Dark'. Within the darkness of the forge the ringing of the hammer on the anvil is accompanied by the 'unpredictable fantail of sparks', akin to the exploding fireworks of poetic creativity.

The final poem in DN 'Personal Helicon' tells that he will 'set the darkness echoing' while the first poem in DD says 'All I know is a door into the dark'. Darkness echoes through his second volume (DD 1969) and the echoes continue over forty years later, 'The door was open and the house was dark' (HC 2010). He said that his choice of 'Death' and 'Dark' in the titles of his first two volumes reflected his view of The Dark as something one needs to traverse to reach a reliable light or reality...the dark night of the soul.

Related to the night of the soul is the origin of poetry, the darkness of the forge where the blacksmith shapes iron to his will at the altar of the anvil. Eliot identifies darkness as a positive element, 'the dark embryo in which poetry originates'. Heaney sees the dark as a place 'where the neophyte sees a continuity between the effect he wants to achieve in his writing and the noise he made when he used to shout down a well shaft to set the darkness echoing'. This too is the dark sky from which the stars shine over the city of Derry and the sky of 'no-stars' over the lane which leads to the house in Mossbawn. From the darkness of the night, of the well, of the embryo, of the forge, words will explode like sparks. In 'Saint Francis and the Birds', (DN 1966), Heaney describes the birds as being like a flock of words. The description could be that of the fantail of sparks in the forge as words 'wheeled back, whirred about his head,/Pirouetted on brothers' capes,/Danced on the wing, for sheer joy played/And sang, like images took flight.' So too the music of words in the poem 'Waterfall' in the same volume. 'The burn drowns steadily in its own downpour,/A helter-skelter of muslin and glass/That skids to a halt, crashing up suds.'

The blacksmith was Barney Devlin. He was born on December 26th in 1919. His obituary (Irish Times March 3rd 2016) tells us that 'his mother was a cousin of Heaney's grandmother'. Barney left school in his early teens and worked with his father in the forge, shoeing horses, making hoops for wheels 'and fashioning church gates and other iron work'. The forge was a meeting place for old and young and when Barney set up 'The Forge Players' in the 1980's the forge was their venue for practice. Pride of place on his living-room wall was an inscription from Seamus Heaney, "For Barney – old friend and good example of how to do good work and stay true." Barney died on Feb 18th 2016. He lived all of his long life within 100 yards of the house where he was born.

Visits to Mossbawn by the thatcher, plasterer and water diviner were rare and individual but once, each autumn, a group of neighbours, a 'meitheal', arrived for the annual threshing of the corn. Wheat and oats, sown in springtime, would have been cut and tied into large bundles or stooks. A tractor, pulling the threshing machine would have arrived in the corn field. Power to the machine was provided by a large belt running from the flywheel on the tractor to the large wheel which powered the shuddering, groaning threshing machine. Many hands were needed to feed the machine as it separated the corn from the chaff, fed the corn into large sacks and coughed out the straw. Men stood high on the platform, caught the stooks thrown up to them and fed the loosened stooks into the thresher. Men fed the supply line while others took away the bags of wheat and oats. Straw was carefully saved and chaff disposed of. All in a smooth efficient operation.

THE NIGHT OF OTHER DAYS

Threshing is described in his poem 'The Loose Box', (E.L.2001), and here Heaney presents a darker and more negative pastoral than those of his first three volumes. He had read the threshing scene in 'Tess of the D'Urbervilles' as a teenager. 'Raving machinery,/The thresher bucking sky, rut-shuddery, /A headless Trojan horse expelling straw...While the big slag and slew of the canvas belt/That would cut your head off if you didn't watch/ Flowed from the flywheel...

This is the scene Margaret walks into carrying tea and thick slices of bread, described in 'Wife's Tale' (DD,1969). She spreads her linen cloth on the ground and pours the tea.[17] 'When I had spread it all on linen cloth/Under the hedge, I called them over'. Her husband directed her to examine the harvested grain. She did so. Meanwhile they lay in a ring of their crusts and dregs. She gathered cups, folded the cloth and went. 'I'd come and he had shown me/So I belonged no further to the work'. This was 'The Wife's Tale'.

Most of the poems in Heaney's first three volumes 'are characterised by an exact evocativeness in the way they handled country themes and by his use of precise agricultural language. His early subjects were natural to one raised on a farm[18]. But Samuel Beckett in the 1930s and later others, like Anthony Cronin, saw images from a country background as 'a derogation of literary responsibility'. Indeed the young Heaney was of the same opinion until he read the work of Patrick Kavanagh.

Patrick Kavanagh was born in 1904, the son of a cobbler who farmed nine acres of grey Monaghan soil south of the border in the Republic of Ireland. For almost 35 years he followed in his father's footsteps. He left school aged thirteen. He read whatever books he could lay hands on and began to write. In 1939, he left Monaghan, walked to Dublin and devoted the rest of his life to writing. W.B.Yeats died that year and it was also the year of Seamus Heaney's birth.

HUGH MULROONEY

Kavanagh's poetry focused on Iniskeen, the rural parish in which he was born. In his writing he conveyed the reality of ordinary, and often conventionally ugly, rural images. He was breaking new ground. 'His intimate, closely focused images of country life were a radically new departure in Irish poetry, where the tradition of peasant romanticization was at least a century old'.[19] In 1936 he wrote the poem 'Iniskeen Road: July Evening' which dramatizes the poet's relationship to his parish. Focussed on the theme of community and communication, Kavanagh presents himself as a figure isolated socially and linguistically, unable to participate in the 'wink-and-elbow' humour of those attending the dance in Billy Brennan's barn and equally out of step with contemporary Irish poetry. In 'The Great Hunger' he paints images of country life which offer 'a shockingly honest and comprehensive portrayal of small-farm Ireland'. Here we meet the elderly Patrick Maguire, wifeless and childless, controlled by his mother...'wife and mother in one/when she died /The knuckle-bones were cutting the skin of her son's backside/and he was sixty five'. In her introduction to 'Selected Poems', Antoinette Quinn, editor, credits Kavanagh with liberating Anglo-Irish poetry from its role as agent of nationalism and cultural separatism. It needed to be freed from its obsession with history, mythology, folklore and the translation and adaptation of Irish language verse. Kavanagh, she says, wanted to find a historyless world, one that began 'this morning'. 'He wanted to celebrate the everydays of nature and the life of the street- to use the rhythms and idioms of contemporary vernacular speech.'

In his poem 'Shancoduff', Kavanagh wrote 'My black hills have never seen the sun rising,/Eternally they look north towards Armagh'. In the final poem 'Bogland', (D.D. 1969), Heaney wrote 'We have no prairies/To slice a big sun at evening-/ Everywhere the eye concedes to/ Encroaching horizon...'. Both poets are indicating that their early poems are rooted in the home place.

THE NIGHT OF OTHER DAYS

The places they describe are in their native countryside and their horizons are the horizons of their own consciousness.

Kavanagh gave us images of ourselves and made our subculture, the rural outback, a cultural resource for all of us. He brought us back to where we came from. In doing so he courageously broke with the established artistic representation of rural people and rural life as portrayed by J.M. Synge, Lady Gregory and W.B.Yeats. He placed the parish at the centre and gave to it the social and artistic value it deserved. He rejected provincialism. 'The provincial has no mind of its own; he does not trust what his eyes see until he has heard what the metropolis...has to say on any subject'.

In 1985 Seamus Heaney gave the opening address 'The Placeless Heaven: 'Another Look at Kavanagh', at 'Kavanagh's Yearly' in Carrickmacross, Co. Monaghan. He recalled that in 1939 his aunt Mary had planted a chestnut seed to mark the year of his birth. The tree grew out of its jam-jar, was replanted, and as it grew it became synonymous with the growing poet. Then, when the family left 'Mossbawn' for 'The Wood', the tree was cut down.

Not for the first time, he recalled the fact that when the tree was gone it was replaced in his mind with a luminous emptiness...a space he identified with. This new space, he said, was a transparent yet indigenous afterlife, a placeless heaven rather than a heavenly place.

Now, turning to Kavanagh, he likened his early poems to the chestnut tree and his later poems to the luminous emptiness. The early poems rooted in his home place; the later poems emanating from the luminous places and spaces within his mind. Years before when Heaney read Kavanagh's 'The Great Famine', in a book lent to him by Michael McLaverty, he realised that the details of his own rural life were worthy of a place in a poem or a book. He read Kavanagh's 'Spraying the Potatoes'; he met Patrick Maguire, 'a thick-witted farm labourer reeking of sour pig-meal and parish piety, somebody who gave me a way of writing about the local sub-culture' and he read the words 'Every old man I see/Reminds me of my father/When he had fallen in love with death/One time when sheaves were gathered.' Heaney saw Kavanagh as opting for a relaxed, casual stance, a momentary benediction of things 'common and banal'. As he expressed it in 'The Placeless Heaven' Kavanagh gave you permission to dwell without cultural anxiety among the usual landmarks of your life.' Heaney knew people like Patrick Maguire and was proud of that fact. Kavanagh was a country poet at home with his country subjects, a poet who linked small-farm life 'to the slim-volume world we (recently graduated scholars) were supposed to live in'. Kavanagh also cultivated ideas of national identity which drew away from the Anglo-Saxon literary vogue and he did not apologise for his fundamental Catholic mysticism.

Speaking to Dennis O'Driscoll, Heaney put it like this: 'Kavanagh walked into my ear like an old-style farmer walking a field. He had that kind of ignorant entitlement, his confidence contained a mixture of defiance and challenge. You were being told that you would never hit your stride if you didn't step your own ground, and you would never hit the right note if you didn't sound as thick as your own first speech'.

When Heaney read Kavanagh's 'Spraying the Potatoes'... 'And poet lost to potato-fields,/Remembering the lime and copper smell...he is not lost' or 'The axle-roll of a rut-locked cart/Broke the burnt stick of noon in two', he felt free to record his own memories of a small farm and of his own childhood.

One such very early memory was of a confrontation at the flax-dam. It is recorded in the second poem of his first volume (DN 1966), and the poem, like the title of the volume, describes the 'Death of a Naturalist'. It begins 'All year the flax-dam festered in the heart/Of the townland;'

The flax-dam was a feature of the countryside right across Northern Island at a time when linen of world-class was produced

THE NIGHT OF OTHER DAYS

there. Linen was exported across the globe and Northern Ireland linen graced the tables, beds and fashion-houses of the world. The production of linen united town and village, factory and farm across the country and Heaney's own for-bears worked in mills as close as those at Castledawson, the town where his mother's people lived.

In 'Irish Folk Ways', (now out-of-print), E. Estyn Evans describes the harvesting of flax[21]. 'When grown for fibre, flax is harvested after the pale blue flowers have fallen, but before the seed ripens, and because it is the stalk that is being harvested it is not cut, but pulled up by the roots.' It is then gathered into sheaves of three handfuls, twenty-two inches in diameter, and tied with two lengths of green rushes.

In the flax-dam, or lint-hole, stagnant bog-water has been warming for days. The sheaves are now placed upright in the dam. For seven to twelve days the sheaves (or 'beets') are weighted down with heavy sods to keep them under water. The beets are now retting or rotting. A foul smell pervades. 'Then the slimy, stinking beets are taken out of the dam and spread on the surface of a newly mown hayfield.' Further drying is achieved by standing the beets in cones that look like tents or skirts (gaits). The gaits are built into two-storey structures with hipped roofs. The weaver then takes the flax through various processes up to spinning and weaving...' This was a scene familiar to child Seamus, a scene long faded. Little flax is now grown in Northern Ireland and all processes are now mechanised.

There was a flax-dam near the house in Mossbawn. Its water continued to stench all year but particularly so when the flax was retting. 'Daily it sweltered in the punishing sun.' As the water 'gurgled delicately' bluebottles 'wove a strong gauze of sound around the smell'. Best of all, a warm thick slobber of frogspawn grew like clotted water in the shade of the banks. Each spring the delighted child would fill jampots of 'the jellied specks' from the flax-dam and put them on shelves and window sills at home and in school. Miss Walls, his teacher, told of how the bullfrog croaked and the mammy frog laid hundreds of eggs and this was frogspawn. The jellied specks would eventually burst into 'nimble-swimming tadpoles'. This was the age of innocence for the young naturalist.

Then one day the angry frogs invaded the flax-dam. Everywhere gross-bellied frogs were cocked on sods 'poised like mud-grenades,/their blunt heads farting...and I knew/That if I dipped my hand the spawn would clutch it.' This was the death of a naturalist. The guileless young boy had progressed from the stage of innocent exploration and discovery, from the stage of fosterage in beauty, to the stage of fosterage in fear. The cosy domesticity of Mossbawn and Anahorish is displaced forever.[22] 'The innocence of childhood is invaded by the violent outer world, and penetrated from within by the emergence of a darker daemonic self'. A hidden and unwelcome emergence is that of an adolescent's revulsion at his own sexuality. Bernard O'Donoghue says that in Heaney's work there is movement from self-discovery to self-consciousness and self-revelation. The 'death of the naturalist' is at the level of the local and is related to the psyche of the child. At the level of the literary there was movement too but to a much more profound extent, as in the course of his poetic life he advances from the familiar and strange to the material and mystical on to the political and poetic and ultimately to the prehistoric and modern.[23]

His encounter with the frogs marks his initiation into fear and this first experience of fear is to last a lifetime. 'Fear is the emotion that the muse thrives on. That's always there' he said to J.Heffenden. He felt real fear later, he tells us, when he wrote about the bog people. And 'Nolli Timere' were his last words to his beloved Marie.

The impulse of the child is to run away from fear. The adult learns to stand and stare. Frogs and rats represent what is liquid, slimey and untrustworthy. The child stares at them and other

THE NIGHT OF OTHER DAYS

creatures of the dark in utter horror. He is frightened by a sense of violence and violation. Yet it may be that in this same world of fear and darkness the growth of poetry begins. It may be that the 'fantail of sparks' comes from here? From the darkness of the forge inside 'Door into the Dark'.

Yeats said that it is in the quarrel with oneself that poetry begins and through which it finally endures. Heaney's quarrel began in childhood as he became aware of separations, of divisions and of boundaries. His poetry emerged from remembered experiences, from the dark centre of the imagination. He said 'I think this notion of the dark centre - the storehouse of insights and instincts, the hidden core of the self - is the foundation of what viewpoint I might articulate for myself as a poet'. The last lines in DN 'I rhyme/ To see myself, to set the darkness echoing' are echoed in the title of his second volume 'Door Into The Dark'. The neophyte sees a continuity between the effects he wants to achieve in his writing and the noise he made when he shouted down a well-shaft 'to set the darkness echoing'. The Door gives entry to the darkness of the forge. The blacksmith works at the anvil which is presented as an altar. Here in the interior darkness is the locus of the creativity, manifest in the 'fantail of sparks'.

The dark and darkness have many meanings in Heaney's work. He intends to see himself, to set the darkness echoing; he intends to explore the buried life of his own feeling. He will advance through the door out of the darkness. He will also explore the dark of Ireland's history and pre-history and he will dig into the darkness of Irish bog and into Irish soil and river-bed. He will encounter the eel and the rat but he will no longer have fear of them. He will fish, dig, probe and peer into the secret and mystery of his own being, his origins, his ancestry and his place in the cosmos.

The fear expressed in DN and in DD lingers, but he gradually gains the courage to explore more deeply into his subconscious mind, into the soil, into the past. As his search continues he conquers his fear of darkness as he finds its source. Beyond the darkness of the soul and of the dark wood he will seek and arrive, in his own words, 'at some kind of reliable light or sight of reality'.

In probing the dark he probes the mystery of fecundity, of sexuality, of birth and of life. He tells us that T.S.Eliot spoke of the dark embryo within the poet which is born as a poem. Indeed the final poem in DD, 'Bogland', is the birth of a major sequence of poems. Another sequence, is found in W.O. where a number of poems concern birth and the role of woman.

Within the confines of the farm at Mossbawn there were places to fear. One such was The Barn. In 'A Poet's Childhood' Heaney wrote 'I was always afraid in its dark heat that something was going to jump out of its corners — a rat, an owl, anything. And sometimes at night I'd be afraid too, if I remembered that place'. In the barn there were dark corners, cobwebs, mouse-grey floors, bats, and this was where 'The two-lugged sacks moved in like great blind rats'.

The poem 'The Early Purges' begins 'I was six when I first saw kittens drown'. He tells that 'the scraggy wee shits' were drowned in a bucket by Dan Taggart. 'Suddenly frightened, for days I sadly hung /Round the yard'. Although he shortly forgot his fear, 'the fear came back' when Dan trapped big rats, snared rabbits, shot crows or pulled the necks of old hens. But, in time, false sentiments were displaced by reality. On well-run farms pests have to be kept down, he observed.

One of his earliest fears was of rats. His instinct was to run from them. Then one day he overcame his fear. Walking along the embankment path he saw a rat slimming out of the water. Then another nimbling up the far bank. His throat sickened in a cold sweat and he turned to run. But stopped, turned and stared the rat in direct confrontation. The rat retreated up a pipe. The child stared after him and walked calmly across the bridge. This surely was 'An Advancement of Learning', (DN).

THE NIGHT OF OTHER DAYS

He learned too of disappointment. When the blackberries were ripe all the able-bodied children, armed with cans, jars, tins and pots went in search of the bountiful harvest. A bath-tub, in the barn, filled with the juicy fruit. But a rat-grey fungus grew on top and the juice was stinking. All the lovely canfuls smelt of rot. 'I always felt like crying. It wasn't fair'. The words of a cruelly disappointed child.

Fear and foreboding lie at the heart of later poems like the poem 'Dream' 1969 (DD) and poems written during the years of 'The Troubles'. He dreamt that he was hacking down a stalk with a hand-forged billhook. He awakened to the horror of his billhook sunk into a man's head. This poem anticipates his translation from Dante's Inferno, 'Ugolino', published in 'Field Work' (FW,1979) and 'Veteran's Dream' (WO 1972), referred to earlier.

Whether he writes of childhood delights or childhood fears, people places or activities, irrespective of the subject matter, the reader of Heaney's work is immediately impressed and delighted by the beauty and appropriateness of his language which makes his poetry totally accessible. He can re-create the actual physical world through the sensuality of his language, through his use of mimetry and through the presentation of simple visual images. His poetry has a re-assuring, homely and unassuming feel to it. It is never obscure, pedantic or affected. There is strength and pride in his presentation of a rural way of life and its attendant crafts and practises. Yet what appears to be simple and effortless is much more as "in a poem, words, phrases, cadences and images are linked into systems of affect and signification". In his conversations with his mother he is humble and sensitive. In describing the expertise of his father as he ploughs and digs, the poet endeavours to raise physical activity to the level of poetry, in particular through his use of the imagery of digging. The poems in his first three volumes have been described as 'Anonymities'.[24] Most of the sentiments could be voiced by any child who grew up on a farm. He records the work of anonymous labourers who are forgotten. Their tools are in museums and their work described by historians: 'The Seed Cutters', the thatchers, the flax-harvesters and the threshers. 'O calendar customs! Under the broom/ Yellowing over them, compose the frieze/ With all of us there, our anonymities'. (North,1975).

In the first volumes, symbolic figures like these 'stand for the poet's recognition of the immemorial nature of the work done on the family farm'.[25] And the language shows his sensuous and evocative power 'in rendering the places objects and processes of his County Derry childhood'.[26]

The fact that Heaney's poems were so available, and so easily read and understood, led one Northern Ireland Protestant politician to suggest that Heaney could be the universal voice of a socially united people. Heaney resented the notion that he could ever be the voice of the arrogant, intolerant and repressive Protestant and Unionist ruling class. He resented the notion that he would be considered the voice of the 'other side'. In fact he used the words 'whatever you say, say nothing' to indicate a deep social divide right across Northern Ireland society.

The publication of his first three volumes led to recognition of his stature. Professor Christopher Ricks wrote of Seamus Heaney as 'the poet of muddy-booted blackberry-picking'. In his review titled 'Lasting Things' he noted Heaney's concern for skills like thatching and salmon-fishing; grievances and injustices like those whose seepage still stained Irish living; the seasons and the hours; the farm-lunch in the fields, the scene Horatian...

Heaney recognised, with Kavanagh, that genuinely parochial poetry was universal because it dealt with fundamentals. Irish farming had been translated into poetry by Kavanagh[27] and Heaney brought it to perfection. His art appealed to both intelligence and emotion, had harmony and beauty which, through the force of his visual imagery, it recorded and illuminated in fulsome measure. And, because his poetry was rooted in personal rural experience,

THE NIGHT OF OTHER DAYS

he could speak for and celebrate silent vanishing rural toil and the language and traditions of craftsmen and labourers no longer living.

He concerned himself with the proper relationship between a poet and his first community even if this brought its own difficulties. From the very beginning he wondered about the possible inferiority of poetry to farming. He also knew that in recording his admiration for rural labour and craft he was recording his rejection of this way of life; as when he noted the reversal of role in the father/son relationship with guilt and regret. He was raised between the bog and the demesne but his place was in neither. His education opened a gap. His poetry-writing took him further. And his use of words and language opened yet another area of concern and worry because words and language are not neutral. They contain depth-charges of meaning and emotion.

In 1992 Heaney noted[28] 'Almost thirty years ago I wrote "my father wrought with a horse-plough" because 'wrought' was still in common use'. Then he had second thoughts and used the word 'worked'. He went on to say that once you think twice about a local language usage you have been displaced from it...you have been translated from the land of the unselfconsciousness to the suburbs of the 'mot juste'. You have moved from the hearth-speech, from the first idiom of a hermetically-sealed, univocal home place, to acquired language. So too with poems. Heaney's poems are primarily not about place, they are about transit. Language is not the representation of a static identity, self, home, nation. Language 'perpetually constructs and deconstructs our given notions of identity'.[29]

In his Beckman Lecture, (Berkeley 1976), Heaney talked of the origins of English speech and its relevance to writers in English who are not English born. He was speaking about himself and about Hughes and Hill and Larkin. He traced the origins of the English of 'here and now' to the English of 'there and then'. From Anglo-Saxon through Anglo-Romanesque, through Norman and Renaissance he traces the influence of Latin, middle-English, French, the influence of Chaucer and Shakespeare and Tyndale down to Robert Burns. There are cultural depth-charges latent in certain words and rhythms, words that delight not just the ear 'but the whole backward and abysm of mind and body'. Poets of a mother-culture other than English, but writing in English, are aware of words not just as articulate noise but as symptoms of human history, memory and attachments. And these writers are afflicted with a sense of history which can be traced back not only to the main channels of language but back to the roots of their distinct dialect. Ted Hughes said in 1971 interview published in London Magazine, 'Whatever other speech you grow into, presumably your dialect stays alive in a sort of inner freedom… it's your childhood self, there inside the dialect and that is possibly your real self or the core of it…Without it I doubt if I would ever have written verse'.

In his lecture 'Through-Other Places, Through-Other Times', Heaney writes "…any account of the Irish poet and Britain must get past politics and into poetry itself…A precis of the content…takes no account of the literary echoes and illusions which can be fundamental to its poetic energy. In a poem, words, phrases, cadences and images are linked in to systems of affect and signification which elude the precis maker."

The verse of Seamus Heaney, written in the language of his home and his origin, combines 'a colloquial prose readiness with poetic breadth, a ritual intensity of music with clear direct feeling, and yet in the end is nothing but casual speech', (Heaney's description of the poetry of Hughes). When Heaney encountered the words "Wee sleeket, cowran, tim'rous beastie", he felt liberated from 'his best verbal behaviour', felt that the emotional and cultural ground had been taken over thus 'dispossessing the rights of written standard English and offering asylum to all vernacular comers'. Burn's language belonged to Scottish and English speech

THE NIGHT OF OTHER DAYS

and it had a place in the language of Heaney's youth. Beast was beastie and Hugh was Hughie! He tells us that in the first encounter with poetry, in school, 'we expected that the language on the written page would take us out of our unofficial speaking selves and transport us to a land of formal words where we would have to be constantly on our best behaviour...Hail to thee blyth spirit!' The language Seamus spoke as he grew up had trace elements of Elizabethan English; English as spoken in his home; the English of poetry and prose as taught in school and through literature; and in addition, the dialect of Lowland Scots. And there were elements of Irish, which he studied in St Columb's as part of the exam curriculum. Irish had been lost as a universally-spoken language but was much-loved by the poet. So the very language used by the poet contained within itself cultural depth-charges latent in certain words and rhythms. He well knew that words are not neutral and will convey stored and hidden meaning. Speaking of an older Ulster poet, W.R.Rodgers, Heaney referred to the 'triangulation of understanding' between London, Loughall and the Lowlands, '...in that three-sided map of his inner being that he provided with its three cardinal points, in all of that there is something analogous to the triple heritage of Irish, Scottish and English traditions that compound and complicate the cultural and political life of contemporary Ulster.'

An added dimension is the fact that, whereas the goal of words in poetry is to grow up to the contents, there is a problem in that much of the psychic energy felt by the poet is lost in the attempt to vocalise it. Putting feelings into words can lead to an emasculation of the strength of the emotion. Language can fail because it is more than a medium of expression. It can be a badge of identity and within its word-hoard, it stores an age un-named.

Heaney forged a link between place-names, identity and language. He linked the geographical country to the country of the mind in a marriage that 'constitutes the sense of place in its richest possible manifestation'. There are a number of lush sentimental poems: 'Anahorish', 'Broagh', 'Toome' and 'A New Song' in 'Wintering Out' (WO,1972). 'Broagh' brings together three languages, Irish, Elizabethan English and Ulster Scots. The place names roll around on the tongue and add a further dimension to language. Most place-names have been replaced by phonic rendering which bears no relationship to their original Irish meaning. But for those who trouble to look, place-names can yield a bounteous harvest.

The question of identity was to become very serious and significant in Northern Ireland. The reality of his own situation was brought home to him one night on Malone Road in Belfast 'some time in 1970'. He went out late one night to the local fish and chip shop. The new assistant there recognised him...'Aren't you the Irish poet? "Not at all dear", said the owner, "He's like the rest of us, a British subject living in Ulster." And Heaney was afraid to contradict her. His silence reflected his fear. 'Like all Northern nationalists of my generation, I accumulated silent things within me whenever incidents like the one in the chip shop occurred.' This was the silence of his ancestry, of his contemporaries, of the silent craftsmen who came to Mossbawn or the members of his Catholic community who said nothing. 'I myself hesitated to face the full force of the sectarian circumstances.'

This expressed itself later when Heaney found his poetry included in an *Anthology of English Poetry*. 'My passport's green' he protested. Although he was writing in English he totally rejected the notion that he was an English writer. He was Irish. An Irish poet writing in English, using the dialect which was rooted in his own history and heritage.

'Anthology of English Poetry', edited by Blake Morrison and Andrew Motion *was* published in 1982 and poems by Seamus Heaney were included. He published an 'Open Letter' which stated his position. He established his identity as an Irishman

THE NIGHT OF OTHER DAYS

writing in English and this did not detract from the fact that he was in the words of Elmer Andrews, 'At present the one undoubtedly major poet in the English-speaking world'.

At that time Heaney was living in The Irish Republic. He left Northern Ireland in 1972 and never returned. Heaney linked his own 'out-of-placeness' to the work of the Irish poet Francis Ledwidge who left his home near Drogheda to join the British army in 1914 and went to war. Home on sick-leave, Ledwidge wrote to Lord Dunsany expressing his ardent English patriotism. But, to his horror, the Rising of 1916 led to the execution of Thomas MacDonagh, Joseph Mary Plunkett and the other leaders. Heaney recognised the dilemma and he wrote 'It's one thing to find yourself in a British anthology at the time of an Ulster crisis, but it is something else to find yourself in the British army at the time of an Irish rebellion'. Heaney referred to his Ledwidge syndrome, where a man is divided against himself. Francis Ledwidge had joined up at the time when Irish Home Rule was on the books at Westminster. He was proud of the British uniform and committed to fight for small nations. But in 1916 an armed rebellion broke out in Dublin. Home Rule was rejected by the rebels who stated their claim to complete freedom for all Ireland. The leaders of the rebellion were executed and this shocked the young poet, Ledwidge, who wrote in appreciation of Thomas MacDonagh: "He shall not hear the bittern cry/In the wild sky where he is lain,/ Nor voices of the sweeter birds/Above the wailing of the rain." In Heaney's words, Ledwidge's Irish patriotism was revealing itself at a poetic and phonetic level. And behind his words was the same dilemma which Wordsworth had encountered when the idealism of The French Revolution was followed by the Anglo-French war. The dilemma of a mind where idealism and reality are conflicted.

The 1916 Rising had a lasting effect on all of Ireland especially as it affected Ulster. The fiftieth anniversary of 1916 was marked in 1966 at the time when Seamus Heaney was writing his first verses and within three short years Ulster was convulsed. Questions of identity, alienation, loyalty and poetic integrity were about to be confronted and primitive passions were about to be unleashed. For Heaney the alienation felt on the domestic and home front was now reinforced by turmoil, violence and hatred on a national scale.

CHAPTER

Earthmother

10

Although most poems in Heaney's first three volumes are locally-based, a number of them lead out of Mossbawn towards the wider world and towards confrontation with issues of major import. This applies to the opening poem in his first book ('Digging') and to the last poem in his second ('Bogland'). The focus shifts from the small world of a child to the wider world of politics, religion, social division violence and hatred. The language becomes more charged, the emotion more intense and the subject-matter more controversial and profound.

His most famous poem 'Digging' describes his admiration for the skill of his father as he rooted out tall tops to expose the new potatoes. But the poem is about more than his father… 'the curt cuts of an edge/Through living roots awaken in my head'. The questions raised are concerned with the relationship between father and son, between poet and his first community, between the external and the internal, between nature and mind, between experience and language. Here is the emergence of displacement, uncertainty of identity and the tension between the living roots in the soil and the thoughts which arise in the poet's head. The father/son relationship has been explored in a narrow context in an earlier chapter. Now seen in a wider context, this poem is about blood, kinship, ancestry, roots, growing up and away and the need to reconcile the boy and the poet.[1]

The father may be simply digging potatoes. But the potato is not just a vegetable. It is an emblem for the suffering of the Irish nation. The potato lies deep in the soil of Irish tragedy. History says that for more than fifty years before the disastrous Famine of 1845 the rapidly expanding population of Ireland was entirely dependent on the potato. Estyn Evans, in his book 'Irish Folk Ways' says that each member of an Irish family would have eaten, on average, eight pounds of potatoes per day. Then the killer fungus, 'phytophthora infestans' struck in the autumn of 1845. The resulting famine 'left the Irish psyche permanently scarred'... one million died and one and a half million emigrated. The spirit of the people was broken, the Irish language went into decline and all the while sufficient food was produced in Ireland, but only for export to England.

Heaney wrote 'At a Potato Digging' (DN 1966). The poem describes a mechanised harvesting of the potato long after the Famine. The digging machine is followed by a 'swarm' of labourers picking the tubers into wicker creels to be piled in pits. The earth smells good and the potatoes are 'white as cream', life-sustaining, wholesome and nourishing. Not so in 1845 when higgledy skeletons 'wolfed the blighted root and died'. That year the new potatoes putrefied in pits; stinking potatoes fouled the land; 'Mouths tightened in, eyes died hard, faces chilled to a plucked bird'. To this day 'where potato diggers are you still smell the running sore'. And 'gaunt ones in their shirtsleeves' who stooped and dug, still haunt the fields, 'apparitions now', and territorial too, as they wonder how far the country of the shades has been pushed back and how long the lark has stopped outside these fields[2].

THE NIGHT OF OTHER DAYS

Heaney wrote of 'The Eliza' as it sailed into Westport harbour and how it encountered a small boat carrying six dying men 'with gaping mouths and eyes bursting the sockets like spring onions in a drill'. How they begged for food and how the Eliza sailed away and left them to die, although there was plenty of flour and beef on board the ship. The captain was obeying the advice from Whitehall, 'Let natives prosper by their own exertions' (DN) 1966.

In those two public poems the poet is lamenting 'the matter of Ireland' which will increasingly claim his attention. The voice is the reflective voice of one who has reclaimed his history and will give voice to it. For the rest of his career Heaney will be involved in this reclamation, digging downwards and inwards as 'he stumbles on mines and myths left over from previous conflicts, which can't be defused by literary devices '.

He wrote 'Requiem for the Croppies' to mark the 50th anniversary of the 1916 rising and it was published in 1969, (DD). The croppies, who had their hair cropped in the manner of French peasants, fought in the rising of 1798 when a poorly armed and savagely repressed Irish population took on the might of the British Empire. They were mown down in their thousands by the cavalry as they 'shook their scythes at cannon'. They were buried without shroud or coffin, their pockets full of barley 'And in August the barley grew up out of the grave'. Heaney saw the 1916 Rising as a harvesting of the seeds of 1798. The publication of the poem coincided with the outbreak of violence which would pulverise Northern Ireland for over thirty years. This violence had an effect on his poetry: 'From that moment the problems of poetry moved from being simply a matter of achieving the satisfactory verbal icon to being a search for images adequate to our predicament'.[3]

In speaking of images and symbols adequate to our predicament he says he did not mean liberal lamentation that citizens should feel compelled to murder one another or fight over the labels of 'Irish' or 'British'. He meant a poetry that would encompass perspectives of a humane reason while at the same time granting 'the religious intensity of the violence its deplorable authenticity and complexity'.

Of the many anonymous voices used by Heaney none is more provocative than that of the buried bodies in the bogs of Ireland and Denmark, and none more varied than the voices of the murdered victims of violence in Northern Ireland. In Part two of 'Wintering Out', Heaney's voice is increasingly a public voice as his attention is forced onto 'The Question of Ireland'. Language now accepts an additional burden as it tries to transmit the poet's emotions in the face of indescribable horror. For language is not merely a transparent medium. Language is self-generating, productive, and it exceeds us as individuals. Heaney believed that we surrender to language rather than master it, that language works through the medium of the author, rather than the author working through the language.

In his early work language is used not to explain but to evoke. Images are used rather than argument. Words convey textures... slimey, scaly, jaggy. The language of DN and DD is sensuous rich and direct as he describes potatoes, turf, blackberries, butter. Sound is used: 'the squelch and slap of soggy peat', 'the pat and slap of small spades on wet lumps', what Philip Hobsbaum called 'the snap-crackle and pop of Heaneyspeak'. But words can also convey threat, danger and revulsion.

Vendler[4] observed that his language is as sensuous as mud and mud was an obsession both in his life and in his language. The very texture of his language is mud-like and the mud is also that of his sub-conscious. There is mud on the bed of the river and here the eel inserts itself in sexual imagery. There is mud at the bottom of wells where sometimes the image of one's face is distorted by the slithering of a rat. The turf in the bog is mud-like and here may be buried the victims of ancient violence.

THE NIGHT OF OTHER DAYS

In 'The Tollund Man' there is a tender description which carries the man's body from a bog-photograph into language (W.O,1972). Heaney will someday go to Aarhus to see his peat-brown head, to stand a long time and recall how the goddess tightened her torc on him and opened her fen. Heaney will risk blasphemy in consecrating the holy ground in Denmark and he will experience hostility when he links the Tollund Man with the naked savagery of the slaughter of four brothers in Northern Ireland (back in 1922). There in Jutland the poet will feel lost unhappy and at home, as he has in Mossbawn. This poem is a forerunner to the controversial connection which Heaney will forge between the sacrificial killings in pre-historic Denmark and the sectarian murders in Northern Ireland.

He also forges connections and meaning between the sound and etymology of place-names and the language and history of their origin. In so doing he advances the idea that the sounds of words could be matter as well as means for poetry. Following the colonisation of Ulster by English and Scottish settlers place names were anglicised. 'Doire', the Irish word for 'oak' became 'Derry' with the loss of any or all meaning. As time went on the Irish language died out in Ulster and only survived in small pockets. The death of a language is one of the most grievous blows that can be inflicted on national identity. From the time of the Norman conquest and more particularly the 17th century plantations, through to the implementation of The Act of Union and the Ordinance Survey of 1824, a central aim of English policy in Ireland was the destruction of Irish culture, language and identity. The Famine was the final blow.

So, when Heaney faced the reality of Northern Ireland, with the outbreak of violence in the late 1960s, he had to find images of suffering, endurance and resistance which would be adequate to the situation. He had to evoke fresh images to present a new political, historical and linguistic complexity. This he first attempted in a number of poems in his third volume, (WO. 1972). He also dealt with the question in his 'Lecture ,Royal Society of Literature' (FK, "Feeling into Words"). In his poems he used an oblique method to represent the increasing chaos, the violence, repression, exploitation and betrayal he saw all around him. From now on voice and language would have to be employed with increasing sensitivity and complexity.

Co-incidentally there was an increased mastery of his own art at this time. He described to Dennis O'Driscoll, (Stepping Stones P147), a creative surge in one week in May 1969. In that week he wrote about forty pieces. It was a visitation, an onset and as such, powerfully confirming. 'This you felt was 'it'. You had been initiated into the order of the inspired...from that point on I felt different in myself as a writer'. The writer of the poems in 'North' is the mature Seamus Heaney speaking from the depths of his being and many of the images in these poems are disturbing, a far cry from the innocence of his two earlier books, DN and DD.

The year that W.O. was published, 1972, was the year of Bloody Friday and Bloody Sunday. The times were bleak and the political scene was deteriorating, but Heaney knew that he was on the move. He had found 'a way in'. His poetry was moving freely to places beyond the comfort-zone of family and friends. 'I was freed up and aware...I had passed the stage of probation and felt confident of vocation...I felt I had to try the experiment of becoming a freelance or full-time writer'. He had passed the stage where just writing poems was enough. It was time to lose the nine-to-five life and to find the poetic life. This was a huge step and given the fact that he was always 'subject to a perverse urge to galumph rather than glide' it came with reservations and guilt.

According to Seamus Deane, Seamus Heaney is always torn between being bold and being timorous. In relation to his writing he boldly masters the art and mystery of poetry. But then feels guilty because he has mastered his mentors. The tension between

THE NIGHT OF OTHER DAYS

mastery and mystery is echoed in the tensions which result from Heaney's newly found freedom. Bold in his decision to move to The Irish Republic but timorous in not staying the course in Northern Ireland. Bold in the politicisation of his poetry yet timorous in holding on to tradition. As some would see it, bold in turning his back yet timorous in walking away. He was constantly torn between two forces.

In the late 1960s poets in Northern Ireland knew that they were 'witnessing a decisive historical moment'. Journalists and reporters were pouring into Northern Ireland. There was a constant demand for statements and interviews. And there was a demand that poets should fashion some kind of response. Heaney put it this way: 'All of us, Protestant poets, Catholic poets – and don't those terms fairly put the wind up you? – all of us probably had some notion that a good poem was 'a paradigm of good politics', a site of energy and tension and possibility, a truth-telling arena but not a killing field. And without being explicit about it, either to ourselves or to one another, we probably felt that if we as poets couldn't do something transformative or creative with all that we were a part of, then it was a poor lookout for everybody'(FK).

He was talking then of the 1960s and went on to tell of how, thirty years later, the Good Friday Agreement of 1996 was prefigured in these subtleties and tolerances. Poets did not feel that it was necessary or appropriate to deal with the political issues because 'the subtleties and tolerances of their art were precisely what they had to contribute to the coarseness and intolerances of public life'. Many poets felt that they should remain silent but, in response to the question 'How with this rage shall beauty hold a plea? Heaney bravely replied: 'by offering befitting emblems of adversity',(Feeling into Words). Some of these emblems he would find in the bogs of Ireland and Denmark.

The publication of 'Wintering Out' in 1972 met with indifferent reviews (a sharp contrast to the publication of 'North'

1976). Some felt that it did not speak directly to the burning political issues of the day, that it only concerned itself with the context. But he did try to reconcile the two worlds and he does invite his fellow artists to confront the violence and to offer hope without ignoring the social distress. Not surprisingly, professor Ricks saw Heaney as a force for civilisation and as a source of comfort at a time of emergency, violence and threat. He identified him as the most trusted poet in our islands.

Professor Ricks noted the subtlety and delicacy of Heaney's language in its powers of observation of actual life and in its power to evoke myth. Using ordinary everyday language Heaney has the ability to evoke a scene, an action or a sensation in a short phrase. 'Were they in uniform, not masked in any way?' 'Open up and see what you've got – pills or a powder or something in a bottle'?[4] These were words used before the ghastly late-night murder of an innocent victim.

Ghosts haunt his later work especially in 'Station Island' 1984 and 'Sweeney Astray' 1983, as had the ghosts of the potato-diggers in 'The Digging Skeleton' (North 1975). 'Sad gang of apparitions… tell me/what farmer dragged you from the boneyard? Or are you emblems of the truth…Even death lies/the void deceives/We do not fall like autumn leaves/To sleep in peace…We earn our deaths; our one repose/when the bleeding instep finds its spade'.[5]

The spade is an important symbol in Heaney's work. Heaney's father, Patrick, is associated with the spade and potato digging and his grandfather dug more turf in Toner's bog than any other man. Heaney's reading of Glob's book led to the bogs of Denmark and a controversial interpretation of the violence in Northern Ireland. Given the centrality of spade and bog it seems appropriate to give a brief description of bog-landscape.

E.E.Evans calculated that one fifth of Ireland is, or was, coated with bog, principally in mountain areas and in ill-drained lowland hollows. Post- glaciation bog formed when as a result of an increase

THE NIGHT OF OTHER DAYS

in rainfall, forests perished and collapsed into wet swampy ground. Here decomposition of vegetable matter was arrested and in the water-logged depths everything was preserved... seeds, grass, pollen, insects and animals. Thousands of years later pathways, tools, field-patterns, monuments and human remains have been uncovered as turf-cutters removed layer after layer of bog to be burned on domestic hearths. Because Ireland lacks other fuel resources there has always been a demand for turf especially in rural areas. When the Heaneys moved from Mossbawn to The Wood they brought with them Turbary Rights to cut turf in Toner's bog. Here for generations turf-banks have been cut into sods, lifted, wheeled, spread and dried before being carted away to heat family homes. When a turf-bank is cut it presents a sheer, straight cliff-like face in which preserved remains are exposed. Finds thus unearthed include bronze-age gold ornaments, metal, wood, leather, cloth and butter, all almost perfectly preserved. This gives another meaning to 'turf-bank', that of a repository. Referring to the custom of burying things in bogs Evans says 'I am inclined to think that a practice which came to be generally adopted for utilitarian reasons had its origin in magic, and the deposits were originally made in the hope of appeasing the powers of evil and inducing an abundant flow of milk from the pastures'.

This fits in with the conclusions of P.V.Glob in his work 'The Bog People' published in English translation in 1969. Heaney bought a copy of the book as a Christmas present for himself! 'Opening it was like opening a gate', he said. In the book he would find 'befitting emblems of adversity' for Northern Ireland.

Glob describes the finding of bodies murdered during the Iron Age and preserved in the bogs of Denmark. He concludes that the bodies were the remains of sacrificial offerings of victims whose throats had been cut to appease the Earth Goddess.

Heaney wrote 'The unforgettable photographs of these victims blended in my mind with photographs of atrocities, past and present, in the long rites of Irish political and religious struggles'. For Heaney the bog bodies were images of slaughter rising to view after centuries of secrecy. And their anonymity allowed his imagination free scope, a freedom it would not have had in describing local contemporary assassinations. The bog bodies convinced him that away back in history ritual killing had been a feature. Later, he linked this with Irish adherence to the myth of Kathleen Ni Houlihan (Ireland). He felt that the recent history of Northern Ireland was insufficient to explain the explosion of anger, violence and atrocity. A possible thread of explanation might be found in P.V.Glob's 'The Bog People', and in particular in one body preserved in a Danish bog, that of 'The Tollund Man'. When he encountered The Tollund Man Heaney found 'a field of force which could accommodate fidelity to the processes and experience of poetry while respecting perspectives of a humane reason and the religious intensity of violence'. [7]

The bog-related poems of Seamus Heaney began with 'Bogland' (DD 1969), followed by 'The Tollund Man' (WO 1972) and 'The Graubelle Man' (N 1975). Each poem reflects changes in his personal life, in his emotional state and in his responses to a rapidly changing political reality.

The first of these poems is 'Bogland', the final poem in (DD,1969). In his lecture of 1974, 'Feeling into Words', he details its importance to him and to us. The poem was written when he returned from honeymoon. He felt that he had discovered the gift of writing lyric poetry. Likening himself to a pilot at the edge of an airfield, looking at the aircraft he is about to fly, he glories in the realisation that a poem, 'Bogland', has been given to him, that it has arrived freely, 'arrived out of old layers of lore and language and felt completely trustworthy as a poem'. He is now confident that he can express his poetry as a public art. And the last line of each poem will lead further, to where he does not yet know. But he knows that he has arrived 'at something different' which he likens

THE NIGHT OF OTHER DAYS

to doorjambs which open to a bright sky rather than 'the dark' of the forge. He looks inwards and downwards to the bottomless centre of Irish history, discovering there the traces and treasures of previous cultures and peoples, because the bogland of Ireland literally preserves historic and pre-historic deposits which can now be released by archaeology and through his poetry.

Speaking of his poems he says that the best moments are those 'when your mind seems to implode and words and images rush of their own accord into the vortex. Which happened to me once when the line 'we have no prairies' drifted into my head at bedtime, and loosened a fall of images that constitute the poem 'Bogland'.

For Heaney bogland landscape has 'a strange assuaging effect', one reaching back to childhood, when he had heard of bog-butter, taken salty and white from a bog after a great number of years. So too with the skeleton of an elk taken from a bog near his school. As a result, the poet came to consider the bog as the memory-bank of the landscape. But 'Bog' is not just the recall of a world of rural toil. Heaney made it central in his exposition of the history of Northern Ireland.

In his first essay in 'Finders Keepers' titled 'Mossbawn', Heaney writes of the immediate and peaceful attraction of green wet corners, flooded wastes, soft rushy bottoms, any place with the invitation of watery ground and tundra vegetation. 'It is as if I am betrothed to them, and I believe my betrothal happened one summer evening, thirty years ago'. That evening with another boy he stripped naked and bathed in a boghole.

Bog is one of the defining symbols of Heaney's work. It is a preserver and a witness to history. It preseves the memory of the landscape as it dies into its own life. Andrews says that the peat-bog treasures help Heaney to feel his way down past words to things. [8] Through his pen he digs to find life below the surface of the level of agriculture, below the level of silt where the eel lives, down to the 'primitive and shaky ground where memory and creation live side by side', a soft womb sucking history into itself, a pollen bin, a sun bank, a melting grave, an insatiable bride.

Heaney credits P.V.Glob with opening a gate to this world of myth. Heaney read 'The Bog People' in 1969 and acknowledges that '... the minute I opened it, and saw the photographs and read the text, I knew there was going to be a yield from it. I mean, even if there had been no Northern Troubles, no man-killing in the parishes, I would still have felt at home with that 'peat-brown head'.

P.V.Glob described the naked bodies of men and women buried in the early iron age in the Tolland area of bogland in Denmark. They had been strangled or had had their throats cut in ritual sacrifices to the Goddess Earth, called Nerthus. The Goddess needed to bed each winter with a sacrificial bridegroom to ensure continued fertility. This archetypical pattern was related by Heaney to the tradition of martyrdom in the cause of Cathleen Ni Houlihan (Ireland). He accepted Glob's interpretation, that of sacrifice, yearly bridegrooms and a mother goddess. But one result is that history is reduced to myth as each disparate event becomes a symbol of an underlying continuity of tribal identity. And myth seems now to offer a rationalisation for conflicts. Violence, terror, murder and conflict can now be institutionalised and aestheticized in myth in the name of right and freedom. This is the means 'to grant the religious intensity of the violence its deplorable authenticity and complexity'.

The writing of 'The Tollund Man' marks the entry of myth and politics into the life and poetry of Seamus Heaney. 'Someday I will go to Aarhus/To see his peat-brown head', he writes, as he makes a connection between the victims of violence buried in a Danish bog and those three thousand victims who will soon die in Northern Ireland. He recalls a photograph which he saw in Barry's book, 'Guerrilla Days in Ireland'. It was of a farmer's family, shot in reprisals by The Black and Tans and left lying beside the

THE NIGHT OF OTHER DAYS

open door of their family home, 'Stockinged corpses/Laid out in the farmyards'. He tells too of 'Tell-tale skin and teeth/Flecking the sleepers/Of four young brothers, trailed/For miles along the lines.' And this brings fear. He tells us 'When I wrote this poem, I had a completely new sensation, one of fear. It was a vow to go on pilgrimage and I felt as it came to me – and again it came quickly – that unless I was deeply in earnest about what I was saying, I was simply invoking dangers for myself'.

'The Tollund Man' transfers from Jutland to Northern Ireland, from the Iron Age to modern times and from sacrificial killing to political martyrdom. It testifies to the fact that we are all dispossessed people and that history is in large measure 'the brutal record of our denial of that fact'. But it should also be said that it is easier to reverence a victim from the Iron Age than it is to reverence the remains of a neighbour being swept into a plastic bag after the bomb he had carried out of his shop had blown up in his face.

PART THREE

'The Night Of Other Days.'

'North' (N), Published 1975.

'Field Work' (Fw), Published 1979.

The origins of the violence which ravaged the people of Northern Ireland for a period of over thirty years and how this violence affected the life and work of Seamus Heaney.

CHAPTER

Northern Ireland

11

Heaney spent a year as a visiting lecturer in Berkeley and returned to Ireland in 1971. Wintering Out (WO) was published in 1972. By then the scene in Northern Ireland was utterly changed and Heaney's poetry would now reflect this.

His poetry began to reflect the identity, history, territory and tongue of his people, the Catholics of Northern Ireland. The reality of the status of a catholic in Northern Ireland was described In 'Feeling Into Words',(FK,1974). He wrote of the sectarianism which existed between Catholic and Protestant, between Nationalist and Unionist at a political level and concluded that the enmity could be viewed as a struggle between the cults and devotees of a god and a goddess. The god represented the seventeenth century Ulster planters whose founding fathers were William of Orange, Cromwell and Edward Carson. The goddess was 'Mother Ireland' or 'Kathleen Ni Houlihan' whose sovereignty had been temporarily usurped by a power now resident in a palace in Westminster.

HUGH MULROONEY

It is interesting to note that Heaney referred to 'Ulster' rather than to 'Northern Ireland'. Ireland consisted of four provinces, Munster, Leinster, Ulster and Connacht. Ulster was the historic northern province of Ireland and was made up of nine counties. The State of 'Northern Ireland' came into being in 1921 and it is composed of only six of the original nine counties of Ulster and excludes the counties of Donegal, Cavan and Monaghan. These three Ulster counties have never been part of Northern Ireland. [1]

The symbols and rituals of this new State of Northern Ireland were almost entirely Protestant or Unionist and these Protestant-Unionist- Orange symbols were meant to be seen, heard and feared by Northern Irish Catholics. The Orange symbol represented William of Orange who defeated the English King James at the Battle of the Boyne in 1690. The Unionist symbol proclaimed the total commitment of Ulster Protestants to union with Britain. The most obnoxious evidence of these was manifest through the actions of the part-time police reserve force, the B-Specials, established in the very first days of the new state. A group of armed Protestant bigots, dressed in a hated uniform, they were a daily and nightly irritant and threat to peaceful unarmed Catholics who were constantly and unremittingly harassed by people who lived as their neighbours. In the poem 'The Wood Road' [2] we meet 'militiaman' Bill Pickering with his gun 'under the summer hedge'. He is part of a road block 'harassing Mulhollandstown'. Bill is a friendly neighbour until he dons the uniform of 'B-Special' and changes character.

The part-time B-Specials were eventually replaced by the Ulster Defence Regiment, the UDR, another almost exclusively Protestant force. The fulltime armed police force was the RUC, the Royal Ulster Constabulary, founded in 1922 and replaced in 2001. It never claimed or received any allegiance from Catholics.

Catholics were also subjected to a vicious Protestant rhetoric, particularly on the July and August days of Orange-Order

THE NIGHT OF OTHER DAYS

celebrations marking the 1690 victory of 'King Billy' at the battle of The Boyne. The expressions of this vituperative anti-popery date back even earlier to the 1640s and the scurrilous writings of Henry Jones, Bishop of Clogher. Addressing the English parliament at Westminster he described what he saw as the 'the ancient hatred the Church of Rome beareth to the Reformed Religion' and a most bloody and Anti-Christian plot by the whole Romish sect, home and foreign, - aimed at the entire extirpation of the Reformed religion and the setting of 'that idol of the Masse, with all the abominations of the whore of Babylon'. The message of Sir John Temple, one of the virulently anti-Catholic New English, was in the same vein. 'He was the first to paint what was to become an enduring picture of the Catholic Irish as untrustworthy dissemblers'.[3] His Calvinist conviction of Catholics as irredeemable traitors became the theme of annual sermons down to the middle of the twentieth century. The belief that Catholics were a threat to the very existence of Protestants led to a Protestant hatred of Catholics in Ulster (and in parts of Britain) which lasted through to the second half of the twentieth century, when it continued in Northern Ireland as an expression of anti-Catholicism through the politically motivated hate-sermons of demagogues like Hugh Hanna and Ian Paisley.

Protestant parades were a constant irritant as the Lambeg drums punched the air and sash-wearing Unionists strode behind their banners through resentful Catholic areas, with arrogant swagger and defiance. And these parades were a feature of Ulster life long before the setting up of Northern Ireland as a state in the 1920s. For much of the nineteenth century Orange parades were aggressively and provocatively anti-Catholic. Marches often ended in rioting, in the deaths of Catholics and in the destruction and the burning of Catholic homes. In one such riot, in 1886, 32 Catholics were killed and 371 injured in Belfast. Between 1852 and 1909 riots leading to death, destruction and burning of Catholic homes are recorded on eight of those years. Persecution of Catholics was a permanent feature of everyday life in Ulster. And it began long before 1969. The oft-quoted notion that the violence in Northern Ireland originated in the twentieth century is entirely false. It was endemic in Ulster for centuries before the setting-up of Northern Ireland in 1921.

Any attempt to provide a short outline of the history of Northern Ireland is hazardous. There are so many contradictory interpretations, all held with absolute conviction. The approach taken here, and elsewhere in this book, is to rely solely on the accounts of professional historians. No personal views are aired. But an attempt is made to link a complicated history with the work of a Nobel poet. The approach is to leave the interpretation of history to the historian and let Heaney's poetry speak for itself.

Professor Lee in his introduction to 'Ireland, Politics and Society' points out that that 'without history the Irish Nation is nothing...and without history Ulster is nothing.' He goes on to say that what the Irish have is a sense of grievance which they choose to dignify by christening it 'History'. It follows that interpretations of events, and the justifications for actions, will vary widely depending on source and prejudice.

The historian Marianne Elliot states that there are four strands which illuminate the situation in Ulster up to the foundation of Northern Ireland as a political entity in 1921. The first concerns ownership and occupation of land. The second strand concerns migration. The third strand concerns the Irish language. The fourth, and probably the most central concerns religion, and not just religion per se, but the perceptions of religion, their own and that of others, held by the members of the two main Churches, Catholic and Protestant. Each of those strands has a bearing on 'identity' and this is the context in which they are considered.

It is necessary to revert to the early 1600s to trace the history of the first strand, that concerning land occupation and ownership. Towards the end of the sixteenth century and almost at the end

THE NIGHT OF OTHER DAYS

of her reign, Elizabeth the First sent her faithful courtier Essex to break the power of the ancient Irish nobility. The seat of their power lay in Ulster, the northern province of Ireland. The lands held by the powerful Gaelic chieftains were confiscated and planted. The confiscated lands were given to three groups, two of them Protestant and non-Irish. Land was granted to Scottish and English undertakers; to English servitors (usually government officials); and to 'deserving Irish'. Derry and Belfast were incorporated and both towns were later designated as Protestant although Derry had a Catholic majority population, then as now. Derry lands were given to London commercial interests and renamed Londonderry. The Catholics of Derry lived outside the city walls in The Bogside.

Numbered among the deserving Irish (Catholic) were many Gaelic gentry some of them unhappy that the historic title to their lands was not written. Title to planted land, now re-granted to the existing Irish tenants, was enshrined in legal documentation, and written in English. This afforded a security which was not given under the ancient Irish oral system. Thus, the English legal system was a contributor to the decline of the Irish language. Tenants under the system felt more secure in the knowledge that their rights were enshrined in written English law.

English and Scottish settlers were settled in Ulster in the ratio of 24 per 1,000 acres and each supplied with a stone house. No Irish or non-conformists (mainly Scottish Presbyterians), were tolerated. On the whole the Irish remained in occupation (as distinct from ownership) of the land. One reason for this was the scarcity of tenants in Ulster. By the 1660s in Ulster fertile land was occupied in equal numbers by native Irish and planters. Infertile land remained with the Irish. Under the Plantation of Ulster Irish chiefs were demoted and dispossessed. Although many Ulster Irish continued to look to the old chieftains for leadership, their power was gone and the Plantation played havoc with 'this intensely status-conscious society'.[4] Ulster-Catholic-Irish were left leaderless, landless and powerless. 'The great were lowered and the middle ranking consolidated'.[5] It seemed that the aim, 'the creation of a secure Ulster Irish population alongside the new planter element... where every man shall have a certain home and know the extent of his estate', had been achieved. Although 40,000 Protestant settlers had arrived, Catholics remained the majority in an Ulster population of between two and three hundred thousand. This was the position mid-seventeenth-century.

But before the end of the 17th century Ireland had become embroiled in English politics and in particular in the power-struggle between the monarchy and parliament. The Irish sided with King James and by 1640 Wentworth had raised a Catholic army, in the royal cause, with many of its soldiers billeted in Ulster. In the area of religion there were two significant developments at this time. Presbyterians no longer felt welcome in the Protestant established church, and a vicious anti-Catholic campaign had been launched in England, led by Henry Jones, bishop of Clogher, and Sir John Temple. It preached that Irish Catholics were party to a Vatican plot, founded on hatred, and aimed at the elimination of all Protestants. It linked together 'Catholic', 'Irish' and 'traitor'. This perception of Catholics as subversives and traitors lodged in Protestant minds and poisoned Protestant thinking in Northern Ireland down to the middle of the twentieth century. Protestants were persuaded that Catholics were inferior, unworthy, treacherous, ungodly, and dangerous. Thus by the time the Protestants achieved political power in the newly created State of Northern Ireland in 1921, their hatred of Catholics had hardened into absolute conviction. Even more alarming was the fact that identity was now a matter of religion. Protestants were now by definition and by perception faithful subjects of the English Crown while Catholics were seen as disloyal, traitorous, inferior and nationalist.

In the poisoned atmosphere of the late 17th century, Ulster became a place of chaos. In this atmosphere of fear, threat and

THE NIGHT OF OTHER DAYS

violence the parties turned on each other. Catholics massacred many Protestants. Counter attacks, reprisals and a vicious civil war followed and all factions bunkered down to nurse their hatred, fears and resentment. By the 1650s clear lines were declared. On one side powerful land-holding Protestants and on the other broken impoverished and defeated Irish Catholics. Ulster had been transformed and worse was to follow.

In the 1690s, following the victory of William of Orange at the battle of the Boyne, there was a massive increase in immigration with the transfer of land from Catholics to Scottish Presbyterians. By 1712 the movement of Protestant people into Ulster stood at 270,000. This represented the greatest movement of people in Europe during that period. As a result, Catholics were now completely overwhelmed, reduced to a minority and in very poor standing. Small Catholic land-holders lost the most. And the fact that Catholics had lost their lands to Protestants created a lasting social, political and religious division between land-holder and tenant which led to some of the lasting political evils of Ireland. This link between Protestantism, land-holding and political power was resented as fiercely in Seamus Heaney's time as it had been in the seventeenth century.

The majority population in what was to become Northern Ireland were now committed loyalists. This contrasted with developments in the rest of Ireland where there was a regeneration of Celtic fervour and a definite policy of republicanism with a push towards a total break with England. In the South of Ireland the nineteenth century was marked by the emergence of a number of issues which challenged the power and authority of the English parliament and Crown. The most pressing concerned land-holding. A concerted campaign led to a series of land acts which transferred ownership back to tenants. The Protestant Church was disestablished and Church lands were taken over by the government and passed on to tenants at favourable terms.

HUGH MULROONEY

A campaign was launched to win back the Irish Parliament, which had been surrendered to Westminster by the Act of Union in 1801. Now Irish nationalist MPs (Members of Parliament) sought Home Rule with eventual national sovereignty and some were prepared to use force. During the course of the nineteenth century various groups and organisations were established (in Ireland outside of Ulster) and many morphed into familiar and feared players in the tragedy of Northern Ireland. A secret organisation called The Irish Republican Brotherhood (IRB), set up in the 1860s, played a central part in The Rising of 1916 and later evolved as the IRA (Irish Republican Army). Similarly in Northern Ireland the UVF, the Ulster Volunteer Force, (set up to resist any move towards Home Rule) was an armed force seen by Catholic Nationalists in much the same terms as the IRA was seen by Unionist Protestants.

Another organisation, The Gaelic League, was established in Dublin, to revive the Irish language and Gaelic cultural heritage. The end of the nineteenth century also marked the triumph of Irish Literary theatre and poetry with the award of the Nobel Prize to W.B.Yeats. Sinn Fein ('Ourselves') was set up in 1905 with the aim of a united Ireland achieved by peaceful means. It is now an established political party in Northern Ireland and in The Irish Republic. Founded by Arthur Griffith and Bulmer Hobson it was organised into clubs and with over 100,000 members it swept into power at the height of the Anglo-Irish war in the 1918 election to Westminster with 73 seats to Unionist 26.

Home Rule, for all Ireland, on the Westminster Statute Book in 1912, became law on September 18th 1914 with implementation delayed until the war ended. Although many saw it as little more than glorified local government, Unionist re-action was furious. Ulster Unionists saw Home Rule as Rome Rule and refused to be governed by what they saw as an inferior breed. They were prepared to unleash violence into twentieth century Irish politics

THE NIGHT OF OTHER DAYS

if that was what was called for. Although Catholics were in a three- to- one majority in Ireland as a whole, in Ulster Protestants numbered 891,000 as against 691,000 Catholics. And in Ulster race, politics and religion were inextricably linked.

As an earnest of their resistance to Home Rule in Ulster 471,414 signed up to the principles of the Solemn League and Covenant and 90,000 joined the Ulster Volunteer Force and took arms, (in April 1914 the UVF took possession of 24,600 rifles and 3,000,000 rounds of ammunition from Germany).[6] There was total commitment to the emergence of a new State in Ulster and henceforth the word 'loyalist' meant Protestant, Orangeman, Unionist and defender of Northern Ireland against Catholic, Irish and nationalist. Both sides in Northern Ireland believed that victory for the other side would lead to persecution and tyranny and in the event their worst fears were realised. The future for the minority Catholic citizens of Northern Ireland looked bleak.

In 1916 a Proclamation was read at The General Post Office in Dublin. It declared 'The Irish Republic'. The Rising, April 24th to 29th, was concentrated in The General Post Office in Dublin and the commanders surrendered at the end of Easter week. Seven commanders signed the Proclamation and all seven were subsequently executed. One commander escaped execution. His name was Eamon de Valera.

The 1916 Rising was rightly seen by Unionists as violently anti-British and as intensely anti-unionist. As they saw it, the signatories had no democratic authority to declare a new state and there was no indication of any compromise. Unionists could point to the fact that they had a clear mandate from their people to resist any attempt to coerce them into a Gaelic, Catholic state. No such mandate they maintained had been indicated in the south.

The power of the Catholic Church in Ireland increased during the nineteenth century especially in Education and in its involvement in all spheres of social life. Catholic clergy had their own training institution in Maynooth. Everywhere the identity of Catholic was re-enforced in its Irishness and in its nationalism.

Language is central to identity. 'The vast majority of Ulster Irish had no knowledge of written language, Irish or English'[7] in the seventeenth century and by the mid nineteenth century Irish had all but died out in Ulster, except Donegal, (and Donegal was never in Northern Ireland). By 1851 only 6.8% of Ulster people could speak Irish and that had decreased to 2.3% by 1911, and this mainly confined to Donegal and Antrim.[8] Over the rest of Ireland Irish had declined. By 1891 less than 15% of the Irish population spoke the native language. The cause of the Irish Language was enthusiastically espoused early in the twentieth century, but not in Ulster.

Seamus Heaney linked the death of the Irish language over much of Ireland to the Famine which ravished the country in the 1840s. One of the consequences was the reduction of the population of Ireland from 8million in 1841 to around 6million in ten years. Emigration, starvation and ruthless subjugation marked English rule in Ireland in the 1840s.

By the nineteenth century identity, especially in Ulster, was a matter of one's religion. There, the identity of Catholic and Protestant communities owed far more to sectarian awareness than to any Irish or British nationalism. The reality of the situation in Ulster by 1900 was that it was a deeply divided sectarian intolerant society which could not be described as either Gaelic or native. And absolute power rested with one group.

In Northern Ireland the roots of the violence of the twentieth century were nourished in the soil of the two preceding centuries which were marked by hatred, intolerance and periodic violence. Leaderless and powerless, the Catholic minority in the North looked to the Church. The Church preached obedience, unquestioning acceptance of an oral theology as interpreted from the altar, suspicion of 'The Book', submission to Church authority

THE NIGHT OF OTHER DAYS

and total rejection of violence. Acquiescence was the hallmark of Catholic Church teaching.

In the South of Ireland the power of the Catholic Church grew stronger in the nineteenth century as demands for national independence grew more insistent. This was anathema to the Protestant majority population of Ulster. Here Protestants and Presbyterians closed ranks to protect the Union and their Protestant Faith. They knew they had little or nothing in common with the South.

With the Rising of 1916 and the execution of the leaders, Ireland, North and South entered a decade of turmoil. Eventually negotiations led to a treaty between Dublin and London. One outcome was the partition of Ireland and the establishment of the state of Northern Ireland.

The state of Northern Ireland was established under The Government of Ireland Act of 1920. Two governments now existed in Ireland. The island was divided or partitioned, with six counties of Ulster constituting Northern Ireland. These were the counties of Antrim, Armagh, Down, Derry, Tyrone and Fermanagh. The Government of Ireland Act recognised a reality. The island was home to two political entities and these entities were mutually repellent, each utterly convinced of its own rightful place. In Northern Ireland those in power gave total commitment to the new State and henceforth the word 'loyalist' meant Protestant, Orangeman, Unionist and defender of Northern Ireland against Catholic, Irish and nationalist. Both sides in Northern Ireland believed that victory for the other side would lead to persecution and tyranny. And this was the State into which Seamus Heaney was born in 1939. Unionist/Orangemen of the north held no sympathy for any of the developments in what became the Irish Free State, whether political, cultural, social or para-military. Questions like Irish independence, the revival of the Irish language, the renaissance of Anglo-Irish literature and drama, or the preservation of the Celtic/Catholic ethos were of no interest to Northern Irish Unionists. In fact they were viewed with great apprehension. They quoted the 'Ne Temere' decree from Rome. Under this decree the children of a mixed marriage had to be raised as Catholics.

In the years following 1916, south of the border, the Anglo-Irish war (1919 to1921) was followed by a civil war, 1922-1923, fought on the matter of the treaty which had divided the country. The civil war was 'bloody, savage and intimate' and it dictated the politics of Ireland for generations. The treaty, which brought an end to the Anglo-Irish war, was signed in London by the Irish plenipotentiaries who had been sent by de Valera, accepting the formation of 'The Irish Free State' and the partition of Ireland, ('The Irish Republic' was named in 1948). Fully absorbed with its own difficulties the Free State was unable, and perhaps unwilling to involve itself with Northern Ireland. Although there were sporadic attacks on police barracks in the border areas, mounted by the IRA, there was no support for the Catholics in Northern Ireland and they were left to their fate.

Figures for the years 1920 to 1922 illustrate the violence and sectarianism which characterised the government of Northern Ireland from its inception. In the town of Lisburn, the mass burnings of Catholic business premises was followed by the expulsion of almost the entire Catholic community. In Belfast following the 12th of July Orange parades the 'pogram' of 1920 was followed by two years of brutality. 453 died in that period; between nine and eleven thousand Catholics were expelled from their work; 23,000 Catholics were forced out of their homes (this represented one quarter of the Catholic population of Belfast).

A sectarian police force, full-time and part-time, was put in place; the proportional representation system of voting was replaced; constituency boundaries were redrawn to Protestant advantage and gerrymandering of votes became commonplace.

THE NIGHT OF OTHER DAYS

Discrimination in employment, education and housing was widespread. All this is borne out in the official English reports of the 1950s and 60s. The Cameron Report of September 1969 found all the claims of the civil-rights movement to have been substantiated (claims related to discrimination of all kinds against Catholics).

In 1969 Seamus Heaney took part in some of the first peaceful civil rights protest marches and meetings which followed the Royal Ulster Constabulary baton-charging of the civil-rights march in Derry on October the 5th.

About to take centre-stage was Ian Paisley, the man many people would consider to have wrecked every attempt to find a just solution to Northern Ireland's problems, the man who in 1969 at a loyalist rally described Catholics 'breeding like rabbits and multiplying like vermin'.

The Civil Rights Movement was peaceful and non-confrontational. But it was met with violence. The initial demands for fairness, justice and equality in housing, employment and education were dismissed. The Catholic population was unarmed and helpless in the face of a fully- armed and hostile majority. Peaceful demonstrations demanding justice were suppressed by armed forces of the State. The time for violent civil war was at hand. What had been started by idealists would be finished by men of violence. The IRA now took centre stage with an armalite-gun in one hand and a ballot-paper in the other.

CHAPTER

Poetry and Politics

12

The upheavals of summer 1969 changed Heaney's life as a poet. 'How with this rage shall beauty hold a plea'? he asked. His answer: 'by offering befitting emblems of adversity'[1,] was variously greeted with approval, with rejection and with absolute condemnation. He discovered with the publication of 'North' 1976 that he was accused of aestheticizing, mythologizing and glamorising violence in poems like 'Punishment' and 'Kinship'. But Heaney stood firm, and caught between Republican bully and public critic, he spoke for himself, as a private poet with a public platform. 'I'm not in favour of stand-off', he said, 'I'm in favour of tension and connection'.

He was entitled to speak as a citizen of all-Ireland.[2] In an 'Open Letter', 1983, following his inclusion as a British poet in 'The Penguin Book of Contemporary British Poetry' Heaney wrote 'My passport's green/No glass of ours was ever raised/To toast the queen.' His passport conferred him with dual citizenship of The Irish Republic and Northern Ireland and gave him the right, within the borders of Northern Ireland, to express an Irish identity even though he grew up and was educated through the British

THE NIGHT OF OTHER DAYS

educational system. Although he never argued for the exclusion of the British connection he did argue for diversity and inclusion within the British Northern Ireland framework to express his Irish citizenship and to speak as a citizen of both political entities... to be allowed to live 'in two minds'.

Questions were raised on Heaney's role as public spokesman, on his right to be involved in politics and public affairs. There was little merit in this. The outbreak of violence politicised every Irish person on the island and Seamus Heaney had experienced this violence at a deeply personal level. Friends, neighbours, colleagues were dead. A vicious reality had manifested itself. Heaney marched with the peaceful civil rights people and he saw how they were attacked, beaten and harassed by mobs led by Ian Paisley. The times demanded courage and Seamus did not shirk.

Poets live precisely at the intersection of the public and the private he said and they should be concerned with examining fundamental assumptions about culture and identity 'to reveal and confirm the existence of a continuous tradition.' With regard to poetry he distinguished civic, public and political. He supported civil rights in Northern Ireland, freedom of conscience in The Republic, anti-apartheid in South-Africa and he was a spokesman for 'The Republic of Conscience'. He believed that 'no poetry worth its salt is unconcerned with the world it answers for and sometimes answers to' with the proviso that poetry, while engaging with public issues, must guard its own private integrity.

In Ireland, he believed, you cannot divorce the literary from the historical, from the political, from normal everyday life and he was fully aware that the words of a poet will be heard, examined and interpreted. Because Heaney wrote in his own inimitable home tongue and because his style is inclusive, non-factional and undogmatic, 'he is the most trusted poet of our islands' (Christopher Ricks). His was the voice of reason, of conscience and of a culture which had been silenced for too long.

HUGH MULROONEY

Heaney was well aware of a possible conflict when the poet assumes a public role and when his poetry is interpreted as political. The publication of Wintering Out, 1972, and in particular the poems 'The Tollund Man', A Northern Hoard', and 'Traditions', thrust Seamus into the limelight at the time when the world's press eagerly sought his opinions. He was now a trusted spokesman but, as he said 'the question was – and remains – to what extent the role of spokesman can or should be exercised in poetry'.

Heaney believed that the poet attunes his poetry to his own consciousness and not to the violent reality around him. Pure poetry is perfectly justifiable 'in earshot of the car bomb'. Competing demands are made of a poet – public poetry is expected to be either propaganda or disinterested truth – but the poet must protect the mystery and integrity of poetry and while 'detachment' may be the desired norm, occasions will arise when direct political poetry is called for.

Two such occasions were the civil rights march of October 1968 and the twenty fifth anniversary of the Bloody Sunday massacre 1972, when thirteen innocent unarmed citizens were murdered by British troops. 'We've gerrymandered Derry but croppy won't lie down' he wrote and 'in the dirt lay justice like an acorn in the winter/Till its oak would sprout in Derry where the thirteen men lay dead'.

In 1973 the poet summarised the situation in Northern Ireland. It was a time of great constitutional crisis. A non-violent Civil Rights movement of protest had been met with savage violence by the police. This led to a campaign of bombing and shooting marking the end of the old order. The Stormont government was suspended, the hated B-Special force disbanded and a power-sharing assembly was being envisaged. When Heaney returned from his year in Berkeley in 1971, 1570 people had been interned without trial and 144 were dead.

THE NIGHT OF OTHER DAYS

His year in Berkeley 1970-1971 opened a new perspective. Free of money worries and enjoying the sunshine, he relished 'the intellectual distinction of the people around us', the vivid environment and 'the genuine glamour and attainment about many of the people on campus'. Occasionally the Heaney family would go out to enjoy breakfast of champagne and hamburgers before returning to campus and the day's work! He tells us that when he went to Berkeley his mind was 'wired to English Literature terminals'. Under the influence of friends like Tom Flanagan with his 'sardonic Hiberno-centric thinking', he found the whole Berkeley experience nourishing and educational. And then it was back to Northern Ireland, the week that internment without trial was introduced and everything had changed.

'People keep asking what it's like to be living in Belfast', he wrote, following his return, Christmas 1971. In reply he said 'things aren't too bad in our part of town' by which he meant that he didn't expect to be killed in crossfire if he stepped into the street. But he told of 'the weary twisted emotions that are rolled like a ball of hooks and sinkers in the heart'. He is fatigued by the continuous adjudication between agony and injustice and feelings of pity and terror. 'We survive explosions and funerals and live on among the families of the victims, those blown apart and those in cells apart'.[3] He described being marched, with his three-year-old son to the police barracks, because his car-tax was out of date (and maybe because he was a Catholic called Seamus). 'By day you are watched by soldiers with cocked rifles; as you drive you are impeded by ramps which will wreck your car; road blocks are thrown up everywhere; it feels like martial law. At night 'jeeps and armoured cars groan past without lights' and the troubled housing estates are in darkness to facilitate the night-sights of sniper and marksman. And then there are the vigilantes. They hold the entrances to housing estates in the name of their religious denomination and these are no-go areas with watchman huts and tea rotas. There are few people on the silent streets at night and those who do venture out to the local fish and chip shop are accosted and questioned by 'gentlemen with flashlights, of mature years and determined mien'. He recalled a bomb scare near the Marks and Spenser Store where he had just purchased socks and pyjamas. A warning had been given 'although there were four people on the Shankhill Road who got no warning".[4] Caution is exercised everywhere and not always effective, as evidenced by the corpses in the rubble of McGurk's bar.

There are hardly any fairy lights, or Christmas trees, and in many cases there will be no Christmas cards.

'But by then the curtain was about to rise on the larger drama of our politics' and Heaney and other writers were to find themselves in a play within a play. All was captured on TV as the world's media converged on Northern Ireland. Nightly bulletins exposed the violent actions of police and Protestant mob. A fierce battle was fought in Derry's Bogside. In August the British army entered Derry and the following year the Provisional IRA was formed in Dublin. Peace was shattered. 1972 was a vicious year. 58 soldiers died and in a period of six months 186 civilians lost their lives. The year 1969 marked the end of almost fifty years of constant anti-Catholic violence. A peaceful movement to gain elementary civil rights had been met with state violence and a peaceful civil-rights campaign to gain elementary justice for Catholics had elicited a murderous response from Protestant officialdom. The IRA stepped into the role of defenders of an unarmed catholic nationalist minority. There was no going back.

Seamus Heaney experienced the violence, knew the fear and could compare the havoc and chaos of Northern Ireland with the ease and civility of life in California. They had two small children and Marie and Seamus made a momentous decision. They left Northern Ireland and moved south to Wicklow. That same year 1972 his third volume 'Wintering Out', was published.

THE NIGHT OF OTHER DAYS

Much has been written about the move to Glanmore in rural County Wicklow. Heaney gives a full account in his conversations with Dennis O'Driscoll. He celebrated Saint Patrick's Day 1972 with 'The Group' and it was his last contact with them. One of his reasons for leaving was his need to break with the consensus that had developed within the Group... although he paid the price of finding himself 'lonelier imaginatively'.

By 1972 he saw his role as a Northern Poet 'more in relation to the wound and work of Ireland as a whole'. The motive for the move was 'writerly'. He knew he needed to move but in his typical way he vacillated between being timorous and bold.[5] Bold in moving south yet timorous in escaping the horrors of the north.

In 1972 Ann Saddlemeyer offered her gate-lodge at the Synge estate in Glanmore, County Wicklow, and the Heaneys moved there. Heaney had listened long enough. It was time to strike his note. He felt that he needed to step away, to keep at a tangent. He had reached a critical stage and he had the confidence to 'go it alone'. Ian Paisley rejoiced that 'the well-known papist propagandist' had moved south and 'The Irish Times' rejoiced that the 'Ulster Poet' had come to Wicklow.

But as Elmer Andrews expressed it, he may have made good his escape from the massacre in the North to a kind of Wordsworthian pastoral romanticism, but he couldn't leave history and politics behind him. He did find respite in Glanmore and he could re-dedicate himself to lyric and poetry, but there would be many references to blood and death, to purple bruises and blood on the pitchfork.

The move to Wicklow was a move from economic security and independence and it could not have happened without the unswerving love, support and devotion of his wife Marie.

Some people criticised the move to Wicklow. It was suggested that he turned his back on the Northern situation; that he should have stayed and expressed himself more fully on the deteriorating situation there. Perhaps as a poetic war-correspondent? Heaney is quite clear on this subject. His reasons were 'writerly'. There was no element of fear or intimidation. He had the offer of Ann Sadlemeyer's cottage. And he had the courage to strike out on his own, to become a 'file' (poet), as he is described in the school records when he enrolled his children in the local primary school.

1972 was a year of appalling violence. On Sunday January 30th thirteen unarmed innocent men were killed by members of the Parachute Regiment of the British army ('the broken arm of the law') in Derry. On Friday July 21st, 26 bombs were detonated by the IRA in Belfast. Eleven innocent people died and 130 suffered serious injury. Seamus Heaney and David Hammond were on their way to the BBC studios in Belfast when they heard the explosions. They turned home because they felt that the recording of songs and poetry constituted a betrayal of suffering.[6] At the top of the road where Seamus lived Mr Lavery was blown to pieces as he carried a bomb out of his 'Ashley Arms' pub. Violence affected every single person in Northern Ireland and Seamus Heaney was no exception.

Bloody Sunday led to the death of a dear friend, Louis O'Neill, 'Casualty' (FW, 1979). Louis was a regular at the pub of Heaney's father in law, where Seamus sometimes helped out. Louis was a skilled fisherman and together they often fished Lough Neagh. He drank nightly and would indicate his choice of drink with wordless mimicry. He ignored the IRA curfew on the night of the funerals of the Bloody Sunday Derry victims – not in his usual pub but one some miles away – and was blown to death. He drank like a fish and that night was swimming towards the lure of warm lit-up places. That same Wednesday night Seamus Deanes' car ran out of petrol on Glenshane Pass and Heaney came upon them on the mountain road. He drove them to a nearby petrol pump attached to a pub which was crowded with after-funeral drinkers. And Louis O'Neill lay dead some miles away. This was the reality of Northern Ireland in 1972.

THE NIGHT OF OTHER DAYS

'Casualty' is an elegy for a victim who did not espouse the nationalist cause. He was a simple fisherman killed by a bomb. 'How culpable was he/that last night when he broke/Our tribes complicity?' 'Puzzle me the right answer /To that one'.

To answer the question and to express the reality presented a unique challenge. Newspapers and news bulletins were reporting daily. But a poem is neither a work of reporting nor a position paper. The challenge for Heaney was to put his feelings into words without betraying his art. In the words of Neil Corcoran '...the questions about poetic responsibility in relation to public atrocity which are raised here...with a painful, even piercing intensity, remain unanswered...only to be raised again and again in the work of this much-haunted and endlessly self-questioning poet'.[7]

His language would now reveal conflict, fear, anger and profound grief. 'The grieving register is always there' he wrote... .'This morning from a dewy motorway I saw the new camp for internees' and 'now our river tongues must rise/From licking deep in native haunts/To flood, with vowelling embrace,/Demesnes staked out in consonants', (A New Song). Although the language in 'Wintering Out' (1972) was more bleak and political than its predecessors, it paled when compared with the language of 'Intimidation', which he had published in Canada in the early seventies... 'how we slaughter for the common good/and shave the heads/ of the notorious/how the goddess swallows /our love and terror.' In the poem-series 'A Northern Hoard' (WO) the fault is opening out beyond each curtained terrace 'to the sound of gunshot, siren and clucking gas'. Questions are posed: must the man in 'No Man's Land' crawl back 'to confront my smeared doorstep and what lumpy dead'?... 'What do I say if they wheel out their dead'?

In dedicating his book to David Hammond and Michael Longley he tells of seeing the new camp for the internees; of the crater of fresh clay in the road left by a bomb, of machine-gun posts and a real stockade. 'Is there a life before death'?

By now he was a public figure and admired as a poet, broadcaster and commentator. He tried to engage at a social level with the stress of a population suffering fear, conflict, murder and betrayal. But he could not escape the political reality of a society rent with division and he could not shirk his responsibilities to his tribe. Events forced him to become a poet of public life, to engage in identity politics. For this he would require new images, renewed language and the courage to defend his poetic integrity.

Seamus Heaney, writing of this in 1989, said poets were being pressed directly and indirectly to engage in identity politics and 'the search was on for images and analogies that could ease the strain of the present'. The poets were needy for ways in which they could honestly express the realities of the local quarrel without turning that expression into 'yet another repetition of the aggressions and resentments which had been responsible for the quarrel in the first place'. Questioned on the role of the poet as spokesman, Heaney replies in kind. To what extent can or should the role of spokesman be exercised in poetry? The poet cannot claim any exceptional wisdom, yet the violence of the moment and the writing of poetry place issues in juxtaposition and now that Heaney has become a public figure he will be asked for his opinion and his poetry will be interpreted in the light of current events. Questions arise. Detachment or solidarity? Artist or activist? Poet or propagandist? Aesthetic or ethical? The reply is unequivocal. A poem is not a position paper. As a poet, Heaney's gift lies in the summoning and meshing of the sub-conscious and the semantic energies of words. This is his gift and the focus must be on the poetry rather than on any implied statement. At the same time, it should be remembered that at any given stage in the life of the poet his writing reflects change, change in the world around him and change within himself and poetry is bound to manifest the reality of change.

A silent record of change is found in 'Bogland'. The poet is unsure when he visits Aarhus. Is he there as mourner, wedding guest or voyeur? And what of the new sensation? "When I wrote this poem, I had a completely new sensation, one of fear", he wrote, ('Feeling Into Words'). "It was a vow to go on pilgrimage and I felt as it came to me …that unless I was deeply in earnest about what I was saying, I was simply invoking dangers for myself". [8]

This poem is the most accomplished in Heaney's search for 'images and symbols adequate to our predicament' and it marks the commitment to myth which, in turn, marks the politicisation of the poet's writing in its combination of historical analogy, intense emotion and bleak reality. The myth-making has been criticised because it is easier to reverence a victim from the distant past than to respond to the 'all-too-immediate horror of the present'.[9] And easier to reverence a figure in a glass case than to sweep the remains of a bomb-victim into a plastic bag. In many quarters it was felt that the transfer of a myth from Denmark to Ireland, was forced as was the parallel between the goddess Nerthus and Caitlin Ni Houlahan. To equate a myth built up around a stone-age figure in a Danish bog with the historical figures in the tragedy of Ireland was totally unacceptable to the majority population of Northern Ireland. Appeals 'to make germinate the scattered, ambushed flesh of labourers and stockinged corpses' was a step too far for many of his Northern Ireland colleagues.

CHAPTER

Poetry and Violence

13

Heaney's fourth volume 'North' was published in 1975. It has been described as the most controversial, mainly because he addresses the violence which erupted in 1969. Conor Cruise O'Brian wrote, 'I have read many pessimistic analyses of Northern Ireland but none has the bleak conclusiveness of these poems'. 'North' opens with two poems, 'Sunlight' and 'The Seed Cutters', which are timeless in their lyrical salute to his beloved Aunt Mary: 'And here is love/like a tinsmith's scoop/sunk past its gleam/in the meal-bin'. The peaceful rites of those two poems contrast with those which follow, especially his 'bog poems'.

As will become clear, some felt that 'North' was not a great book while others[1] wrote 'it is clear that thousands of readers have found their feelings defined in that volume'. Heaney wrote that he knew himself to be symptomatic of a new confidence in the nationalist minority... and I was conscious that an Irish dimension was at last beginning to figure in the official life of the North'.

With the publication of 'Wintering Out' (WO,1972) and 'North' (N,1975) came recognition that Heaney was now accepted

THE NIGHT OF OTHER DAYS

as the spokesman for the Catholic peaceful repressed minority. 'WO' was also the first step in the mythologizing and politicising of his poetry, dating back to the first of his 'bog' poems 'Bogland', the final poem in 'Door Into The Dark', (1969). It opens with the lines 'We have no prairies/To slice a big sun at evening'... but we do have bogs. Crusting between the sights of the sun, bogs have yielded the preserved remains of a Great Irish Elk, trunks of great firs and firkins of white salty butter. And as the pioneer turf-cutters strike inwards and downwards they reveal layers which have been camped-on before. Bog preserves material elements, swallows everything, and remembers everything that has happened in it and to it. 'Bog Oak' (WO, 1972) links the uncovering of a seasoned piece of wood with a roof-beam supporting a first thatch but also with the ruthless deforestation of Irish great forests by colonists like Edmund Spenser. The poem 'Belderg' (N, 1975) tells of the field-patterns under the bogs of north county Mayo and the yield of quern-stones, flint, iron and bronze. The 'Bog Queen' lay hidden between the demesne wall and the turf-face until she was barbered and stripped by a turf-cutter's spade. She has a less violent history than the 'murdered, forgotten, nameless, terrible/Beheaded girl, outstaring axe.../What had begun to feel like reverence' ('Strange Fruit', N,1975).

The poems, which were inspired both by Heaney's search for images and symbols and his reading of Glob, were also the poems which gave rise to the most strident criticism, particularly 'The Tollund Man', included in the volume 'Wintering Out' 1972, and 'The Graubelle Man', 'Kinship', 'Strange Fruit' and 'Punishment', published in 'North' 1975.

Two volumes are considered here, Wintering Out (WO,1972) and North (N,1975). Field Work (FW,1979) is considered later. The focus is on the political nature of poems, the re-action to them and the questions and criticisms to which they gave rise. These three volumes reflect the changes in Heaney's circumstances. They reflect his temperament, his disposition, focus, entrancement and impulses over a period of more than a decade. They reflect a changing reality, and a confrontation with questions, choices and decisions which were mediated in the full glare of public scrutiny and which were subjected to harsh criticism. Heaney was now a public figure and he always had the courage and conviction to face with honesty any questions raised. He always insisted that his poems should reflect his current circumstances and he tells us that after his move to Glanmore he was 'living up to his neck in complication', living in the Republic but feeling the call of Northern Ireland and all the while conscious of the value of poetry as a consolidating element. He found poems arriving now from an older, deeper, cleaner spring and the writing of certain poems 'took me to the bottom of something inside myself, something inchoate but troubled'. The poems he mentions are 'Oysters', 'Singer's House', 'The Harvest Bow' and 'The Gutteral Muse', all included in Fieldwork (FW,1979).

'Funeral Rites' included in N described his participation in wakes and funerals. Heaney had attended death ceremonies in more peaceful days. Before the violent deaths of 'The Troubles' he had encountered death at domestic and local level and had often represented his parents at wakes. A reading of 'Funeral Rites' (N) will familiarise the non-Irish reader with the funeral customs. 'I shouldered a kind of manhood/stepping in to lift the coffins/of dead relations./They had been laid out//in tainted rooms,/their eyelids glistening,/their dough-white hands/shackled in rosary beads.' At this time people pine for 'ceremony, customary rhythms' as news comes in of each neighbourly murder. He returned to the description of Irish wakes in 'Route 110' V11, (Human Chain, 2010) as he describes funeral customs now long gone. '...Right through the small hours, the ongoing card game/Interrupted constantly by rounds//Of cigarettes on plates, biscuits, cups of tea'. And of the funeral of his beloved aunt Mary he wrote 'They

THE NIGHT OF OTHER DAYS

bore her lightly on the bier. Four women,/Four friends - she would have called them girls - stepped in/And claimed the final lift beneath the hawthorn.'[4]

Death and religion were always intertwined and Heaney mythologised both. But when he referred to 'the long rites of Irish political and religious struggles' he was accused of mythologizing current savagery. Longley said 'A struggle is not a rite, and murder, like that at Vinegar Hill, is not heraldic when it happens. The decorative tinge that Heaney imparts to violence and to history derives from a ritualising habit, which itself derives from his religious sensibility'.

From the poem 'Funeral Rites' it is a short step from ceremony and customary rites to the world of megalithic doorways, charming noble barbarity, and to 'The Tollund Man' (WO,1972). The poet tells us that this bog figure seemed almost an ancestor. 'I felt very close to this. And the sacrificial element, the territorial element, the whole mythological field surrounding these images was very potent... a sacrificial, ritual religious element in the violence of contemporary Ireland'.

Because Heaney fused the physical and the metaphysical some critics saw poems in 'North' as overly ritualistic and many felt that they have had a petrifying effect on his lyrical poetry. Some members of the Belfast Group felt betrayed. Significantly he says 'I created a stand-off when I left and they said their piece. You get my side in the poem 'Exposure'.[5]

Neil Corcoran identified 'Wintering Out', 1972 as 'the seminal single volume of the post-1970 period of English Poetry'. Combined with the exactness of description and evocation of his first volumes there now came a more precise sense of political context, not surprising given that Heaney had experienced it 'bomb by bomb'.

Although he was now accepted as a trustworthy and honest spokesman for the Catholic nationalist population his interpretation of the 'Northern situation' was rejected by the Protestant unionist citizens. They questioned the basis of his interpretation and rejected his reliance on myth. A storm of criticism developed and continued with the publication of 'North', 'Field Work' and 'Station Island'.

Heaney made his position clear. A good poem was a paradigm of good politics, a site of energy and tension and possibility, a truth-telling arena but not a killing field and after the 1969 riots 'from that moment the problems of poetry moved from being simply a matter of achieving the satisfactory verbal icon to being a search for images and symbols adequate to our predicament'. And a political poem has to 'outstrip the condition of tract or propaganda.'[6] In the words of Helen Vendler poems are 'provisional symbolic structures' not position-papers.

Turning now to the individual volumes, attention is immediately drawn to the violence in the dedication of 'Wintering Out' to David Hammond and Michael Longley. 'This morning from a dewy motorway I saw the new camp for the internees... a bomb had left a crater...' But it is a group of five short poems titled 'A Northern Hoard' that alerts the reader to the impact of the violence on the sensitive poet. The fault is opening 'out there beyond each curtained terrace' to the sound of gunshot, 'siren and clucking gas'. Must the poet crawl back 'to confront my smeared doorstep and what lumpy dead'? 'What do I say if they wheel out their dead'? 'Why do I unceasingly/ arrive late to condone/ infected sutures/and ill-knit bone'?

Neil Corcoran, in a chapter titled 'A Northern Hoard'(WO,1972) refers to a number of rather indifferent reviews which criticised Heaney for his lack of engagement with the political situation in Northern Ireland, in that he addressed the context rather than the conflict, but for Corcoran, probably the best commentator on Heaney's work, the book 'displays that peculiar charge and vibrancy' of a poet coming into possession

THE NIGHT OF OTHER DAYS

of his unique destiny. Two poems illustrate this, the opening dedicatory poem and 'Whatever You Say Say Nothing'. Heaney poses a direct question: 'What do I say if they wheel out their dead?' 'WO attempts to find a voice for this abjection and to find images of suffering, endurance and resistance which will not seem already seen. Heaney was hurt into poetry by the Northern Ireland scene and, especially in the 'Northern Hoard' sequence, he fingers the cold beads of conflict. The poems 'hover' between the symbolic and the literal, realism and allegory, politics and philology as they probe the bonds between a people and their history. Most of those he writes about have been marginalised and suffer isolation, exploitation and betrayal. But the figure who towers over the book is 'The Tollund Man'.

In his attempt to find answers to contemporary questions, Heaney sought rationale in the bogs of Ireland and Denmark. He had read P.V.Glob's 'The Bog People' and now he vowed 'Some day I will go to Aarhus/To see his peat-brown head...' Bridegroom to the goddess, the Tollund Man had been sacrificed to the goddess of fertility in an annual ceremony to ensure rich harvests. The poet will go to Jutland and in the old man-killing parishes 'I will feel lost,/Unhappy and at home'. These are the words of a man who has entered the political arena and the domain of myth.

Corcoran comments: 'This use of the word home, which goes beyond irony and sadness into tragedy, is utterly comfortless and desolating.' And in Jutland his utter isolation is emphasised by his inability to speak the local language.

There are six poems in 'North' (N,1975) which can be described as 'bog poems'. 'Kinship' is Heaney's hymn to bogland where, 'kinned' to the strangled victim, he uncovers the cooped secrets 'of process and ritual' with each bog-bank a gallows drop. Soft and feminine as the fall of windless rain the bog is an insatiable bride 'casket, midden, floe of history'. Heaney stands at the edge of centuries facing a goddess. This is the soft 'vowel' of earth

HUGH MULROONEY

'composing the floor it rots into'. But bog is also our mother ground 'sour with the blood of her faithful' and the place where the goddess swallows our love and terror.

Four exhumed figures are described, 'Beheaded Girl', 'Tollund Man', 'Bog Queen' and 'The Grauballe Man'. The Bog Queen was barbered and stripped by turfcutter's spade on Lord Moyne's estate in Northern Ireland. Their throats had been cut. The murdered, forgotten, nameless terrible girl had been beheaded, ('Strange Fruit').

'Punishment' is the most disturbing poem. 'I can feel the tug/of the halter at the nape/of her neck, the wind/on her naked front'. The wind blows her nipples to amber beads. Blind-folded and with her hair shaven she was weighted down and drowned in the bog. Heaney declares that he could almost love this beautiful young adulteress but would probably remained silent. Then he makes an astonishing declaration. 'I who have stood dumb/when your betraying sisters,/cauled in tar,/wept by the railings,//who would connive/in civilized outrage/yet understand the exact/and tribal, intimate revenge'.

Volumes have been written in reaction to 'Wintering Out', 'North' and 'Field Work'. Clive James suggested comparison with WB Yeats. Robert Lowell saw Heaney as 'The greatest Irish poet after Yeats'. John Carey identified 'The one undoubtedly major poet in the English-speaking world'. Elmer Andrews welcomed a scholar, a critic and a poet. Denis O Donoghue spoke of the remarkably profuse welcome extended to 'North' and the consolation of hearing that there is a deeper, truer life going on beneath the bombings and the torture and says that interpreted form an archaeological point of view his poems 'offer a perspective of depth upon local and terrible events'. Mark Patrick Hederman in comparing parts one and two of 'North' talks of poems more daring, works from the heart and the singing of a song that shatters itself even in the sounding. Approval is voiced by Michael

THE NIGHT OF OTHER DAYS

Hartnett, Richard Murphy, Christopher Ricks, John Jordan, Denis Donoghue and many others.

But Heaney was subjected to much criticism, often from former fellow poets in 'The Group'. He took a philosophical view: 'I've been overwritten with praise and to a lesser extent with blame', he said adding that he has learned to inspect criticism 'to see if it is salutary objection or shitty backlash'. He might also have heeded Clive James' observation that there are occasions when the main purpose of criticism is to draw attention to the commentator or the columnist rather than the work in question. And there was the advice of Ezra Pound: pay no attention to the opinions of those who have not themselves produced notable work. 'I've had my own Star Wars defence system against certain attacks' Heaney said.[6.]

Blake Morrison accused Heaney of granting respectability to sectarian killing and suggests that whereas it might be going too far to say that the poem 'Punishment' and the 'Bog-poems' generally offer a defence of Republicanism 'they are a form of explanation'. Indeed, he says, the whole procedure of 'North' is such as to give sectarian killing in Ulster a historical respectability which is not usually given in day-to-day journalism. But he concedes that Heaney excludes inter-tribal warfare by concentrating on the Catholic psyche as bound to immolation and within that immolation to savage tribal loyalties. The source of current troubles lies deep in mythic history and unavoidable cycles result... love and terror; casualty and sacrifice; myth and history; land-possession and political subjugation...all inextricably mixed. On the subject of his poetry, Morrison says it is less comforting than is supposed, far from being 'whole' it is torn, tense and divided against itself. Far from being archaic 'it registers the tremors and turmoils of its age, forcing traditional forms to accept the challenge of harsh intractable material'. He wrote as a Wordsworthian about traditional labourers and craftsmen but he is also shaped by 'the modes of post-war Anglo-American poetry'.

HUGH MULROONEY

According to James Simmons, Heaney offers a barren nationalism that descends into vanity and self-pity. He is accused of violent nationalism, reactionary politics and he is a poet 'without moral centre' who will become irrelevant! David Lloyd says that Heaney's typical poetic paradigm serves 'to reduce history to myth, furnishing an aesthetic resolution to conflicts constituted in quite specific historical junctures by rendering disparate events as symbolic moments expressive of an underlying continuity of identity'.

Ciaran Carson identifies Heaney as a laureate of violence, a mythmaker, an anthropologist of ritual killing, an apologist for 'the situation' and in the last resort a mystifier who, in applying wrong notions of history, fails to see what is before his eyes. Along with Lloyd he objects to what he sees as the dangerous conflation of myth and history. According to Lloyd and Carson, Heaney is saying that suffering is natural, inevitable and without political consequences. It belongs to the realms of sex, death and inevitability. They say that Heaney presents horrific acts of mutilation and killing as inevitable recurring natural cycles. He leaves us, they say, with no sense of why or how they happened.

A. Alvarez is less than impressed and his criticism is oblique and a little surprising. He describes Heaney's poetry as 'steady, discreet, reliable and highly successful' in its appeal to contemporary English taste. The poet is besotted with words and his fine way with words is a mark of his Irishness. Maybe the universal praise heaped on him reflects the fact that he is the token Irish star on the British literary scene and he adds, he writes so eloquently about 'that troubled and troublesome sore on the British conscience', (Northern Ireland).

Blake Morrison, while acknowledging that Heaney has cultivated a self-image of a relaxed traditional craftsman in his interviews and lectures, points out that one does not have to look too deeply to see that his work is less comforting and comfortable than has been supposed. "Far from being 'whole', it is tense, torn,

THE NIGHT OF OTHER DAYS

divided against itself; far from being straightforward, it is layered with often obscure allusions; far from being archaic, it registers the tremors and turmoils of its age, forcing traditional forms to accept the challenge of harsh intractable material".

Heaney's most strident critic, Edna Longley[7], wrote...'and does the idea of the North really provide an umbrella for the not very Nordic north of Ireland, fertility rites and capital punishment in prehistoric Denmark, and the conquests of the Vikings in Ireland – coming to and from the north?' On the relevance of 'The Tolland Man' as victim and Christ-surrogate whose death might redeem 'the scattered, ambushed/ Flesh of labourers' and whose image reminds Heaney of his ancestors, she criticises his failure to distinguish voluntary from involuntary martyrdom and accuses him of sitting on the fence, not in the political but in the artistic sense.

Longley places Heaney in a tradition which 'travels a rich boundary between conscious and unconscious and fuses physical and metaphysical explorations'. In his earlier poems he probes the darkness, sets it echoing but does not switch on a light. In reaching political conclusions he does light a candle but Longley objects. Most of his poems in 'North', part one, have a factitiously ritualistic quality she says while those in part two 'tend to either accommodate and collaborate with the clichés they aim to express or to become melodramatic and over-literary'. The imaginative failings in 'North' result from its gestures of Catholic and Nationalist commitment, and his view of the deeper tragedy is fixed and pre-ordained. Longley wonders if this has any petrifying effect on poetic life. She claims to grant to poetry some kind of transcendent power and force. Seamus Deane grants the same but in his case it is granted to the Irish resistance to English tradition, influence and oppression.

Much comment has been expressed on the final poem 'Exposure' in 'North'. Murphy [8] surmises that the poem may be

HUGH MULROONEY

an admission of failure to trace in large-scale, grand, ostentatious mythical gestures 'the diamond absolutes of Northern Ireland and its history'. It seems certain that by the end of 'North' the exhumed bodies have lost their appeal. Fascination with myth can distract from the real horror and atrocity. The poem 'Strange Fruit' faces the reality of a beheaded girl and this is no romantic dream. The fore-going is sample of the re-action to 'North' and 'Wintering Out', especially their mythical linkage with contemporary violence in Northern Ireland. The harshness of some of the criticism, especially from former friends and colleagues must have been deeply wounding.

CHAPTER

Integrity

14

'Field Work' (F W) was published in 1979. Many commentators have traced the progression from his first work 'Death of a Naturalist' (DN, 1966). They have noted the movement from the rich sensuousness of DN and DD to the myth-making of WO and N. A plainer style emerges in FW and 'Station Island' (SI, 1984) leading to the parable-style 'Haw Lantern' (HL, 1987).[1]

There are no traces of consoling or explanatory myth in FW. The victims of violence are friends, relations, acquaintances, not distant myth-beautiful images.[2] In this volume the violence is not tamed; crisis is not domesticated. The dead and their killers live in the same house and together they hear the same wild goose pass overhead. The response to violence is now highly-charged nervousness and split-second tenderness as atrocity is experienced at a close level. The poetry now yearns towards a possible peaceful future. Forgiveness must find its nerve and voice. Prophesy should replace nostalgia. Questions, guesses, voices, answers are the order of the day. The monologue of the self becomes a dialogue with others. Choices must be made and responsibilities must be shouldered. By the time of the publication of 'Field Work', Heaney's work was increasingly seen in terms of the Yeatsian conflict between artistic freedom and public responsibility, with the acceptance that artistic freedom must allow for 'social and familial responsibility too'.[3] He turns from ceremonial communal response to the issue of 'individual pain and individual outrage'. The dominant register of many of his poems in FW is interrogative as he questions 'the inherited political, cultural and religious truisms of his community.'[4] Given that the late 1970s and early 1980s were among the worst years of violence in Northern Ireland, with hunger strikes and prison protests, it is little wonder that Heaney, having agonised over his personal 'responsible tristia' in the poem 'Exposure' (N), would continue to feel a responsibility to speak for his community. He knew that he was now expected to address the question of Northern Ireland as he had in WO and N but on different terms. In FW he returns again and again to the political scene. From Glanmore in the Irish Republic he looked over his shoulder as he struggled not only to find the words adequate to the predicament in Northern Ireland but also to address the question of his own responsibilities in the situation.

In 'The Toome Road' (FW), he records the bitterness of the farmer who encounters a British army convoy, 'How long were they approaching down my roads/ As if they owned them'? Asked if he resented the presence of the British army in Northern Ireland, Heaney's response to Dennis O'Driscoll was measured. On the one hand he recognised that 'the squadies' were simply doing their job while on the other he was angered by the constant harassment. And he recalled his recurring dream that someday the Russians would water their horses by the shores of Lough Neagh.

He always sought a soil 'that will cultivate the creative', the life-giving, the hopeful, the creative and the sexual.[5.] But even this creative soil is divided. Catholic nationalist soil is of the earth itself. That of Protestant loyalist belongs to 'the earth cultivated'

THE NIGHT OF OTHER DAYS

and Heaney's Ireland is torn between the two. This is shown in the struggle between 'rationality and mythic atavism' in 'Hercules and Antaeus', where some commentators would connect Hercules with the Nationalist viewpoint while connecting Antaeus with a primitive, tribal bigoted view of Northern Ireland.

The inside cover of the 1979 paperback edition of FW notes that the central themes of the collection, which includes groups of elegies and love poems, include the individual's responsibility for his own choices, the artist's commitment to his vocation and 'the vulnerability of all in the face of circumstances and death'. In 'Field Work' a new territory is opened up. Poems to craftsmen not only commemorate lost innocence, they attempt to restore lost wisdom as Heaney's journey continues towards personal integrity and civic consciousness. There are personal meditations on history and on Ireland, and elegies dedicated to dead friends and artists. As the work proceeds 'the worlds of art, history, domestic life and politics appropriate each other'. The covenant between art and life is most clear in his elegies for murdered friends and the hope is expressed that it may be possible to transcend the conditions of one's fate. 'How perilous is it to choose/not to love the life we are shown'?

The progression from DN to 'The Hawthorn Lantern' (HL 1987) is an advance from earth to air. In the early poems 'his people are bent over towards the ground, processional stooping through turf, victims, solidarity, digging'.[6] But In "Station Island', 'Sweeney Astray', 'Seeing Things' and 'The Spirit Level' there is a man transformed into a bird, visions to lighten the heart, children sliding, kites flying, cars flowing, ships drifting through the sky; drifting, flotation, light-hearted liberating upward movement. By then the poet is walking on air.

Seamus Deane sees the progression as a journey to personal integrity and civic conscience.[7] FW is meant to be read as a book - a useful structure reflecting a unity of purpose where poems deal with all aspects of his existence - mind, voice, body, spirit.

HUGH MULROONEY

Heaney's idea of healing through poetry has been shattered by The Troubles in Northern Ireland. Now a new territory is being opened up in pursuit of 'a reconciliation so far denied, although so nearly achieved'. He begins to consider his literary heritage, to interrogate it in relation to his experience of violence in Northern Ireland and 'to elicit from it a style of survival as a poet'. He feels that his writing must face confrontation with the ineffable in order to vindicate its authenticity.

His poetry in and after FW tries to move from Antaean darkness into Herculean light.[8.] The Antean influence has produced his most powerful and original poetry, straight from the heart, 'it shatters itself in the sounding'. Now dawns the realisation that 'The way we are living/timorous or bold,/will have been our life…' Choosing one's life is a matter of choosing the bold course, that of not being overwhelmed, not driven by the weight of grief or the glare of atrocious events. This he believed but was sometimes inclined to 'galumph rather than glide'[9]. Choosing between timorous and bold was not easy. His boldness and that of his wife Marie is not in doubt when the risks are considered in leaving Belfast, in throwing up the security of a prestigious university post and in becoming a freelance writer. This confidence and boldness comes from his poetic mastery. His timorousness originates in the face of the creative mystery. Heaney never doubted the wisdom of their move to Glanmore but it was not due to boldness, it was due to 'sleepwalk rather than spasm'. When he returned from Berkeley in 1971, he knew that some shift had to happen. There was also the fact that although his move involved a stand-off with The Group in Belfast it also produced a measure of empowerment. Glanmore marked a new stage; it was a retreat; it marked a renewal; a hedge-school; two people recommitting to their chosen way of life. After a couple of years it became 'a locus that was being written into poems'. This started with 'Exposure' and continued with the sonnets.

THE NIGHT OF OTHER DAYS

Heaney said that in his earlier works he was burrowing inwards. Now came a period of self-interrogation and inner struggle. 'I wanted to turn out, to go out, and I wanted to pitch the voice out'[10]. He no longer wanted a door into the dark, rather one into the light. The light which he sought 'derives from clarity of expression, from plain speaking. In 'Oysters' he expresses anger 'that my trust could not repose/ In the clear light, like poetry or freedom/ Leaning in from the sea'. He longs for amplitude and freedom of mind, but is aware of the drag of conscience related to history and politics.[11] In conversation with Dennis O'Driscoll he spoke of how the unwritten poem is always going to be entangled with your own business, part of your accident and incoherence – which is what drives you to write. 'But once a poem is written, it is, in a manner of speaking, none of your business'[12]. Asked about poetry as prophesy, Heaney noted that, because he had been nurtured within the magisterium of the Roman Catholic Church and tuned to Gregorian Chant, he was 'less likely to be a voice in the wilderness'. Nonetheless the poet can reach for the stars, can shake free of entanglements, can walk on air.

'Field Work' opens with the toasting of friendship in the eating of oysters and closes with the eternal eating of a living head. The reticence of 'North' is gone and Heaney 'is back to the verbal showman's sleight of hand'.[13]

A controversial interpretation of 'Oysters' has been written recently.[14] Certainly, the author says, it strikes a radically different note from the 'responsible tristia' of 'North'. The whole poem and its intricate acoustics, is 'a paean to taste, to the tongue and to the pure verb itself'. While it touches on history, geography, politics, astronomy and poetry itself, its language is emphatically erotic. For the author in question there is 'something profoundly, tragically and truly unresolved in this poem'.

'I ate the day/Deliberately, that its tang/Might quicken me all into verb, pure verb'. In Andrew's words the poem 'Oysters' 'opened at once the oyster, the mouth, the meal and the book'! Closing the book is 'Dante's insatiable avenger and the hideous devouring of a living head through all eternity. 'Oysters' circles elegantly around on itself until it ends where it began, with language. But Heaney's real strength and originality is not in flashy rhetorical pieces, but rather in modest perfect little poems like 'homecomings', the short sequence 'Field Work', or the closing stanzas of 'The Skunk'.[15.]

Heaney translated 'Ugolino' so that it would be read in the context of the 'dirty protests' by IRA inmates in the Maze prison.[16] It is an underground poem, the expression of creativity in the face of history, and also reflective of his personal experiences and relationships. Being a work of translation, and in its placing at the end of the volume, it also indicates the direction of his future poetic work.

The poet's personal life seems happy but politics, power and violence intrude and FW includes elegies and tributes to dead relatives, friends and colleagues. The elegies record questions, reflections and recollections, penned years after the events and in moments 'when the bird sings very close/To the music of what happens'. Some poems revert to the home ground at Mossbawn, but it is the public poems that predominate and in these it is the social rather than the political voice that is heard. Public, local, political and aesthetic now merge. And there is his claim to artistic freedom and the efficacy of poetry. He says that whereas no poem ever stopped a tank, poetry can change existing feelings or create new ones, especially in times of violence and stress like those prevailing in Northern Ireland in the 1970s. This theme is fully developed in 'Crediting Poetry', his Nobel Lecture, 1995.

Elegies in FW record friendships with Robert Lowell, Sean O Riada, and Francis Ledwidge. Two of the elegies are considered among the very best of Heaney's writing: 'Casualty' and 'The Strand at Lough Beg'. In 'Casualty' Heaney is most emphatic about

THE NIGHT OF OTHER DAYS

a public event, and this is his only poem about Bloody Sunday in 1972. On that day thirteen unarmed men were shot dead and one hundred and thirty seriously wounded by members of the Parachute Regiment. 25years later, in The Sunday Times of February 2nd 1997, he marked the anniversary with the words 'And in the dirt lay justice like an acorn in the winter/ Till its oak would sprout in Derry where the thirteen men lay dead'. These words recorded his revulsion at the Bloody Sunday massacre and also his utter rejection of the conclusions of the Widgery Enquiry, which in its conclusions added serious insult and injury.

'Casualty' is an elegy for one man. It is not Heaney' reflections on nationalist sentiments.[17] Louis O Neill was a personal friend, a regular drinker at Heaney's father-in-laws's pub at Ardboa and a seasoned fisherman with whom the poet spent many hours on the water. On the Wednesday evening of the burial of the Bloody Sunday victims, the IRA imposed a curfew on pubs. Louis, finding the pub at Ardboa closed, went to a pub some miles away, where he met his death. The fatal bomb was not planted by the IRA.

'Casualty' honours a personal friend and the poem is back-lit by the poet's awareness of the historical moment and the political circumstances[18]. The violent death of the amiable drinker would have been recorded as just another casualty in the statistics of Northern Ireland. But he is saved from anonymity without mention of his name. The final section of the poem is concerned with the rhythm of life, death, funerals, poetry and memory. The purring of the hearse' motor, the purling of the fishing-boat' screw …'Dawn-sniffing revenant, /Plodder through midnight rain,/Question me again'.

"'Casualty' is a public poem of the sort that I'd aspire to" was Heaney's own verdict. For some 'The Strand at Lough Beg' marks the high-point of FW. Images of a peaceful pastoral countryside contrast with the outrage of the mutilation and death of Heaney's cousin, Colum McCartney, driving home from a football match. Colum was the victim of a random killing by Loyalist paramilitaries. Heaney was in Kilkenny at the time and he did not attend the funeral. He later said he felt something between unease and guilt. In the elegy he washes away the blood and the muck, lays his cousin flat and plaits a Green Scapulars 'to wear over your shroud'. He returned to the death in 'Station Island', (SI 1984), and allowed his cousin to allege that he 'confused evasion and artistic tact'.

The delightful friend, Sean Armstrong, is remembered in 'A Postcard from North Antrim'. In his dedicated social work, Sean had crossed the divide between communities in Northern Ireland and his 'candid forehead stopped/A pointblank teatime bullet'. Reciter of ballads, singer of songs, a man who enjoyed wine and dance, he is remembered especially for the night in his kitchen when Seamus first danced with Marie. Sean had been a student at Queen's when Heaney was there. He spent some time in communes 'of one sort or another' in California. Describing him as a wonderful, colourful, original man 'half-hippy, half-artist, wholly committed to trying to do some good in Belfast', Heaney surmises that he might have been regarded by the hard men as some kind of spy.

'Triptych' tells of two young men with rifles on a hill. Christopher Ewart-Biggs, British ambassador to the Republic of Ireland was killed when his car was blown-up by the IRA near his residence on the outskirts of Dublin in 1976. Violence spilled over the border in the seventies. The British Embassy in Dublin was burned to the ground and several bombs were detonated with major loss of life. In 'After a Killing' there is ambiguity in relation to the gunmen. Are they real or hatched from memory? Are their guns weapons or instruments? Are they innocent hunters or IRA? The violence of the event contrasts with the normality and trust of the girl delivering new potatoes, three tight green cabbages, 'and carrots / With the tops and mould still fresh on them'. She

THE NIGHT OF OTHER DAYS

looks cynicism straight in the eye and represents 'The pined-for, unmolested orchid'.

In the second 'Triptych' poem, 'Sibyl', there are images of explosions, cracked gables and fouled magma. Sibyl said that our very form is bound to change. Unless forgiveness finds its nerve and voice and the fouled magma incubates bright nymphs our island will remain full of comfortless noises and the sound of the helicopter 'shadowing our march at Newry/The scared, irrevocable steps'.

In 'Elegy' the way we are living, timorous or bold, will have been our life, with Seamus Heaney and with Robert Lowell. He 'drank America like the heart's iron vodka, spent a night in Heaney's kitchen and spoke with love and arrogance. 'Will we meet soon again? Heaney asked as they bade goodnight outside the door in Glanmore. 'Unlikely' came the reply. Ten days later he was dead. 'I'll pray for you.'

'In Memoriam Francis Ledwidge' describes a young man in his Great-War Tommy's uniform. His haunted Catholic face reflects the inner turmoil of an idealistic young man who followed from Boyne waters to the Balkans. 'To be called a British soldier while my country has no place among nations!'.

FW contains elegies, love poems and a sonnet sequence. In the love poems and sonnets Heaney is following Wordsworth rather than Yeats. In October1974 he delivered a lecture, 'Feeling. Into Words' to The Royal Society of Literature.[19] 'I was getting my first sense of crafting words and for one reason or another, words as bearers of history and mystery began to invite me'. Each one of the sonnets records a liberation of feeling after stress, of feeling which is the greater because it has absorbed stress.[20] What is celebrated above all in the sonnets is relief from the stress of the Northern Ireland conflict. The peace of an inscape is established and held in the face of a violent landscape. Each verse turns like a plough on a headland as the words move from the music of the unconscious to

HUGH MULROONEY

the music of what happens[21]'vowels ploughed into other: opened ground'. Juxtaposed is a sense of beauty and a sense of dread; a sense of loss and revival; ominous and brilliance; a black rat and a human face; a gale warning and a peaceful haven; words entering almost a sense of touch...'These things are not secrets but mysteries...small ripples across our drinking water and now across my heart' and a wild white goose heard after dark above the drifted house.

Sonnet number one is written for Ann Sadlemeyer 'our heartiest welcomer'. It marks the end of four years living in the cottage at Glanmore, their 'hedge-school'. Ann is Augusta in 'Glanmore Eclogues'. She was Professor Emeritus in the University of Toronto and she rented the cottage in 1972. Heaneys purchased the cottage in 1988.

In October 1975 Heaneys moved to Dublin and Seamus joined the staff of Carysfort College of Education. The College, under the management and control of the Archbishop of Dublin and the Sisters of Mercy, was 'a little lean-to that would shelter me with a salary and leave me alone'. He felt that it would allow for a less public role than a university. Carysfort launched its B.Ed programme that year and Seamus was eventually appointed Head of the English department. He served there until 1981 at which stage in addition to feeling himself 'crumbling down into administration again' he felt that the Irish Catholic forms and presuppositions of the institution seemed to be demanding from him 'a degree of ratification which he felt increasingly unable to give'. Be that as it may, it must be said that Carysfort allowed him total freedom to pursue his American ambitions and to continue writing, lecturing and broadcasting. When Carysfort College was closed in 1988, under a political decree which must rank as one of the most stupid decisions by an Irish minister of education, Heaney, from America, marked the occasion with a poem which

THE NIGHT OF OTHER DAYS

was presented to all students and all members of staff at the final graduation ceremony in 1988.[23]

Elmer Andrews considered FW to be a better book than N. It is more profoundly exemplary, she said, and could only have been written by a poet who is trusted and this was especially important in an Ireland torn by distrust.

The poem 'The Harvest Bow' was one of the first things he wrote after 'North' and he described the texture as being richer than many of the other poems in FW. Evans described the harvest bow as 'decorative twists of straw finely plaited and tied into loops or interlaced'. Girls wear them in their hair and boys in their coats. They are exchanged as a sign of mutual attachment or given as tokens of love or luck. They are made from wheat, flax or fine wild grasses.[25] As Heaney contemplates the 'frail device' he has now pinned to the deal dresser, his motto is 'the end of art is peace'. In the poem plaiting the love-knot of straw tongue-ties the father but his son can glean the unsaid off the palpable. As they walk together, a homesick boy and his father, whacking the tips off weeds with his ashplant, it is left to the boy to contrast, balance, repair and articulate on a lost rural heritage, on love and on the art of a poet.

'The Skunk' is an unlikely subject of a love poem. If disturbed it can emit an atrocious smell, enough to clear an entire neighbourhood. The poet is sitting on the veranda of the house he occupies in California. Marie is in Dublin. Heaney's desk light picks out the oranges on the tree nearby and the air is rich with the scent of eucalyptus. The skunk comes by with her black and white striped erect tail as she snuffs the boards just feet away. The poet's mind is oceans away as he hears 'the sootfall of her things at bedtime' and her 'head-down, tail-up hunt in a bottom drawer for the black plunge-line nightdress'. This is an exquisitely comic love poem,[26] based on reciprocal trust and love. There is no offence intended. What might be considered inappropriate is a confident expression of affection and love. Heaney talked of an intimate experience being transformed into an object to be inspected. 'It calls you close and the intimacy is not embarassing'. In 'The Skunk' there is a playfulness and 'a definite serious engagement' and he still associates the waving of the black and white plume with the erotic!

CHAPTER

Voices

15

When Seamus Heaney moved to Glanmore from Northern Ireland in 1972, he set himself the task of translating the medieval Irish poem Buile Suibhne (Sweeney's Rage). He relied on the translation of J.G. O'Keefe which had been published in 1913. The original was based on oral tradition dating back to the battle of Moira in the year 637 and a manuscript written in County Sligo in the 1670s. Heaney made use of the O'Keefe translation rather than the Irish language of the original.[1] Although he completed the work he was unhappy with the result and he filed it away, ('sixty pages in a drawer...The pay-off came a decade later with the 'Sweeney Redivivus' poems'). He completely revised, improved and published it in 1983 under the title 'Sweeney Astray'. In the earlier version he stayed too close to the original translation and forged too close a link between Sweeney and Heaney[2]. There was also the guilt and stress of his years in Belfast. Heaney brought his own dark historical moments from Ulster – random bombings, 'dirty protests', hunger strikes – as he wove them into the public and private lives of 'Sweeney Astray' (SA 1983), 'Station Island' (SI, 1984) and 'The Haw Lantern' (HL 1987).

For years, Heaney tells us, he was bound to the desk attempting to carry his portion of the weight of the world – blowing up sparks for a meagre heat. Eventually he straightened up and made space in his imagination for both the marvellous and the murderous. He saw glimpses of the ideal intersecting with natural process and 'manifesting that order of poetry where we can at last grow up to that which we stored up as we grew'. He also knew that one's sense of justice and reality change over time and his mind remained fluid and responsive.

Poetic thinking is not static and a poem is a reflection of reality at a particular time and in a specific space. Some critics complained that he continually hesitated between the timorous and the bold but Vendler[3] pointed out that a poem is not a position paper and is a reflection of the poet's feelings, responses and emotions to a particular situation at a specific time. A poem provides a focus where our power to concentrate is concentrated back on ourselves[4]. It allows the presentation of the private mind and heart caught in the changing events of a geographical space and a historical epoch. Sheamus Heaney has done this for himself, his country and his time'.[5] Asked by Dennis O Driscoll: What has poetry taught you?, he replied, "That there's such a thing as truth and it can be told – slant'. Subjectivity is worth defending; poetry itself has virtue; poetry he said is a ratification of the impulse towards transcendence and represents the need for an ultimate court of appeal. [6]

A crucial element is the language. After the publication of 'Wintering Out' it was inevitable that he would confront the political situation in Northern Ireland and this, in turn, had implications for the language of his poetry. Because he was 'involved in the tradition of the lyric' he would have to 'take the English lyric and make it eat stuff that it had never eaten before'.

THE NIGHT OF OTHER DAYS

[7] Given his role as public spokesman this led to greater scrutiny of his lyric, his responses and his language. In 'Feeling Into Words' he spoke of his search for appropriate images and symbols which, without abandoning fidelity to the processes and experience of poetry, would present a humane perspective while granting the religious intensity of the violence its authenticity and complexity. The publication of 'Sweeney Astray' (SA, 1983), 'Station Island' (SI, 1984) and 'The Haw Lantern' (HL, 1987) marked further progress in this search. And as he later observed, in relation to his visit to Burnt Norton, 'I realised that I did not really want a landscape to materialize since I had long since internalised a soundscape'.

Central to his situation was the question 'can an English-speaking poet do justice to the translation of an Irish-language medieval document?' and 'what is the relevance of a medieval Irish saga to the life of a Northern Ireland Unionist, or for that matter a member of the IRA?' Writing in 'Poetry Ireland Review', Spring 1989, in a piece 'Earning a Rhyme', Heaney wrote that in that situation the translator must respect historical, cultural and political contexts. In the 1960's, Ulster poets were being pressurised towards identity politics which might have led to sectarian expression. How then could a medieval Irish poem engage with a Northern Irish Unionist or 'the wild men of the IRA'? Perhaps naively, Heaney hoped that the medieval poem might lead unionists to look with sympathy at their Irish heritage and find areas of common ground.

His own ancient Irish heritage led Heaney back to medieval Ireland but by now he was also reading Viking and Icelandic sagas and this was to lead to a rich harvest. Asked if he considered ancient Irish writings to belong in some way to himself he pointed out that many poets in Ireland, north and south, were 'ploughing up the ground of the classics in translation'. He himself was following the footsteps of Eibhleen Dhubh Ni Chonaill, Brian

HUGH MULROONEY

Merriman and Nuala Ni Dhomhnaill. In his translations he was also incorporating the contemporary violent political scene and his emotional response to it. And he was indicating future paths, short and long-term, in poems like 'At the Water's Edge, (FW,1979)... .'to bow down, to offer up, to go barefoot, foetal and penitential, and pray at the water's edge'.

'Sweeney Astray' along with 'Station Island' raised three issues: poetic freedom, religious practises and public responsibility. In turn questions were raised in relation to guilt and answerability. Of his work 'Sweeney Astray' Heaney wrote, 'It is possible to read the work as an aspect of the quarrel between free creative imagination and the constraints of religious, political and domestic obligation'.[8] It tells the story of Sweeney, son of Colman Cuar, king of Dal-Arie, who was defeated at the battle of Mag Rath near Moira in 637. On hearing that the saintly Ronan Finn was surveying land with a view to the building of a monastery Sweeney rushed naked from battle (his wife Eorann snatched his cloak in an attempt to restrain him), killed a psalter with his spear, pierced the bell hanging from Ronan's neck and threw the holy book into the lake. Ronan cursed him: he would be a homeless bird-brain, naked among branches and he would die at spear-point. For seven years he wandered, flying from tree to tree and from place to place. In Heaney's own words this is '...the tale of a petty king from 7th century Ulster, cursed by a saint, transformed by the shock of battle into a demented flying creature, and doomed to an outcast's life in the trees'. Sweeney speaks of a depoliticised poetry drawing from nature. This birdman is the figure of a poet divided between freedom and social attachment, a lonely figure savouring solitude and freedom but 'gazing at his coffers of absence', looking over his shoulder at what he has lost and where he has been, weightless but aware of the appetites of gravity. 'I almost forget what it's like/ to be wet to the skin or longing for snow'. Now he yearns for the power of the albatross 'gliding for days without a single wingbeat'

THE NIGHT OF OTHER DAYS

and the concentration of the heron. In the Introduction to the 1983 publication, Heaney tells us that Sweeney is a literary creation, an historically-placed character, caught in the tension between an ancient culture and the power of an emerging Christian ethos. Sweeney is also the figure of the artist, displaced, guilty 'assuaging himself by his utterance' and through his free creative imagination raging against the constraints imposed by religious, political and domestic obligations. Heaney says he was attracted by the double note of 'relish and penitence'. Sweeney wanders over lands familiar to Heaney, which is why the fundamental relation with Sweeney is topographical. There was also a family of tinkers, called Sweeney, who camped under a keeled-up cart along the road to Anahorish school. Heaney's fundamental relation with Sweeney, however, is topographical. Sweeney's kingdom lay in what is now South County Antrim and north County Down, and for over thirty years Heaney lived on the verges of that territory, in sight of some of Sweeney's places and in earshot of others...One way or another, said the poet 'he seemed to have been with me from the start'.

The original poem has laments, dialogues, rhapsodies and curses and Heaney's interest is further stimulated by his familiarity with the ditchbacks, the trees and the landscapes so close to his home and by the clash between an ancient culture and an overbearing church. The immediate impact on the reader lies in its local power and in its descriptions of the beauty and power of nature. But the more permanent impact on Heaney was the writing of 'Sweeney Redivivus', part three of 'Station Island' (SI, 1984).

There is a real sense of rebellion, a sense of lashing out, in the twenty poems. A sense of things being said that might not otherwise have been said. 'I got a lot out of my system', Heaney said, especially in relation to the hostile reception in the north to his volume 'North' and to his resentment at being treated as a 'runner-in' in the south, (The Scribes).

HUGH MULROONEY

The poems are 'strictly dramatic monologues' and he found great satisfaction in writing them. He felt 'up and away', at full tilt...'Reckless and accurate and entirely Sweenified, as capable of muck-raking as of self-mockery. The poetry was in the persona'.[9] Sweeney achieved complete freedom and Heaney too aspired to be as free, even at the expense of a purgatorial element. He also inhabited Sweeney's voice and wanted Sweeney's voice to inhabit him. For years Heaney 'stalked around' the idea of kidnapping mad Sweeney into his own time and place' [10] As he did with 'Mycenae Lookout'. "When I finally pounced, both Sweeney and the watchman started singing like stool-pigeons".

The figure of Sweeney dominates all three sections of 'Station Island'. He achieves a freedom to roam but at the loss of an anchor. The sense of place replaces the sense of self. Heaney's description of him is that of a figure of the artist, displaced, guilty, assuaging himself by his utterance. It is possible to read 'Sweeney Astray' and 'Sweeney Redivivus' as an aspect of the quarrel between free creative imagination and the constraints of religious, political and domestic obligation'.[11] Taking on the characteristics of a bird and using the tree-perches of his boyhood Heaney/Sweeney subjects his own world to scrutiny in the 'Sweeney Redivivus' dramatic monologues. As the wet ball of twine/memory unwinds, he sees the rivets of the landing aircraft, the advance of tanks along roads near Mossbawn and the figure of a man alone in a car, driving lonely roads. Anger boils to the surface. The anger of the artist, 'a dog barking at the image of himself barking'; the poet who blew hot and cold in the face of the two-faced accommodating seed, breed and generation of the pious, exacting and demeaned; always whacked down to make sure he did not grow up; his faith in priest and God weakened; surveying the old icons of priest, patriot and informer. He will roost many nights on the slab of exile, he will migrate to the deepest chamber condemned 'to gaze at my coffers of absence'.

THE NIGHT OF OTHER DAYS

Heaney agonised on questions of artistic freedom and public responsibility and he used the voice-mask to express his innermost feelings and his revised world view. He strove to write 'a bare wire'. Sweeney is present in all three parts of 'Station Island', in the autobiographical lyrics of part one, the narrative of part two and the drama of part three and Heaney is the directing ventriloquist. The short poem 'Widgeon' can be read as an allegory of the voices in 'Station Island'.[12] Like the victims in Northern Ireland the bird has been cruelly shot. The voice of Seamus Heaney is activated in the voice-box of the dead bird and in the words of Sweeney. This is the Voice-Mask. The Mask is not used consistently in 'Station Island' and there are poems clearly in Heaney's own voice: 'The Artist', (Cezanne); 'In Illo Tempore, (loss of religious faith) ; 'The Old Icons' (Republican Politics). In 'The Loaning' (SI) Heaney is in the limbo of lost words as the loaning breathed on him 'When you are tired or terrified/your voice slips back into its old first place/ and makes the sound your shades make there' he writes, as he hears the snap of a twig in Dante's bleeding wood and the click of a cell lock.

Using the Mask of his own opposite, reality is revealed, art is created and hidden struggles are aired. This Mask is used to challenge authority and to assert his autonomy. Sweeney/Heaney expresses his dissatisfaction with work already completed and his doubts about his present fame and reputation. Doubt is a permanent condition as he revises earlier attitudes, beliefs and conditions. He doubts the value of a reputation based on acclamation 'I blew hot and blew cold' he wrote and his opinion of 'The First Kingdom' is harsh. He talks of 'glimmerings of the soul', sermons in stones, bitterness in gin, the pull of grief in a flying kite, the click of a cell door in Magilligan prison while his own insignificance is exposed in the binoculars of a prison guard viewing him from across the bay. The metaphor of the head as a ball of twine allows in its unwinding a review of his life and reputation. This review questions and sometimes abandons ideas and images from earlier poetry, ideas on politics, culture and religion pursued to the font of exhaustion. 'In the Beech' he uses the airy listening post to observe himself on the boundary between a small farm and the wide world. All this in public. Little wonder that he wrote in1983 'I've got so much attention that my impulse is to retreat rather than go forward at this stage'. But Heaney is quite clear in his verdict on 'Sweeney Redivivus'. He considered it to be the real harvest for his work on the medieval document. Having completed the task of translating 'Sweeney Astray' he felt a great burst of freedom in writing 'Sweeney Redivivus' because he was now tired of his own 'mournful bondings' to the matter of Ulster and he valued more 'the otherness of 'Buile Suibhne' as a poem from beyond'. He was up and away. Now 'I would meditate/that stone-faced vigil/ until the long dumb-founded/ spirit broke cover/ to raise a dust/ in the font of exhaustion'.

'Station Island' records a poet in transition as his voice-mask gives vent to his dis-satisfaction with the modes, manners and practices which have been the foundation of his reputation. He now risks a change of direction which, in the event, will be fully vindicated. The work includes many sermons, much moralising and advice on lessons to be learned. It deals with politics, penitence and mysticism. It recalls friends from childhood, neighbours, victims of sectarian violence, figures from history, legend and literature as it registers the examination of conscience of a poet punishing the lyric side of himself. For years he had been 'writing poems where I meet ghosts and shades'. They are among the ones he liked and valued most, he said, and he named 'Casualty, 'Station Island', 'The Tollund Man in Springtime' and 'District and Circle'... 'where I more or less ghostify myself.[13]

'Station Island' refers to a small island on Lough Derg in County Donegal. It has been a place of pilgrimage since Saint Patrick prayed there in the fifth century and is often referred to as

THE NIGHT OF OTHER DAYS

purgatorial and penitential. In the 1950s, the pilgrimage involved fasting for three days, with dry bread and drinks of cold tea or salty water, one night without sleep and a night and day walking barefoot around the stoney stations on this small windswept island. Heaney explained why he went there three times. He was curious; he liked the outing and the company and he relished the challenge of the strenuous cathartic ritual. As to his personal religious convictions he admits that Saint Patrick was never a spiritual figure for him and God the Father was a figure who occupied a realm of light…'a world ceiling that was a heaven-floor, a loft full of distance and translucence where he had absconded'. Heaney was losing his childhood faith and he regretted this. It happened offstage. 'You can lose your belief in the after-life, in religious dogma, but it is harder to lose the sense of an ordained structure…The infinite spaces may be silent, but the human response is to say that this is not good enough, that there has to be more to it than neuter absence'. [14] The spaces are far from silent and sometimes standing under a starry sky we can feel a primitive awe at the muteness of the vault. Heaney's pre-occupation with questions of space lasted his lifetime and were closely aligned with absence, displacement, death, emptiness and dis-illusionment … and with its relevance to wider questions related to religious practice and eternity.[15] 'Infinite spaces may be silent but they are continuously alive and fluent in their own wordless language'.

Space is a central theme: the absence of the felled chestnut tree; the place of his absent mother in his life; a heavenly place and a placeless heaven; displacement from his Mossbawn world, from the life academic and poetic; the reality, politics and poetry of displacement, of famine, of emptiness, of violence, social unrest and death. From the peaceful cottage in rural Wicklow he subjects himself to a rigorous examination of conscience as he walks barefoot around the penitential stations of Lough Derg. The space around had been emptied and from the interior of that space we hear many voices, voices of source and subject, of god and goddess, of poet and muse.[17] This is the space of clearances, of plantation, of famine, of the limbo of lost words of a dying hunger-striker, ('this voice from blight and hunger died through the black dorm...'). It is important that this space be desacralized.

Heaney had read accounts of Lough Derg by William Carleton, Kavanagh and Sean O' Faolain but they left him 'feeling anxious'. He turned to Dante's Purgatorio. The pilgrimage to Lough Derg becomes a series of meetings with ghosts. Ghosts could have historical identity but be scrutinised a-historically. Above all they would have a voice. This would allow a personal perspective and interpretation. It would allow the revenants to teach and advise on questions of ethics and art.[18]

He turns to Dante, a scholarly just man who honours peace in an environment corrupted by politics 'and rife with murderous betrayal'. His Divine Comedy describes a series of encounters with the dead where they explain their fate and offer advice and encouragement to Dante and his companion Virgil.

'Lough Derg' allowed Heaney to walk at a tangent around Northern Ireland's 'strictures and structures'. He had noted as far back as 1966 an interest in 'Lenten Stuff' and what he conceived as 'a poem cycle, with a central protagonist on his fixed route through the pilgrimage'... Dante's three-part journey scaled down to one. By the 1980s Heaney needed to write a poem to clear the blockage caused by his dislocation and his guilt related to Northern Ireland. He needed to be as free as Sweeney to tell his story fully and thoroughly. 'I wanted readers to open the book and walk into a world they knew behind and beyond the book...where they (and Heaney) might find coherence and integrity in a world of constant disintegration and slippage' he wrote in his introduction to the paperback edition of the book.

In Part One of 'Station Island' Seamus Heaney relies on objects and occasions he has encountered and experienced, and he subjects them to scrutiny. Sermons are given on stones and gin and the voice is his own. 'Stand still. You can hear/everything going on… And always the surface noise of the earth…till a twig snapped' and the blackbird stopped singing as it did when Dante snapped a twig in the bleeding wood and a voice sighed like sap 'at the end of green sticks in a fire'. There are times when Heaney cannot clear his head of lives in their element, when he is tongue-tied, timorous and bold, stretched between 'contemplation of a motionless point and the command to participate/actively in history'. But he must protect the soul's awakening. 'Don't break its flight again, /don't deny it; this time let it go free'. There is nothing to hide.

Poems speak of memories, locked in the sandstone keepsake, as he views lights on the prison-perimeter-fence across the bay; memories of a woman spitting on the stored danger of the hot smoothing–iron and aiming it like the resentment of women, feeling dragged upon and buoyant; old pewter and reminders that 'glimmerings are what the soul's composed of–Fogged-up challenges, far-conscience glitters/and hang-dog, half-truth earnests of true love'. Memories crowd in as he pauses to speak his morning offering that 'I may escape the miasma of spilled blood, govern the tongue, fear hybris, fear the god/until he speaks in my untrammelled mouth'. But fear not…the deer of poetry is standing 'in pools of lucent sound' and clandestine winds are stirring in the lyric wood. There is the bird's eye view of a single white egg; a loving message to his daughter, "So tender, I said, remember this…when you have grown away and stand at last/at the very centre of the empty city"; shadows on a workshop wall which recall a simple Christmas gift and 'a doorstep courtesy' to shun a uniform and a gun'.

'The Railway Children' was written between lectures while Heaney served as head of the English Department in Carysfort. One writer [19] compares its lucidity and the exhilarating aptness of its images to the 'limpid, ingenuous pieces' 'Mid-Term Break' and

HUGH MULROONEY

'Blackberry Picking' saying that 'it bears witness to and inscribes within itself' a chastened but entirely inevitable self-awareness. There is more than meets the eye in this poem, she writes, and the railway children know all they need to know. And for those of us whose childhood spanned the nineteen forties, the telegraph wires did hum, words did travel along them in raindrop pouches and although we thought we knew nothing we saw little difficulty in streaming through the eye of a needle.

It was in 1976, when he moved to his Dublin house that Heaney wrote about the loss of friends. He remembered Mr Lavery, blown up as he tried to carry a bomb out of The Ashley Arms, on the corner of the Avenue where Heaneys lived in Belfast. He never forgot Louis O'Neill the fisherman and friend from Ardboe. All the shades that he meets on Lough Derg have lived in the actual world and can offer advice on questions of ethics and aesthetics. In an inner courtroom of his being he vigorously examines his conscience as he tries to relieve different pressures. He uses different voices to lift different mental weights and to accomplish this he turns to Dante as the poet who transforms the personal into the universal, the social and the theological. He meets his own dead and is chastened and comforted by them. In the three parts of 'Station Island' he meets three groups: the living echoed in lyrics singing of ordinary lives; the dead translated (translate: 'to crossover') in visionary encounters; a blending of the two as Sweeney surveys human life from the treetops and speaks in various voices of hate, love, art, war and religion. The imagined pilgrimage to the Island becomes a series of encounters with ghosts who inhabit his own conscience.

His first encounter is with Simon Sweeney whose advice 'Stay clear of all processions' he is about to ignore. This Sweeney of the bow-saw has been dead for many years. There are shadows of Patrick Kavanagh in his admonition 'When they bade you think of

THE NIGHT OF OTHER DAYS

tinkers camped under a heeled-up cart you shut your eyes'. And Heaney turned, saw a crowd of shawled women and followed them.

Heaney gets out of his car to confront a raving man on the high road. He is Carleton, a spy, in religion a turncoat and in politics a traitor. "Your 'Lough Derg Pilgrim' haunts me" says Heaney. "O holy Jesus Christ, does nothing change', comes the reply. Heaney counters: I have no mettle for the angry role...and always Orange drums and neighbours on the road at night with guns. 'Remember everything and keep your head...We are earthworms of the earth and all that has gone through us will be our trace' says Carleton and leaves the poet alone.

Now the voice of the priest who perished in tropical forests because he wasn't able to meet the demands made on a young missionary. Glossy as a blackbird, Terry Keenan stands before the poet who remembers him as a clerical student home on vacation, raising the siege on god-fearing households, drinking tea and praising homemade brown bread. 'I was young and naïve' says the priest...'but what brings you here? ...Unless you are here taking the last look'.

Next his old teacher in the school at Anahorish, Master Barney Murphy, coming early to school each morning, to give extra unpaid tuition to the young Heaney, even if the young scholar felt uneasy and indifferent. Then the poet master : 'For what is the great moving power and spring of verse? Feeling, and in particular, love'. And Kavanagh, the one who had already written about the sacred isle: 'In my own day the odd one came here on the hunt for women'.

An essential requirement of the pilgrimage was the confession of sin at the foot of a priest. As he knelt, erotic thoughts crossed his mind. 'Freckle-face, fox-head, 'where did she arrive from?' Don't tell. Don't tell'. The breathed-on grill became a dress keyhole through which he glimpsed her honey-skinned shoulder blades and the wheatlands of her back, as the priest spoke about the need and chance to salvage everything, to re-envisage the zenith and glimpsed jewels of any gift mistakenly abased. 'Read poems as prayers and for your penance translate me something from Juan De La Cruz'. He made the poet feel there was nothing to confess, free to return to that eternal fountain...'I know its haven and its secrecy although it is the night'...and Heaney pens a poem of beauty, a hymn to the source of his own creativity...'But not its source because it does not have one, which is all sources' source and origin although it is the night'.[20] ... 'within this bread of life I see it plain/ although it is the night'.

The brutality and naked savagery of assassination and death through cowardice and hatred are voiced in the deaths of William Strathearn, Tom Delaney and Colm McCarthy, while the lonely deaths of ten hunger-strikers are focused on the death of Francis Hughes. In Lough Derg, Heaney had walked to the water's edge when he heard his name being called. He turned and felt a shock which is still with him. Standing before him was William Strathearn. He had been awakened by a persistent knocking on the door of his downstairs shop. He looked out and recognised two men. 'There's a child not well. Open up and see what you've got- pills or a powder or something in a bottle'. Ignoring the pleas of his wife, 'why didn't they go to a chemist'? William pulled on his shoes and his sportscoat, went down stairs and was killed in cold blood by two off-duty policemen whom he knew to see. He was still the same rangy midfielder 'in blue jersey and starched pants' killed by 'shites thinking they were the be-all and the end-all'. Heaney is surprised to hear himself saying 'forgive the way I have lived indifferent – forgive my timid circumspect involvement'. 'Forgive my eye; all that's above my head' came the reply as the ghost of William Strathearn trembled and faded.

This sequence reflects the influence of Dante, 'the first mover of the sequence'.[21] Heaney had read 'The Divine Comedy' in the 70s. His poem 'Ugolino' is described as preparatory press-ups

THE NIGHT OF OTHER DAYS

for the writing of 'Station Island' and both are placed in the Irish contemporary context. In 1979 Heaney returned from Harvard to mark final-year papers in Carysfort and 'Station Island' took shape in his head. The early 1980s marked a time of crisis in Northern Ireland. In The Maze prison, inmates covered their cell walls with their excrement in what became known as 'the dirty protest' and a hunger-strike led to the deaths of ten IRA prisoners. This was the context in which Heaney was writing. He believed that as the creative act is witnessed by history, and as the writer writes to be read, his poetry is always in context. Horace and Dante are his spiritual fosterers, 'Shades of the Sabine /On the beds of Saint Patricks Purgatory'.[22]

When he returned in 1979 Heaney went to visit his friend Tom Delaney who was in hospital in Belfast. The visit was not a success even though there was warm friendship between them. Heaney could not take his eyes off the heart-monitor screen, the conversation was forced and he hurried back to Dublin 'guilty and empty, feeling I had said nothing and that, as usual, I had somehow broken covenants, and failed an obligation'. Tom died shortly after and now he appeared briefly on Lough Derg reminding the poet of a long gaze and a last handshake. He fades and is replaced by the shade of Colum McCartney.

Colum was a second cousin and the only relation to die in the violence. He lived on the shore of Lough Beg, a lake familiar to Seamus Heaney and one that reminded him strongly of the lake where Dante and Virgil emerged from the murk of hell. He is the subject of 'The Strand at Lough Beg' (FW, 1979) where Heaney turns to find him on his knees 'with blood and roadside muck in your hair and eyes'. The poem describes how the poet washes him with handfuls of dew, lays him flat and plaits a scapulars of green rushes to wear over his shroud. (Virgil had wiped the mud from Dante's face with the dew of Purgatory).

HUGH MULROONEY

Colum died at the hands of a group, dressed in uniforms of The Ulster Defence Regiment, when he was stopped at a roadblock on the high road taken by Sweeney and by Carleton. Heaney was attending the 1975 Kilkenny Arts Week. He did not leave Kilkenny to visit Colum's family or to mourn him at his funeral. Now, in Lough Derg Heaney is confronted by 'a bleeding, pale-faced boy, plastered in mud' who says quietly 'you were there with poets when you got the word and stayed there with them, while your own flesh and blood was carted to Bellaghy from the Fews… the poets showed more agitation than you did'. In his defence Heaney pleaded that he was dumb, encountering what was destined. He felt like the bottom of a dried-up lake and could only see a deserted strand at Lough Beg. There follows a torrent of accusation: What you wrote was a lie; I accuse the Protestant directly of shooting me in the head, but I also accuse you; you confused evasion and artistic tact; you whitewashed ugliness and saccharined my death with morning dew.

Years later, when questioned by Dennis O'Driscoll, Heaney said that his feelings at the time were somewhere between guilt and unease.[23] He also said that this dialogue between Colum and himself was set up to explore the whole idea of public poetry and to raise the question of interweaving the creative and the responsible. This is the crucial debate voiced on the island of Patrick's Purgatory but first raised on 'The Strand at Lough Beg' when it was admitted that 'yours and mine' fought shy, could not crack the whip or seize the day, timorous, not bold. This is the strongest Dantesque poem written by Heaney and the voices go to the heart of the matter.

Hungry, footsore and weary the pilgrims sleep on their final night on the island. A voice from blight and hunger died through the black dorm, not in Lough Derg but in The Maze prison where two hunger-strikers were already dead and many more would follow. A stillness settled around Francis Hughes as he lay under

THE NIGHT OF OTHER DAYS

the safety of his prison blanket. His voice is heard, 'Often I was dogs on my own track of blood on wet grass...' In reply 'Unquiet soul, they should have buried you/In the bog where you threw your first grenade'. Now he lies 'laid out with a drift of mass cards/ At his shrouded feet', the firing party waits in the yard, his voice is silent and the voice of the poet cries in self-disgust, 'I repent/ My unweaned life that kept me competent /To sleepwalk with connivance and mistrust.'

The Station Island poems were written during a period of extreme tension and violence in Northern Ireland yet the poet subjected himself to 'the sternest form of self-analysis within the Heaney canon'.[24] The whole business of the dirty protest and the hunger-strikes weighed heavily. His silence sprung from his inner unease. He didn't want to put a spring in the step of either side but it was impossible not to feel something like guilt in the face of appalling tragedy. In the words of Milosz he was 'stretched between contemplation of a motionless point and the command to participate actively in history'. Maybe he should have gone into the prison and written something about it? Maybe, but the reality was that he was living in Dublin, holidaying in France and far from it all. He did not know Francis Hughes but he did know his parents and elder sisters. A neighbour's son, Thomas McElwee, was the eighth hunger-striker to die and Heaney did attend his wake. The family knew that he was not an IRA sympathiser, but he was a neighbour. They appreciated his gesture and he got some relief from his own guilt, although a week later the poet attended a dinner in Oxford and occupied the bedroom of a serving Tory minister. In his address to the Nobel Committee in 1995 Heaney admitted to his personal shock that he had once speculated on the possibility that violence might be justified if it helped in the birth of a more just future.[25]

Morning breaks and the pilgrims get up. Looking at his own face in the shaving-mirror the poet mouths the words, 'I hate

HUGH MULROONEY

how quick I was to know my place. /I hate where I was born, hate everything/ That made me biddable and unforthcoming'... as if the eddy could reform the pool. So ends his infantile peasant pilgrimage. As he stepped off the boat onto the mainland a tall boney man took his hand. 'What you must do must be done on your own so get back in harness. The main thing is to write for the joy of it...take off from here...let go, let fly, forget. You've listened long enough. Heaney is about to express his creativity in total glorious freedom.

'Station Island' is a volume full of departures and returns. The émigré is just visiting and experiencing displacement as freedom, away from it all and 'on the road'. In his imagination the poet is taking a last look and is bidding farewell. Like the priest he realises that what had appeared to be a vocation was in fact suffocating social, cultural and religious convention imposed by a besieged, oppressed and dispossessed regime and it should now be rejected and renounced. It is from outside the field, from the treetop, maybe even from a windswept island that the operating forces can be identified. 'Now I can only find myself in one place/Low back island on an inland lough'.

Through the use of his poetry he scrutinises his commitments, attachments, responsibilities and failures to find his identity, to find himself. Where 'Fieldwork' remained with the living, 'Station Island' 'performs an anthropology of the dead', and it uses symbols and myth to do that. The tree is a major site and symbol in the Sweeney poems. It is rooted in the earth and reaches into the air. Mired in attachment until they accused him of being 'a feeder off battlefields' he climbed to the top of his bent in the chestnut tree. The tree is Nature, is Ireland, is femininity, is a presence which when felled remains a luminous emptiness in the land of the dead.

With the writing of 'Station Island' Heaney began to consider his literary heritage and to place it in the context of

THE NIGHT OF OTHER DAYS

his own experience of Northern Ireland with its ineffable and unspeakable violence.[26] Bog bodies in Denmark had featured in the mythology of 'North'. The myths in 'SI' were pre-Christian, Christian, medieval, Renaissance, Irish and European. Soon there would be frontiers, islands, flags, emblems and songs. But however deeply he indulges in myths, he never loses sight of the Mossbawn landscape... myths can be false and misleading. They can emancipate and enrich but also subscribe to tribal bigotry and close out alternative interpretations.

The pilgrimage does not lead to a confirmation of his early faith. On the contrary the result is closer to Carleton than to John of the Cross. 'Up to my early teens I dwelt entirely in the womb of religion, hardly out of the cot before you envisaged the deathbed' he told Dennis O'Driscoll. Then the myths of the classical world and of other cultures provided a matching cosmology. Poetic imagination provided a world of light and a world of dark 'a shadow region, not so much an afterlife as an afterimage of life'.

At a fancy dinner in Chicago months before his death "He leaned over to me and said - very quietly; he seemed to me feeble – that he felt caught between the old forms of faith that he'd grown up with and some new dispensation that hadn't yet emerged, that was trying to emerge".[28]

From 'SI' onwards his poetry shifted. Its proper element is no longer earth or sea but rather the ascent into light, air and freedom. The tree reaches for the light but the chestnut must be prepared to be uprooted, to be immaterialised and purified, to be spirited away to a transparent afterlife. So too poetry 'must be translated into a new spirituality, a different tonality, a neuter allegiance'. The challenge will be to be faithful to the collective historical experience and to be true to the emerging self.

Loss and death are central concerns. With the removal of the chestnut tree Heaney felt the silence of a space utterly empty and beyond it a bright nowhere where souls ramified and renewed.

HUGH MULROONEY

Some have suggested that Heaney leaned towards the notion of nothingness.[30] Others see the moment of death as 'being carried beyond feeling into the aboriginal ice'. In all of his late work Heaney will return to all of those concerns mainly because much of his interest lies in their connection to the source and expression of his own creativity.

CHAPTER

Parables

16

'The Haw Lantern' (HL,1987) and 'The Government of the Tongue' (GT,1988) were published just short of Heaney's fiftieth birthday, (April 13th 1939). It is opportune to take stock of his life and work from 1966 when he was appointed lecturer at Queens University Belfast, when he replaced Philip Hobsbaum, published 'Death of a Naturalist' (DN,1966), and won the Eric Gregory award. Even then he had established himself as speaker and lecturer at teacher conferences and as a presenter of educational radio programmes. He also took part in Civil Rights marches and toured with Philip Hammond presenting a cross-community programme of poetry and song. In 1969 he read to an audience in Richmond Virginia from his second book, 'Door into the Dark' (DD, 1969) and winning The Somerset Maugham award facilitated a summer in France and Spain with his family. 1970-71 was spent in Berkeley with his family and on his return 'Wintering Out' (WO,1972) was published.

1972 was a year of vicious terror in Northern Ireland. In January, 13 unarmed men were murdered in Derry by British

HUGH MULROONEY

troops. On July 30th 26 IRA bombs were exploded in Belfast. Eleven people were murdered that Sunday. Seamus and Marie left Northern Ireland with their two young children in 1972. They moved to Glanmore in County Wicklow, twenty miles south of Dublin. It was a very brave move. Seamus had resigned his permanent post as lecturer and Marie gave her unwavering support. He was now a 'poet', a Gaelic 'file'. He signed up for a weekly book review programme with RTE the Irish broadcaster. 1973 was a year of awards, travel and meetings with well-known literary people, particularly with P.V.Glob author of 'The Bog People'. Then came the publication of 'North' (N,1975) and a deluge of abuse/criticism. That year he was 'head-hunted' and agreed to join the staff of Carysfort College of Education, Blackrock, Dublin, first as lecturer and subsequently as Head of the English Department. He was given generous leave of absence while in Carysfort, where he was universally loved by students and teaching colleagues. He served in Carysfort until his resignation in 1981. He was granted leave of absence in 1976 to return to Berkeley as Beckman professor. He became part of an international circle of literary notables and established his reputation as an outstanding poet. He published 'Field Work' (FW,1979) and began his involvement with Harvard which was to last until he resigned in 2007 following a mild stroke. There was a big rent in the family fabric with the death of Margaret in 1984 and the death of Patrick in 1986. He tells us that his first four books were published in America to 'considerable silence' but now the publication of "The Haw Lantern, (HL, 1987) and 'The Government of the Tongue' (GT,1988) were eagerly anticipated.

1988-89 was a sabbatical year. By then 'the smiling public man' was bestriding the literary world. But he was hurt by the expulsions he had suffered from the 'tried, tested and trusted world of his childhood', from the ranks of 'The Group' in Northern Ireland and from the land of his birth and early manhood. These

THE NIGHT OF OTHER DAYS

estrangements hurt him into a poetry of evocation, yearning and elegy.[1] 'The Haw Lantern' (HL, 1987) marked the beginning of a final phase leading to artistic freedom, uninhibited creativity and world fame. But by then he was 'keenly aware of the chemistry that alters a writer who has gained fame and transforms him from what he is to what his reputation is'[2,] or, as he put it 'And there I was incredible to myself,/among people far too eager to believe me/ and my story, even if it happens to be true'. Now a world figure, he visited Japan and was granted audience with Crown Princess Michiko in Tokyo. In 2005 The Emperor and Empress visited the Heaney family in their Glanmore cottage.

The 1990s and subsequent years are bewildering in their claims and rewards. Glanmore cottage was now their own property and Heaney used it as a retreat from an increasingly demanding world. He was awarded the Nobel prize for literature in 1995 and featured on stamps issued by the Irish and Swedish postal services in 2004. Then in 2006 he suffered a mild stroke and cancelled all engagements for twelve months. In 2007 he resumed an exhausting life of writing, lecturing and participating in poetry readings and festivals around the globe. He died on Friday August 30th 2013.

'The Haw Lantern' (HL,1987) was received with little enthusiasm, apart from 'the wonderfully lucid sequence of elegies,[3] 'Clearances', for his recently dead mother. Some, like John Baley, had seen the poems in his previous work, (SI) 'as beautiful as anything he had written and wider in breadth'. Paul Muldoon called 'Sweeney Astray' a 'masterful action of re-possession' by comparison. Michael Allen asked 'what has happened to Heaney?' Many were disappointed and felt that this slight book was badly written. Significantly, when Heaney published 'Opened Ground', Poems 1966-1996, thirteen poems from HL were omitted. Up to 1987 there had been no question about his gift, but now there was a question about how his gift should be used. His very vocation seemed under scrutiny and doubts remained until the publication of 'Seeing Things, (ST,1991).

Meantime the 'Haw Lantern' is held aloft. It is a small light for small people, wanting no more from them than that they keep the wick of self-respect from dying out, although in the hands of Diogenes it is scanning in the search for one just man. The haw 'embodies strength, maturity and integrity and becomes a classical golden mean against which the poet measures himself'. Poetry reflects a new despair of country and of self while cautiously advancing a vision of a new reality in Ireland but only if social, religious and historical perceptions should change. Under the rigorous scrutiny of the haw lantern much of contemporary practice failed the test.

Helen Vendler identifies the centrality of classical references[4] in HL. Hermes, she says, may be considered the presiding genius of the volume. In Greek mythology he leads the dead to the underworld and he stands in the centre of a cairn built of stones thrown by the gods as they find him innocent of the killing of the dog Argos. 'Innocent' will also be the verdict when the silent Patrick Heaney stands with his stick in his hand and the broad hat on his head at the place of judgement. Hermes is also the god of stone and of writing and he is a prominent figure in poems of ethical scrutiny and inspection. In HL a resisting stone god replaces the soft yielding bog goddess of the bog poems and the poet tells us that although he has been grinding the same stone for fifty years, what he undid was never the thing he had done. The reward for his efforts was darkness at a mirror, full circle, like the ripple perfected in silence.

Many poems in HL 'bristle with citation' and establish Heaney as a learned poet in the classical sense. The volume is full of secret meanings, classical references, parables and coded messages, which allow the poet to use the voice-mask as he has already done in SI and SA, even to the extent of making Heaney strange to himself.

THE NIGHT OF OTHER DAYS

'As a consequence, the lyric becomes what it has never been in Heaney's work before: abstract, diagnostic, analytic, dispassionate, admonitory, forensic, post-mortem'. And there is the question of potential creative resources. The book's dedication to Bernard and Jane McCabe reads: 'The riverbed dried-up, half-full of leaves./ Us, listening to a river in the trees.' Has the early spontaneity and unerring poetic instinct been replaced by calculation? Has the river of poetic inspiration dried up?

In 'The Government of the Tongue' (GT,1988) some answers may be found. In this work poet and critic unite in governing the tongue; prose enlightens poetry, as 'essays and poems form part of a single, even systematic effort of consciousness...(while) the sharpened and unremitting scrutiny of the politics, ethics and aesthetics of writing to which it gives rise is an attempt to answer some of the most difficult questions of all'. One such question is the nature of past experience as it is recollected.

Experience says Vendler is not so much re-created as replaced, 'Vanishings' are a central concern of all his work.[5] 'I made a small hard ball/of burning water running from my hand/just as I make this now /out of the melt of the real thing/smarting into its absence.' Although it may be true that deep personal experience can only be recalled using words which offer little consolation for their inadequacy, nevertheless it is also true that Heaney can locate sensation in language and powerfully reinforce recall through the use of words, links and images...the sting of the hailstones becomes more acute when linked with nettles and the unstingable hands of Eddie Diamond and Eddie's surname links, in turn, to 'the diamond absolutes'.

The idea of 'Clearance' features prominently especially in the series of poems under that title. The 'Clearance' poem-series, already discussed inchapter 3, are among the finest poems written by Seamus Heaney. A clearance is a space emptied of all obstacles and in the case of his mother's death there is a double clearance as the emptiness empties itself into those standing at the deathbed and the poet finds himself in a space utterly empty. Heaney identified with that space when the dead are spirited away to a place where the spirit can flourish. It might be added that this vision of disintegration and removal to 'a placeless heaven' is not in line with traditional Catholic teaching. 'The reality and idea of death become an entirely undesired, but nevertheless necessary enlargement of imaginative capacity...'[6]

The 32 poems in HL were published two years after SI 1985. Heaney was approaching his fiftieth birthday and absorbing the natural losses of middle-age. His parents were both dead. He was now a global public figure. But education and literary success had set him on the road to exile. He was changing direction and seeking to abandon his former self and to become light, airy and free. Meantime he continues to be a poet of rich tactile language while experiencing emptiness, absence and distance. He felt cautious and was aware of 'contradictory apprehensions of the nature of poetic language'. His early volumes sang close to the music of what happens. Then in poems like 'Limbo' he became aware of the lunar distance between reality and words. He turned for inspiration to 'the eternal fountain' and found reality in the melt of the real thing into its absence. With the Sweeney poetry he sensed the early beckonings of freedom. But first came unresolved questions which he tried to address in HL and with greater success in Government of the Tongue (GT 1988) and Seeing Things (ST 1991).

The Haw Lantern shows a retreat from metaphor, which characterised the earlier volumes. Now he tries to avoid the stain of words and the greed of language. Words retreat from the truth like melting hailstones into the silence, emptiness and vacancy of the land of the unspoken. There is a disjunction between the word and the world. Like 'an intermittent outsider' he plays with the spoken and the written word and questions the power of language to express either meaning or identity. He is displaced from his origins and has just emerged from sustained self-scrutiny and interrogation. He now subjects language itself to inspection.[7] He makes use of codes, social, tribal, professional and domestic, which he then scrutinises. He places himself in a space where no one code is dominant. Asked if he was pushing boundaries he replied that it was more like sliding screen doors and trespassing in strange rooms, especially in the parable-poems. These poems also show the importance of analogy-making. For him meaning is a linguistic act, not a natural event. Heaney's language of displacement is designed to make us see things in a new way; through writing it defines us. His writing doesn't just create a poem, it defines an identity.[8]

HL is Heaney's first book of the virtual, sited at the frontier of writing on the border between two worlds. There is no map. But there is a line he must have crossed and he knows that this Parable Island is occupied. The elders have told him stories, like the tale of the man who took to his bed and died convinced that the cutting of the Panama Canal would drain the ocean and cause the island to disappear by aggrandisement. The poet is familiar with borders, boundaries and roadblocks and he has learned to carry two buckets.

The Frontier of Writing is like a roadblock. At a roadblock the driver is constrained by the menace of armed soldiers. Once he passes inspection, he is waved through. He is then on the road to freedom. For the poet, once the words are written the critics/marksmen train their guns on the author and he is constrained until he emerges, as if from behind a waterfall back on to the freeway. Poems can mark the physical and psycho-social stages through a physical roadblock as well as those through to the frontier of writing and the three stages are found in the poetry of Heaney. There are poems marking the condition of subjugation and endurance. There are poems of protest, penitence or conscience, and hopefully there are poems leading to ultimate freedom. At the heart of the poem 'From the Frontier of Writing' is the notion of scrutiny before earning the right to proceed. The location of the action is at the intersection of the real and the surreal; the concrete and the abstract; the public and the private.

Loss, as a theme, is the subject of more than five poems. Loss of religious faith in the poems 'The Mud Vision' and 'Spoonbait'; loss of faith in patriotism in 'Wolfe Tone' and 'The Disappearing Island'; Loss of faith in the language in 'The Riddle', In 'The Mud Vision', the melt of real faith smarts into its loss as people of a simple frugal world of faith fade into a desacralized consumer universe of theory-speak where they lose their history and identity, and words in the word-hoard are dematerialised. The original stimulus for Mud Vision was a wall-mounted set of hand-prints by Richard Long and the location for the apparition was changed from Count Tyrone to the Irish midlands. The crowd have been moved from the world of moving suns and supernatural dimensions; from sacred worlds, precious word-hoards and miracles, to a demystified world of media -speak and consumerism. But so too has the poet. In 'The Mud Vision' he is unwilling to separate his 'believing youth' from his sceptical middle-age. We are presented with a dismal landscape and the complacency of an impotent nation concealing indecisiveness beneath a veneer of political formulae. The style adopted by Heaney showcases his qualities and values, territorial pity, visual wit, reflectiveness, anger and his ambition for a better Ireland. But the truth of the conclusion remains: What might have been origin gets dissipated in news. The other poems in this group portray the doubleness of Irish experience: a dwindling nation, a dying language, a dispersed people whose history is 'a sensation of opaque fidelity'...as they ride away from whatever might have been towards what will never be. The possibility of regeneration and renewal remains even when scrutiny before the haw lantern exposes weakness and failure. 'All I believe that happened there was vision'.

THE NIGHT OF OTHER DAYS

The poetry in HL has grown in density with more inclusion of classical and mythical references but always remains Irish. 'In Ireland, you cannot divorce the literary from the historical, from the political, from the usual self'[9]. His poetry is increasingly multi-layered. In 'The Spoonbait' he builds a bridge between poetry and fishing...the Daylight Art. Finding a spoonbait in a child's pencil-case gives a glimpse of a soul, shifting to the reeling and casting of a line, the burning of a shooting-star, a plea from Dives for one drop of water, a river, a hero, a helmet, a boat, a funeral ship and the resurrection of the soul of a dead hero. 'Alphabets' traces progress with the formation of numerals and letters leading to understanding of rules, the opening of distances, the widening of horizons, the bulldozing of the old, the creation of new worlds, the tensions between the limitations of the present world and the perfection of a world which was created but never existed. The poet stands bareheaded under the banked clouds of a world in which fog is a dreaded omen and where 'lightening spells universal good and parents hang swaddled infants in trees during thunderstorms'.

The Haw Lantern is another step in Heaney's progression towards transcendence. He has advanced from the darkness of 'North' through the healing of 'Field Work', the penitence of 'Station Island' to the dawn-light truths of 'The Haw Lantern'.[10] His next work will be a book of revelations. 'Which would be better, what sticks or what falls through? Or does the choice itself create the value?

CHAPTER

Seeing

17

This chapter is concerned with the 'Stepping Stones', in poetry and in prose, principally with publication of 'Seeing Things' (ST 1991) and 'The Spirit Level' (SL 1996). 'The Government of the Tongue' (GT, 1988) and 'The Redress of Poetry' (RP 1990) are the complimentary prose works in which he addressed the question: 'what gives poetry its governing power'?

In his introduction to GT he recalls the evening in Belfast in 1972 when David Hammond and himself abandoned a planned BBC recording of song and verse to the horrific sound of exploding bombs. How could they celebrate their art in the face of grave human suffering? This reflects the tension which all artists experience, the tension between art and life. How to reconcile song and suffering? 'Why should the joyful affirmation of music and poetry ever constitute an affront to life? By 1988 and the publication of GT Heaney had found peace in relation to the social and political situation. GT is his most concentrated critical book of essays and is a 'sustained exploration of the rights and obligations of the writer' (O'Donoghue). Like 'Preoccupations' in prose and

THE NIGHT OF OTHER DAYS

ST in poetry the main focus is on polarities and the double nature of poetry. The abandoning of the planned BBC recording raised the questions of Art versus Life, of song versus suffering, of poetry and politics, rhetoric and reality, beauty and truth, alterity and identity and conscience versus confusion. In his writings of the late seventies and early eighties he moves from solid objects, rural implements like the pitchfork, to lives of people, from seeing to imagining, sensing and the afterlife, from the concrete task to the imagined burden. A beggar shivering in silhouette on the doorstep and just old truth dawning...there is no-next-time-round.

Heaney discusses poets who wrote of the beauty of life and the savagery of death in the wretchedness of world-war trenches. Wilfred Owen was a conscientious objector yet he led men to their deaths and wrote poetry. 'True poets must be truthful...all a poet can do is warn'. This gentle man of violence, with a machine-gun in one hand and a 'mea culpa' in the other 'performed his patriotic duty so that he could, with authority, question whether it was his duty at all'. Wilfred Owen is 'a poet as witness' for whom the truth-telling urge and the compulsion to identify with the oppressed becomes necessarily integral with the act of writing. He would elevate truth above beauty and above art. The question is: in the presence of the unfree, the wounded and the hurt, is the expression of lyric poetry in its jubilation, truancy and glorious freedom a source of embarrassment? Is it an affront?

In his T.S.Eliot Memorial lectures Heaney addressed some of the questions raised. Eliot's poetry marked a complete break with what Osip Mandelstam described as 'purveyors of readymade meaning', poets who wrote poetry that made sense and that met with public expectations. By contrast Eliot wrote poetry which drafted images and textures from subconscious inspiration. This poetry got its inspiration and its validation from itself, from its ability 'to open unexpected and unedited communications between our nature and the nature of the reality we inhabit'. Here the poet is an antenna capturing the voices of the world, 'a medium expressing his own subconscious and the collective subconscious'. The poetry has an authority all its own, derived from imagination and with the right to govern through the tongue, which here means both the language and the organ. Unfolding by delight the poem 'begins in delight...runs a course of lucky events...ends in a clarification of life...not necessarily a great clarification...but in a momentary stay against confusion'.

Art should never be constrained by rule-book. Some people have seen Dante's 'Divine Comedy' as bound by a system based on the numerical figure 3, three lines in each stanza, three books, thirty- three cantos in each book etc. This is rejected by Mandelstam. 'The three-edged stanza is formed from within, like a crystal, not cut on the outside like a stone'. The poem emerges from a space which has emerged from space, like a honey-comb created by bees. Poetry is a creative, intimate, experimental act subject only to the Government of the Tongue.

But Government of the Tongue can also mean a denial of freedom, with the tongue 'knowing its place', with the clapper removed from the bell and obedience to a system of rules and regulations. It can imply denial, containment, conformity, taking a secondary position to religious, state or public order. Hopkins abandoned poetry when he joined The Jesuits. 'Here it is the common expectation that the writer will sign over his or her venturesome and potentially disruptive activity into the keeping of an official doctrine'. In this system poetry and art are related to licentiousness, heresy and treason. Poets of Eastern Europe have experience of this as have many of Heaney's own Irish generation under censorship. Under such regimes, an order has been handed down, 'the shape of things has been established' and the tongue is governed. Even under a lenient form of such regimes, poets like George Herbert have surrendered to 'a framework of belief

THE NIGHT OF OTHER DAYS

and an instituted religion' and yet produced poetry which was 'intellectually pure, emotionally robust and entirely authentic'.

Whether the tongue is given free range or is constrained, the governor is different in each case, authoritative in one, and light, inventive and carefree in the other. But is free lyric expression in its self-gratification an affront to a troubled world? Should it govern its own joy; take the clapper from the bell; moralize its song? The answer is 'no' because lyric poetry carries feeling and truth into the heart. Lyric poetry fortifies our 'inclination to credit promptings of our intuitive being'. Here is the paradox of poetry and of the imaginative arts in general. 'Faced with the brutality of the historical onslaught, they are practically useless...In one sense the efficacy of poetry is nil – no lyric has ever stopped a tank'. In another sense it is unlimited. Poetry takes a break from the usual life, it does not abscond from it. For a space it focuses attention and directs concentration back on ourselves. 'This is what gives poetry its governing power. At its greatest moments it would attempt, in Yeats's phrase, to hold in a single thought reality and justice'. In 'The Redress of Poetry' (Oxford Lectures 1989) Heaney recommends that poetry should balance the scales of justice by adding weight to the lighter side. Poetry should press back against the pressure of reality, should be involved in cultural and political realignment, but not at the expense of its own integrity.

In 1980 ('Preoccupations') Heaney posed the question: 'How should a poet properly live and write? What is his relationship to be to his own voice, his own place, his literary heritage and his contemporary world'? His answer: 'The fact is that poetry is its own reality... and the ultimate fidelity must be to the demands and promise of the artistic event'.

The publication of ST in 1991 came in the wake of a highly productive stage in the poet's life. The death of his mother Margaret, remembered in the beautiful series 'Clearances', led to the opening of spaces around him, while the death of Patrick in October 1986 was the final unroofing of his world, 'and I'm certain it affected me in ways that were hidden from me then and now.' He was to enjoy a sabbatical 'year' (July 1988 to Spring term 1990) from Harvard. The cottage in Glanmore was their own and is celebrated in 'Squarings" ii, 'Sink every impulse like a bolt. Secure/The bastion of sensation. Do not waver/Into language. Do not waver in it'. There was a powerful surge through the system felt in the writing of 'Fosterling': 'Me waiting until I was nearly fifty/ To credit marvels. Like the tree-clock of tin cans/The tinkers made. So long for air to brighten, /time to be dazzled and the heart to lighten.' [1] His bid for artistic freedom is now clearly stated and placed at the heart of his life. This is a decisive move and must count as one of the firmest positions he has ever taken and it indicates a move away from his East European mentors and back to Wordsworth. He wants to abandon his 'heaviness of being. And poetry/Sluggish in the doldrums of what happens'. He is also making a significant choice between artistic licence and public responsibility. He is inclining towards the visionary but in the context of the reality of everyday living. The political scene was changing with the 1994 IRA ceasefire and hope was in the air as in the beautiful parable of a vision at Clonmacnoise where two worlds an infinity apart collaborate as the stranded crewman, with the assistance of the monks, climbs back up to his airbourne ship.

The central theme in ST is 'harmonised contraries'.[3] In the title poem Heaney looks down from an aerial boat and observes the panic of the passengers, especially himself, as the small boat headed for Inishbofin. 'What guaranteed us – that quick response and buoyancy and swim – Kept me in agony'… insecurity and security, possibly false in the both cases. In the words of Henry Hart: 'in ST, limits are crossed, natural and supernatural wedded, confused infused with the sublime, and everywhere a sense of omnipresence, equilibrium, brim'. Poetic language mediates things and ideas 'transforming both into an artificial medium

THE NIGHT OF OTHER DAYS

that is simultaneously abstract and concrete... the visionary and the real are symbiotic rather than exclusive as Heaney calls for a synthesis of the imaginary and the real and 'repeatedly explores the dynamic relations between them'. He has moved away from the bodies buried in the bog and from the hum of the funeral hearse and is now concerned with the other worldly figures of ghosts and spirits. Increasingly this is an approach which benefits the middle-aged poet; it allows him to rise above sectarian strife to luminous spaces within his own mind and to find a middle way[4]. Memories push back against each other as he releases tensions and counter-tensions. His mind confronts borders and transcends them, as the footballers continue to play in their heads long after the pitch has darkened and long after they are released from the rules of the game. 'As the light died and they kept on playing/Because by then they were playing in their heads.' His poetry now runs free into 'free-flowing music and discourse'. Gates, thresholds, borders, limits, lines, doors, ceilings, roofs, circles and squares, all are 'lightened', set and squared. 'The Golden Bough', 'sayings where clear truths and mysteries were inextricably twined' is an apt introduction to the work and foresees the 'negotiations with the afterlife and the underworld in 'Seeing Things".[5] Paul Muldoon spoke of the ascent of Heaney's poetry from the earth to the sky and Heaney said that for days he felt 'like an inhabitant of the house where the man sick of palsy was lowered through the roof, had his sins forgiven, was healed, took up his bed and walked away'. Many of the lines just wafted themselves up out of 'a kind of poetic divine right;I was subject to the poems and not the other way round;I learned what inspiration feels like but not how to summon it'. Poems kept coming like flat stones skimmed at sunset. These are Heaney's own words referring to the visionary power in poetry to see things in transcendent vision as we have not seen them before. 'All these things entered you/ As if they were both the door and what came through it./They marked the spot, marked time and held it open'. The poet tells us he despairs of the power of language...'what the reach of sense despairs of as it fails to reach it, especially the thwarted sense of touch'.

Nevertheless very strong images are painted; the memory of his father crossing the yard, hatless and drenched when the horse bolted and tossed all into the river; Patrick, pegging-out lines in the garden or reaching out in feebleness to clutch his ashplant, or bending to a tea-chest, packed with salt and bacon, in the light of a lantern held at eye-level; memories of a gentle man all yellow boots and stick and soft felt hat and the emptiness felt when the poet walked away from his death-bed; the woman in the wheelchair...'she never lamented once and she never/carried a spare ounce of emotional weight' yet under her gaze the field behind the hedge became more distinctly strange. 'The places I go back to have not failed/ but will not last', he says, yet he summons remarkable memories of his schoolbag, the cot, the settle-bed and The Biretta. The first time he saw a biretta 'I heard a shout/As an El Greco ascetic rose before me/ Preaching hellfire, Saurian and stormy/ Adze-head on the rampage in the pulpit', enough to put the wind up the poet and his generation. His memory of holding a biretta by its central fin is still there between his finger and his thumb. Now it is a paper boat or the boat of imagination that Dante launches in the opening lines of the Purgatorio, or the boat in Matthew Lawless's painting, 'The Sick Call'. The pitchfork in its polished smoothness suggests a javelin, warrior, athlete and a far-off space-probe with perfection in the opening of the hand of peace and reconciliation.

'The Spirit Level' (SL,1996) has been described as a book of balances which pays tribute to the ordinary while highlighting deficiencies and advancing self-justification. Everything trembles and flows with give and take. Artistic vision is now vindicated and balance achieved between artistic freedom and ethical responsibility, 'so walk on air against your better judgement'. Two

THE NIGHT OF OTHER DAYS

poems, 'The Flight Path' and 'Weighing In' provide an over-view of the poet's way of life and his way of thinking in the 1990s. Fight Path records the paper airplane shaped by his father and connects the New York red-eye special, the Dublin-Belfast train, Glanmore and Rocamadour. He recalls a dream in which he is directed to plant a car-bomb at Pettigo and on the train to Belfast is confronted by a real IRA figure. 'When for fuck's sake, are you going to write something for us'? 'Whatever it is I will be writing for myself', comes the reply, and that was that, just as it had been all his life.

'Weighing In' places balancing weights on either side of the scales representing the measure of tolerance, 'bearing-up' and passive suffering which ensures peace on earth and goodwill to all men. 'And this is all the good tidings amount to: We should balance the intolerance of others against our own'. Passive suffering makes the world go round. Or does it? Is passive tolerance and acceptance the true measure of justice and peace? 'Still for Jesus' sake...just this once...prophesy, give scandal, cast the stone'.

This pent-up anger is stated more clearly in 'Mycenae Lookout' the principal poem in ST. The language in the rape of the innocent is so strong that Helen Vendler recoiled. For Heaney the anger is a snarl in response to 25 years of killing-fest and his tongue feels numb, like the dropped gangplank of a cattle-truck, as he rages for order. He connects 'Mycenae Lookout' and 'The Republic of Conscience'...no such thing as innocent by-standers, referring to the world we have inherited as citizens and writers in the wake of 'The Twin Towers' and the invasions of Iraq and Afghanistan. His tongue is ungoverned as he looks back 'in apoplectic anger at the calamitous years of The Troubles'.[6] In four searing monologues 'soaked in blood and betrayal' he rages in direct comment on the events of a quarter of a century. Only in the fifth section is there an expression of hope, 'the ladder of the future turned waterwheel' feeding the bountiful round mouths of iron pumps and gushing taps. It is time to walk on air against your better judgement. The parallels between the peace at Troy and the cease-fire of 1994 'jut out like bones in the grass'.[7] And this was the time of Heaney's visit to the original resting place of The Tollund Man and the formation of 'Second Thoughts'. Meantime he will continue to claim that 'a virtuous political standpoint is simply a matter of claiming to be in doubt'.

Agamemnon comes home to be slaughtered in his bath. There is a premonition of civil-war. Brother will confront brother. This is the dark side of SL. On the lighter side is the delicate imaginative heart of the book as it explores possibilities, sees small visual stirrings, hears small dulcimer pluckings, ticking of clocks, a whiff of mint, the shaking of the poplars, a tailor threading a needle and a rich man entering heaven through the ear of a raindrop. There is fluidity, balance, give and take, translations, transformations and most of all the transition from earth to air through the 'poetics of listening'.[8]

Nevertheless, the expression of anger, pessimism and hopelessness in 'The Flight Path', 'Weighing In' and 'Mycenae Lookout' is based on a despairing world-view, his concern with ageing and an ever-present awareness of death and what lies beyond it. The poem 'Keeping Going' is dedicated to his brother Hugh and it integrates the domestic, local and public domains. Two tragic events left their mark on Hugh. His daughter had died earlier in a tragic accident and now Hugh witnessed a terrible murder at The Diamond. He parked his tractor and saw a car slowly closing in on the lone figure of a reserve policeman who died in a hail of bullets…'Grey matter like gruel flecked with blood/in spatters on the whitewash'. Now Hugh keeps going and is a regular cheerful visitor to The Diamond. This is the man who led a merry parade of Heaney children with an upturned chair as bagpipes and the kitchen sofa as a steam-train hurtling through darkened fields at night. Now his cheerful greetings hail the possibility of hope and peace while his brother dares to walk on air. But even Hugh must

THE NIGHT OF OTHER DAYS

question; 'is this all'? He will keep on going but he cannot make the dead walk or right wrong. Is the train a ghost train, a death-gondola or heaven-bound? No matter. The secret is to keep rising to your own occasions, to ride the current until the next surge. Another poem which is concerned with ageing is 'The Rain-stick'. Heaney tells us that it is as much about middle-age as it is about the music of rain being created by the driest of elements. 'Listen now again'. Asked if 'The Rain-stick' was a reprising of earlier themes, he quoted George Herbert: 'And now in age I bud again...I once more smell the dew and rain and relish versing'.

There are two lorries. One pulls into the yard in Mossbawn. The tidy coalman carefully folds the empty bags and laughingly invites Margaret 'to the cinema, no less!'. Now forty years later a lorry groans up to the bus-station in Magherafelt. A bomb-blast later and Margaret sweeps ashes into her shopping bag as she waits for the bus from Derry and her schoolboy son, Seamus. Margaret died in 1984. Ten years later the IRA declared a cease-fire at exactly the time that Heaney visited the Jutland bog from which the body of The Tollund Man was taken. All through SL there is the convergence of memories, of current events, of unease with the state of the world and fear of the advance towards old age and death. In 'To a Dutch Potter in Ireland' there is recall of the second world war, awareness of oil-wells burning in the desert and 'Omnipresent, imperturbable/Is the life that death springs from'.

The final poem in the volume is 'Postscript', 'a glorious exultation of air and sea and swans', recalling a drive along the southern coastline of Galway Bay. Seamus and Marie along with Brian and Anne Friel drove out west along the Flaggy Shore when the wind and the light worked off each other, past the swans on a slate-grey lake. They were neither here nor there 'As big soft buffetings came at the car sideways...to catch the heart off guard and blow it open'.

HUGH MULROONEY

'Now and again a poem comes like that, like a ball kicked in from nowhere…there are some poems that feel like guarantees of your work to yourself…they leave you with the sensation of having been visited…'

CHAPTER

Contradictions

18

Heaney always insisted that his creative work mirrored his life in the real world and took into account changes and 'second thoughts'. In the Preface to 'Finders Keepers' (FK 2001) He asks the question; 'How should a poet properly live and write? What is his relationship to be to his own voice, his own place, his literary heritage and his contemporary world'? These were his abiding concerns and it is hardly surprising that his stringent self-examination often resulted in conflicting second thoughts.

It might be thought that his life was that of a poet living in peaceful seclusion in a cottage in county Wicklow. This was far from being the case. He remained an active teaching academic all his life and was admired as a poet, a scholar, first rank poetry critic, a dramatist, a writer of great prose and a much sought-after speaker on matters literary, social and political. He was a world figure who had a library named in his honour at Queens University Belfast; was elected as 'saoi', the highest honour of 'Aostana', the Irish Academy of artists; elected as Foreign Honorary Member of American Academy of Arts and Letters; became professor of poetry in Berkeley, Harvard and Oxford; was awarded honours from Japan to South Africa, from Ireland to Eastern Europe and featured on postal stamps in Ireland and Sweden. He spoke with authority and insight on the politics of Ireland Kosovo and Palestine. Everywhere he was accepted as an honest, sincere, sensitive and troubled man who shared his creative genius with a mainly appreciative world. He followed a bewildering timetable of travel, writing and lecturing and ultimately his health paid the price. He was too gentle for the world of politics and violence but spoke out as his conscience dictated. His words were respected and he was much loved.

As he grew older he was tasked with memorialising the work of poets he knew and loved and many of his tributes are recorded. 'Preoccupations' was published in 1980 and Heaney wrote with insight about Wordsworth, Hopkins, Yeats, Kavanagh and Larkin. J.W.Foster[2] remarked that each Heaney collection accrues value from previous volumes 'by a kind of compound interest'. And each volume records increasing increments of loss and of grief: Heaney's anointed father, 'Ghost drover from the start' reminded him of Hopkin's Felix Randal who brought home the dead body of his uncle by car-ferry; David Thompson...'whose injured eyes saw waves and waterfalls in young girl's hair'; Zbigniew Herbert, 'the herald of Apollo...you learned the lyre from him and kept it tuned'; Joseph Brodsky, 'repetition is the rule', repetition of ice cold, of pepper vodka, of jokes involving sex and sect, of drinking, smoking, laughing...'but nothing will bring back the colour to your cheeks or to your jokes'; in memory of Ted Hughes, pounded like a shore by the roller griefs, in language that can still knock language sideways.

A central question is posed in 'Electic Light'. Is passive grief and suffering disallowed as a theme for poetry? Like the grief of King Hrethel? 'Fragment' draws on the optimistic and spiritual 'Song of Creation' which in turn is drawn from Beowulf. Hrethel must seek redress from the son who had accidently killed his older brother. As a consequence, the king 'lives to see his son's body swing on the gallows'. But he is denied the full freedom to mourn because some things, like a father's grief, are to be left unsaid, left 'for the aye of God and for poetry'. Some things are past oneself. What was is no more. Soul has its scruples; things not to be said; a dividend from ourselves, a thing allowed.

The Title 'Electric Light' is ironic and tinged with grief and tragedy. Rural electrification had a warming demystifying effect but it also brought light to the morgue. The volume is dominated by the pastoral but it is a pastoral seen as grim politics. Some poems like 'Known World' make a bid for freedom but 'That old sense of a tragedy going on…never left me once' and tragedy is dominant in elegies for friends and relatives: Hughes, Brodsky, Herbert, his father, grandmother and murdered Sean Brown. The melancholy of Beowulf (B, 1999) fits grimly well into EL.

Kavanagh had spoken of the health and worth of talk about the properties of land and Heaney wrote: 'The main thing is/ an inner restitution, a purchase come by/by pacing it in words that make you feel/you've found your feet in what sure-footed means/and in the ground of your own understanding'. He would eventually walk on air but his feet were on his own ground and in his own understanding. It was with the captured weight of the rural world that Heaney made his reputation[1], but whether it was a railway sleeper, a harrow pin, a sledgehammer or a biretta the weight is a challenging contrast to the lightness and wonder which he ascribes to them, and he can switch between the cosmic and the micro cosmic 'in a trice'. Things, like people, are translated into the elements of light and air and 'sailing into the longed-for'. Saint Kevin is linked into the network of eternal life, his arm outstretched as his palm is nesting the blackbird's egg. To labour and not to seek reward is his prayer.

HUGH MULROONEY

An overview of Heaney's work shows that he retained the alert eye and the linguistic precision of his first books to the end. The early volumes placed the centrality of self at the core, a revelation of the self to the self. His knowledge of 'dinnseanchas' (a genre of Irish writing which draws on the lore of place-names) led him back to a rich heritage which had been ravished through colonisation. This broken heritage of place-names led to a growing historical awareness, a heightened social conscience and the responsibility to speak out. He found a voice when mastery of the craft of poetry transcended mere skill and developed into technique. When his poetry addressed the violence of the 70s and 80s it drew hostile criticism as the public/local locked with the political/aesthetic. SA and SI are confessional in nature but do not hide the conflict between artistic freedom and public responsibility. Heaney placed himself between those two stark alternatives and he was criticised for his uncertainty. He even accused himself of confusing evasion and artistic tact, of whitewashing ugliness. But he always chose to do the decent thing.

In 'Fosterling' (ST 1991) he declares his freedom 'me waiting until I was nearly fifty to credit marvels'. Yet in SL 1996 there are expressions of pessimism and anger at the political scene at both local and international level and this view is expressed again later especially in the Eclogues in 'Electric Light' (EL,2001).

'Electric Light' is described as giving a cautious welcome to peace; in Northern Ireland terms it is 'a peace-process book'. Some would see it as a book of denied consolations, viewing the peace process as being under permanent challenge and expressing a light-heartedness which cannot be sustained against the angel of death. Balance is sought but 'the conciliatory nature of art is in direct relation to the rage which produced it'. Balance is achieved at a price. Although he argues that poetry can be of help and bring redress, yet his poetry often seems to lack confidence, to be threatened by violence, disaster and tragedy, never settling for

THE NIGHT OF OTHER DAYS

the conventional, the idyllic or the easy[3]. The poetry in his final books revisits and revises what he had already versified, often in language that is elemental...air, light, space that is transformative and unrestrained[4]. The domestic, the cosmic, the political and the violent are ever-present. 'I'm on a roof/That overlooks forever... Cows snuffle at feed buckets in the byre,/the stall-chains clink.' One terrible night in Mossbawn as Margaret is rocking and oching a raiders lorry is hammering on for the Monaghan border, blood loosed in a scrim from the tailboard, the volunteer screaming 'O Jesus, O merciful Jesus'. Bobby X, a little tiny boy/Shut up inside him...and the doctor shouting, 'Bobby, for Christ's sake, Bobby, catch yourself on'. All babies came from a Dr Kerlin's bag but 'overhead/The little pendent, tear-hued infant parts/strung neatly from a line up near the ceiling'.

There is wine, song and laughter at The Struga Poetry Festival, 'we hardly ever sobered', while pilgrims and refugees crowded the roads and there was an opportunity for a cigarette and wine on the flight home. 'I had been there, I knew this, but was still/ haunted by it as by an unread dream'.

Bernard O Donoghue[7] in an essay titled 'Heaney's Classics and the Bucolic' tells of Heaney's gift for incorporating classical mythological figures into his own world and this is especially seen in the Eclogues in EL. 'Bucolic' from Greek means 'song about herdsmen' is now used to include country concerns of all kinds. But in the eclogues the pastoral or bucolic is devastated by violence, pity and tragedy. Even his earliest poetry which evokes rural serenity and optimism sounds a negative note, as blackberries rot and great slime kings threaten revenge. From the publication of Field Work (FW, 1979) there is constant tension between terror and rural harmony. The eclogues are pastoral but it is a grim bucolic which faces eastwards. EL is a book of elegies and eclogues which is dominated by tragedy, despair and foreboding...'that kind of thing could start again'. The eclogues are a central form in

HUGH MULROONEY

EL and they reflect their origins in the work of Virgil, in travels in Greece and in Heaney's own reading and scholarship. Virgil's poems are concerned with land grievances while other themes in EL concern artistic/secular authority, military power/poetic silence. The eclogue is set up to be shot down. Even the title poem begins with excitement but finishes among the beads and vertebrae of the Derry ground. The early Glanmore Eclogue with its celebration of high summer expresses optimism of the 1970s which is quickly dissipated over the following thirty years. The Bann Valley Eclogue celebrates the birth of a child but ends in the sluicing of the milk-house floor. The poem exudes 'an atmosphere of anxiety, uncertainty and lack of conviction'. 'The Augean Stables' ends with the hideous murder of Sean Brown. The entire book is one of denied consolation; a challenged peace-process and 'where negative ions in the air are poetry to me'. 'This pattern of subverted pastoral – of the positive denied or questioned – is everywhere in EL'.[6] As Moeris says in Eclogue IX; 'An outsider has claimed our lands. These kid-goats are his…Songs and tunes can no more hold out against brute force than doves when eagles swoop'. Lycidas, the Heaney figure, expresses surprise that the poetry of Menalaus has not saved all land from confiscation; poetry does not hold sway under military rule.

In 'Preoccupations' Heaney told of a dream. 'I was shaving at the mirror of the bathroom when I glimpsed a wounded man falling towards me with his bloody hands lifted to tear at me or to implore'. All his life he subjected himself to scrutiny only to find uncertainty, conflict and fear. And there were forces to tear at him as well as to implore.

CHAPTER

Overview

19

Seamus Heaney missed the Cavan bypass, stopped the car and took stock, 'the who knows and what nexts and so be its', (DC, 2006). Taking stock was second nature and in his writing he always had the tendency to view from a new vantage point material already explored in an earlier work, a tendency to 'circle his district'.[1] As expressed by Foster, the publication of each collection accrues value from previous volumes 'by a kind of compound interest'.[2] Much of Heaney's later poetry is revision or revisiting, 'now with love and affection and an appreciation of what poetry has done for him'. This applies in EL, DC and HC, his last three volumes, and was expressed by Czeslaw Milosz, (Krakow,Lithuania,1911-2004. Heaney described him as 'The giant at my shoulder'): 'The purpose of poetry is to remind us/how difficult it is to remain just one person, /for our house is open, there are no keys in doors,/and invisible guests come in and out at will'.

To summarise the poet's thinking or his poetry is not feasible. 'Heaney is not rural and sturdy and domestic, with his feet planted firmly in Irish mud, but instead an ornamentalist, a word collector, a connoisseur of fine language for its own sake'[3]... and to attempt to describe the magic of his poetry is, in the words of Theo Dorgan, 'to spear satellites with a pitchfork'. Kirkland[4] wrote about 'the resonances of his talk, the mastery of his language and the searching restlessness of his mind' and all this is echoed in his prose and poetry. When editing her book 'The Poetry of Seamus Heaney', Elmer Andrews structured the work to address Place, Identity, Language, Politics, Gender, Nationalism and Colonialism. As late as 1995, in his Nobel acceptance speech, Heaney told of how he had only recently made space for the marvellous as well as for the murderous, for the air to brighten and the heart to lighten. At all times his poetry reflects his changing state of mind, the historical context and the circumstances of the immediate present, and none of those elements remained static.

In addition to twelve volumes of poetry, several works of drama and major works of translation, Heaney published a number of significant prose works in which he wrote with insight on his own poetry and that of fellow poets, living and dead. In 1980 he published 'Preoccupations: Selected Prose 1968-1978' followed by 'Finders Keepers: Selected Prose 1971-2001'(FK). "Government of the Tongue' (GT) in 1988 was followed in 1995 by 'The Redress of Poetry' (RP). All of these works incorporated lectures delivered from professorial chairs in Berkeley, Harvard and Oxford. And all the while he produced drama, translated Beowulf, (which won The Whitbread Book of the Year award in 1999), and wrote letters, articles and comments for a variety of magazines and newspapers.

His place of refuge remained Glanmore. Here there was no telephone and no contact with the outside world, in contrast to his Dublin home where Dennis O'Driscoll witnessed the daily arrival of 'a sackful of requests, invitations, proofs, academic enquiries, personal letters, manuscripts in progress and glossy new books to a house where neither phone nor fax enjoys a moments respite'. Not that he could ignore calls from the outside world. A glimpse

THE NIGHT OF OTHER DAYS

of his travel itineraries for any given period is awe-inspiring. From Ireland to Japan, Eastern Europe, South Africa and North America he read his poetry, delivered lectures, gave public addresses and spoke of dead colleagues and friends. Ian Hamilton remarked that Heaney was the most interviewed of all living poets, although in response Dennis O'Driscoll believed that most of these interviews were too narrow in scope 'to present a comprehensive portrait of the man and his times'. Patrick Crotty noted that since the turn of the millennium books by Heaney have made up almost two thirds of the total sales of contemporary poetry in the United Kingdom.

In 2006 he suffered a mild stroke which led to the cancellation of all engagements for one year, (the only exception was The Ted Hughes Memorial Lecture which he delivered at Dartington). Three poems 'Chanson d'Aventure' (HC, 2010), describe their journey to the hospital, unable to feel the hand that lovingly held his limp hand in hers and his recovery like the Charioteer at Delphi between two shafts of a walking-frame.

His prose works led to Heaney's recognition as an authorative literary critic whose writing is readily available to the non-specialist reader. He is severely critical of 'the mystification of Art and its appropriation by the grandees of aesthetics'. This might be read in the context of Heaney's belief that the audience for poetry is usually smallish while the potential public for it is very large.

On the broad front he saw poetry as a force, almost a mode of power, certainly a mode of resistance' and an individual poem as a ploughshare that turns time up and over. The best that poetry can do is 'to give us an experience that is like foreknowledge of certain things which we already seem to be remembering'... 'Strange how things in the offing, once they are sensed, /Convert to things foreknown;/And how what's come upon is manifest/Only in the light of what has been gone through' (ST 1991).

'Finders Keepers' (FK 2002) reprints extractions from 'Government of the Tongue (GT,1988) and The Redress of

HUGH MULROONEY

Poetry, (RP,1995) and several hitherto unpublished pieces. In Part One, which is largely Belfast-based, he talks of the difficulties in expressing feelings in words; in accurately capturing local cultural nuances in translations, and in transmitting the humanising power of poetry which is 'full of noises, sounds and sweet airs, that give delight and hurt not'. Significantly he says: 'The essential professing that poets do usually comes about at moments of crisis in their lives; what they have to say about problems they endure or resolve gets expressed first in terms which are personal and urgent, and then those 'ad hoc' formulations about the art or the life become familiar points of reference, and may even attain the force of prescriptions'.[5]

Part Two is rich in its depth and reach. Kavanagh is considered as is Yeats, Auden, Lowell, Sylvia Plath, Edmund Muir, Christopher Marlowe, Philip Larkin, Elizabeth Bishop, Dylan Thomas and Hugh MacDiarmid. Questions are raised. Is 'Creativity' awakened by sexual stimulant, an inner flamenco or a deep sleep? Who is best regarded, Larkin as if he stuck his pale face out on a skewer from behind the graveyard wall? Or Yeats 'always passionately beating on the wall of the physical world in order to provoke an answer from the other side? Or 'Men puddling at the source/ through tawny mud, then coming back up/deeper in themselves for having been there... finders, keepers, seers of fresh water/ in the bountiful round mouths of iron pumps and gushing taps?[6]

T. S. Eliot's literary work is haunted by shades of Dante and 'ultimately involved with the universal sorrows and penalties of living and ageing'. Dante's language takes him away from what is contingent to the imaginary; in its latinate origin and expression it unites the local and the universal; it takes us from the 'brazen world of nature' to the plane of the transcendent. Eliot was attracted by Dante's concentration on states of purgation and beatitude, his system of beliefs and his faith in a world where Christ and Caesar walk hand-in-hand. The commanding voice is that of Virgil, the

THE NIGHT OF OTHER DAYS

prophetic figure who has envisaged the world of allegory and encyclical and now comes as master, guide and authority to offer relief from the toils and snares of self. The figure who emerges from Dante's work is the poet, thinker and 'expresser of a universal myth that could unify the abundance of the inner world and the confusion of the outer'.

Reading Heaney's prose works one realises that much of what he writes about others can be applied to own work. This applies whether he is engaged with Patrick Kavanagh, Osip Mandelstam, W B Yeats or Dante. Heaney is the figure at our shoulder as he faced the question: 'How should a poet properly live and write'?

Seamus Heaney has always been 'in a haphazard pattern of work and worry, fits and starts of highs and lows' (his own words). Early on, when he read Glob's 'The Bog People', he realized that in his search for images and symbols two dominant images emerged: The solitary driver and the door or gate. These may represent his journey into the sub-conscious or into a dream (nightmare?) world. Either way this world is frightening and threatening. He has gone from observation of his first world to feelings of alienation, fear and detachment as he turns inward to find his identity. Allied to the dominant images are two recurrent features: Heaney as driver insulated in the cab and the self-inwoven simile or reflexive image: 'The burn drowns steadily in its own downpour; the breakers pour themselves into themselves'; 'You had to come back/to learn how to lose yourself'. Heaney the driver, cut off by the windscreen, locked in silence...'I drive by remote control'. 'When you have nothing to say, just drive/For a day all round the peninsula...' you will come home with a reservoir of images, (DD). He returned to this theme in 1996, 'Postscript', 'And some time make time to drive out west/Into County Clare, along the flaggy shore... when the wind and the light are working off each other...you are neither here nor there... big soft buffetings come at the car sideways'. Humans touch the land in silence; soft voices of the dead are whispering by the shore; in Brodsky's words: 'if art teaches anything, it's that the human condition is private'.

Heaney's gifted use of language, oral and written, continued to be his hallmark, from his first work. 'I was gripped by the diversity of his phrases, the intricacy of his word relationships and the luminosity of his thought. He used no word that wouldn't be at home on his Derry farm...but the words and phrases were formed by a rare golden vision'(John Keys). Patrick Crotty[10] wrote of the extraordinary breadth of appeal of his work and its success in speaking simultaneously to specialist and non-specialist audiences. But while he criticises Heaney's use of words as if words offered a one-to-one replication of things, he credits the way in which he brings us 'inside'; his use of English as it is spoken by ordinary people; his use of mimetic gift to bring immediacy. 'Funeral Rites' is chosen to illustrate the poet's power to evoke an action or sensation in phrases which use ordinary language. In an overall appraisal of a lifetime's work Elmer Andrews argued for the primacy of the auditory, the passive and the sub-rational 'as modes of cognition' in Heaney's work. Henry Kart sees a career trajectory of deepening mysticism while John Wilson Foster says that his work of verse and criticism taken together raised poetry towards the cultural eminence it had enjoyed from classical antiquity to the Romantic era. Others, including Neil Corcoran, admire the way the work stands out by virtue of its scope, scholarship, seamless transitions between text and context and sustained elegance of style.

The poetic process is a subject of great interest to Heaney. It begins with the ingestion of experience and continues as the imagination sieves that experience for its significance. The significant experience spends a period in the depths of the mind forming relationships with other material similarly collected and stored. And then it lies ready, in a kind of ever-saturated solution, to be 'crystallised out' at the moment of inspiration.[11]

THE NIGHT OF OTHER DAYS

'What is always to the credit of poetry is its power to persuade that vulnerable part of our consciousness of its rightness in spite of the evidence of wrongness all around it, the power to remind us that we are hunters and gatherers of values, that our very solitudes and distresses are creditable, insofar as they, too, are an earnest of our veritable human being'.[12] In 'The Redress of Poetry' he goes on to say that poetry cannot afford to lose its fundamentally self-delighting inventiveness, its joy in being a process of language as well as a representation of things in the world. The demand that poetry gives voice to hitherto denied expression in the ethnic, social, sexual and political life, that it be an agent for proclaiming and correcting injustices, this demand is constant and must be remembered. Poetic imagination seeks to redress whatever is wrong or exacerbating in the prevailing conditions, seeks to find and enforce a correspondence between the procedures of verse and the predicaments of the spirit. The fact is that poetry is its own reality and no matter how much a poet may concede to the corrective pressures of social, moral, political and historical reality, the ultimate fidelity must be to the demands and promise of the artistic event.

Faced with the reality of history there are times when it is difficult to suppress the thought that history is about as instructive as an abattoir and that peace is merely the desolation left behind after the worst has been done by merciless power. Indeed, Heaney admitted to entertaining the thought that violence might be justified if it led to a positive outcome (he quickly scotched the thought). The right way is that of friendship and trust, sympathy and protectiveness between living creatures. Violence may be a reality in Palestine, Bosnia, Rwanda and Northern Ireland but that should not lead to the conclusion that human nature lacks constructive potential or that there is little positive in art. It may be that a poem never stopped a tank but 'The only reliable release from the tension between geographical place and place of the mind is the appeasement of the achieved poem or work of art'. The artist makes contact with the plane of consciousness where he is at once intensified in his being and detached from his predicaments. The mind longs to repose in the 'stability of truth' and the poet longs to write a poem which will create an order true to the impact of external reality and sensitive to the inner laws of his being.

On the question of creativity W.B.Yeats believed that sexual excitement and creative excitement are near allied and Lorca seemed to imply that poetry requires an initial inner flamenco; that it must be excited into life by something peremptory, some initial strum or throb that gets you started and drives you further than you realised you could go. Heaney said of creativity and the birth of a poem 'I didn't quite know where it came from, but I knew immediately it was there to stay'.

His final three books are informed by his work of criticism and translation. He steps on lands already cultivated and is now partially free to walk on air even if he is now walking in the shadow of death. EL, published in 2001, travels widely in time and space, with images of the marvellous grounded in the everyday, poetry, criticism and translations. As described on the cover of the paperback edition, the book visits the classical world, revisits poetry and electrifies a lifetime. It is concerned with the origins of words and oracles, with the origins of human understanding, the power of memory, recall and word-hoard. But it is dominated by tragedy, not with the anger of SL, rather with despair. All Heaney's interests come together in that shadow.

DC,(2006), 'reinforces the death-shadowed theme', is dominated by the chthonic and the transition to the afterlife, as related 'not just to his ageing but his pessimistic view of international politics'.[7] Charon is the dominant figure, the ruined twin-towers are stark reminders of defeat and many poems are set in the underworld. The book finishes on a note of foreboding; 'I never liked yon bird'. The title poem includes many themes

THE NIGHT OF OTHER DAYS

including the buoyancy of Charon's boat balancing a recalled Sunday-morning boat-trip, repetition of the word 'heel', the sense of solid reliability in grabbing the 'roof-wort' and being transported to the plane of the transcendental. On a Saturday night in Louden's butcher shop, rib-roast and shin, plonked down and wrapped up are carried, seeping blood, onto the street where lurk local 'B-men', unbuttoned but on duty', neighbours with guns' who couldn't seem to place Patrick Heaney. The sense of menace is always there.

'Normal life' continued and historical markers were laid down. Heaneys were killing pigs when American troops arrived in Mossbawn and Barney Devlin hammered twelve blows on the anvil to mark the millennium. His nephew heard it in Edmonton Alberta as the cellular phone was held high as a horse's ear and 'Barney smiling to himself'. Nostalgia carried its risks and could mislead. Mint held the promise of renewal and could evoke powerful memories. But it grew in the refuse dump. 'My last things will be the first things slipping from me/ Yet let all things go free that have survived'. The poet coffined in Krakow said 'the art of oil-painting /daubs fixed on canvas/ is a paltry thing/compared with what cries out to be expressed', and in 'A shiver' Heaney noted that 'A first blow could make air of a wall'. He says of Mandelstam of Pasternack et al 'They are the ones who toed the line, not just the verse line but the line where courage is tested, where to stand by what you write is to have to stand your ground and take the consequences'.

In 1999 Heaney published his translation of Beowulf and it has been observed that Beowulf bears the same relation to EL as SA does to SI in its profound melancholy. But Heaney noted in GT that for an Irishman to translate from a tongue other than Gaelic brings with it its own problems. 'It seems self-evident that what the reader who does not speak Russian experiences as the poem in translation is radically and logically different from what the native speaker experiences, phonetics and feelings being so intimately related in the human make-up'.[8] He quotes a line from Brian Friel's play: 'a civilization can become imprisoned in a linguistic contour that no longer matches the landscape of fact'.

Seamus Heaney's final work 'HumanChain' (HC, 2010) won the Forward Prize for Best Collection. Its dust-jacket cover noted 'continuities and solidarities between husband and wife, child and parent, then and now', everyday continuities like bags passed from hand to hand. Here we have the craft of the early scribe, the technique of the classical scholar and the poet singing songs 'at the crossroads of the oral and the written', of the past and of the present, of inheritance and transmission, of Route 110 and of the descent into the underworld. A poetic 'Herbal' puzzles over the world of speechless things. What in the end was left to bury of Mr Lavery, blown up in his own pub or of Louis O Neill who defied the curfew the night they buried the innocent Derry 13? Are graveyard plants different to the grass elsewhere? Less peaceful? Is the funeral bell the only sound that makes them tremble? Must rats' tails and nettles poison the undergrowth? Crush a leaf or a herb between your palms and inhale its smoothness...you gained your knowledge of the universe because you observed, felt, looked into yourself. 'I had my existence in that world of touch, smell, sight...I had my existence.[8] I was there./Me in place and place in me./Where can it be found again'? In the graveyard grass? In the wood canopy that talked in its sleep? With the age of ghosts on route 110? With Colin Middleton, Aligieri, Plato's Er, Odysseus, Orpheus? Did I seek the Kingdom? Will the Kingdom come?

Take a ride down the Wood Road. See Bill Pickering with his gun...special militia man, harassing Mulhollandstown, Heaney on top of a cartload of turf, or walking to the hunger-strikers wake, or seeing the stain at the end of the lane where the child died. And is that the bus stop, overgrown but still standing?

THE NIGHT OF OTHER DAYS

Speaking of Yeats[9] Heaney said: Every good poem could be an epitaph, 'But in certain great poets...you could sense an ongoing opening of consciousness as they age, a deepening and clarifying and even a simplifying of receptivity to what might be waiting on the further shore. It's like those rare summer evenings when the sky clears rather than darkens. No poet can avoid hoping for that kind of old age'. The final question 'Is this all? As it was in the beginning, is now and shall be? Wordsworth answered long ago... It is on this earth we find happiness, or not at all. Which is one reason for 'keeping going'.

'As I age and blank on names/ As my uncertainty on stairs... as the memorable bottoms out /Into the irretrievable'...he can still imagine 'That slight untoward rupture and world-tilt/as a wind freshened and the anchor weighed'. And so Aibhin's Kite climbs higher and higher, carrying further and further the longing in the breast and planted feet. 'The kite takes off, itself alone, a windfall.'

BIBLIOGRAPHY

Chapter One

I gratefully acknowledge the assistance of Chief Inspector Tony Callaghan, area commander, Magherafelt PSNI and Paul McKearney, Cookstown Library. Through them I was furnished with the report on the tragic death of Christopher Heaney.

1. O'Driscoll, D. *Stepping Stones. Interviews with Seamus Heaney*. London: Faber and Faber, 2008.
2. Heaney, S. *District and Circle*. 'The Blackbird of Glanmore' p.75. London: Faber and Faber, 2006,.
3. O'Driscoll, D. *Stepping Stones. Interviews with Seamus Heaney*. p408. London: Faber and Faber, 2008.
4. Feeling into Words, in Finders Keepers Faber and Faber 2002 P15
5. Parker, M, Heaney, S. *The Making of a Poet*. Dublin: Gill and Macmillan, 1993
6. O'Donoghue, B. *The Cambridge Companion to Seamus Heaney*. Cambridge: Cambridge University Press, 2009.
7. O Donoghue, B. *The Cambridge Companion to Seamus Heaney*, p. 184. Cambridge: Cambridge University Press, 2009.
8. Bogland. Final poem in 'Door into the Dark', Faber and Faber, London 1969. Also Elmer Andrews P 10

9. Heaney, S. *Preoccupations. Selected Prose* 1968 - 1978. London: Faber, 1980
10. Finders Keepers, Learning from Eliot, p36
11. Ibid.
12. Door into the Dark 1969.
13. Feeling into Words, Finders Keepers, op. cit

Chapter Two

1. The Nobel Lecture 1995...Crediting Poetry, The Gallery Press, Loughcrew, Oldcastle, County Meath, Ireland. 1995.
2. Seeing Things, Faber and Faber,1991
3. Parker, Michael, Seamus Heaney, The Making of the Poet (Iowa City: University of Iowa Press,1993.
4. The Spirit Level, Faber and Faber, 1995. The Strand p.62
5. Station Island, Faber and Faber, 1984. Making Strange p.32
6. Seeing Things op. cit.
7. Finders Keepers, Mossbawn p.7
8. Stepping Stones pp135 and 402
9. Stations, Faber and Faber, Opened Ground, Poems 1966-1996. The Wanderer. Also Parker op. cit. p9
10. Ibid p33
11. Feeling into Words op. cit
12. Things 1991 Seeing Poem The Ash Plant.
13. Deane, Seamus: Seamus Heaney: The Timorous and the Bold. Chapter 4 in Michael Allen, ed. New Casebooks, Seamus Heaney. St.Martin's Press, Inc, New York, 1997
14. Ibid Album iv
15. Man and Boy, Seeing Things 1991
16. The Haw Lantern, Faber and Faber, 1987
17. Seeing Things, 1991 Poem Fosterling, Man and Boy.
18. '1.1.87', perhaps the only 'Haiku' by Heaney, ST 1991
19. 'Man and Boy', Seeing Things, 1991
20. Michael Parker op. cit.
21. Feeling
22. into Words, in Finders Keepers op. cit. p15

Chapter Three

1. Stepping Stones P39
2. Clearances in The Haw Lantern 1987
3. Quoted in Michael Parker, The Making of a Poet, Gill and McMillan, Dublin 1993. P3
4. Stepping Stones P310
5. Stepping Stones P309 and P135
6. P28
7. Poem Album II in Human Chain 2010 22. Parker

Chapter Four

1. Parker, op cit P178
2. Interview with Blake Morrison quoted in Parker P211
3. Vendler P114
4. The Aerodrome in District and Circle (2006)
5. Quoted, Parker P211
6. Elmer Andrews, The Poetry of Seamus Heaney, Icon Books, Cambridge 1998
7. Squarings, Seeing Things, 1991.
8. Finders Keepers p26 Learning from Eliot.
9. John Carey, Quoted in Elmer Anderson op cit p25
10. 10 Squarings.

Chapter Five

1. References in this chapter refer directly to Heaney's poems or directly to his words as spoken/written in reply to questions from Dennis O Driscoll in 'Stepping Stones'. Stepping Stones is identified as SS and the poems are identified by abbreviated volume title e.g. Death of a Naturalist as DN, Door Into The Dark as DD and Wintering Out as WO.

   Heaney pays a warm tribute to Michael McLaverty, a man he admired, in SS pp50-52. He later wrote an introduction to McLaverty's volume of short stories and wrote his obituary in The Times. He also tells of incidents like the one where McLaverty comes to Heaney's classroom and asks 'Mr Heaney' if he can recognise in the photograph of a rugby team the one who writes poetry. Mr Heaney answers 'Yes".
2. ibid Introduction xxiv
3. P 103
4. P24
5. Michael Parker, P6
6. 'Mossbawn' in Finders Keepers pp3-13
7. 'A Peacock's Feather for Daisy Garnett' in The Haw Lantern HL 1987
8. Dennis O Driscoll SS xi
9. Seeing Things ST 1991 xli
10. ibid The Cot, Glanmore Revisited. ST 1991
11. SS p 25

Chapter Six

1. Finders Keepers (FK) P414 where he speaks of Incarnationin, his essay on Milosz.
2. Elmer Andrews op cit. p26
3. Chukwu is a supreme God in the belief of the Igbo people from the eastern region of Nigeria. In the traditional Igbo spiritual belief system Chukwu is the infinitely powerful, undefinable supreme deity encompassing everything in space and space itself. The Igbo people believe that all things come from Chukwu, who brings the rains necessary for plants to grow and controls everything on earth and the spiritual world.
4. El Andrews p34
5. FK p472
6. W.B.Yeats 'The Cold Heaven'
7. FK p327
8. Stepping Stones (SS), 471
9. The People's University 1858-2008, 150 years of The University of London and its External students, Christine Kenyon Jones, University of London 2008. P182
10. M.Parker p115
11. Nicholas McGuinn, quoted in M.Parker p114
12. M.Parker p145

Chapter Seven

1. Squarings xxli Seeing Things 1991.
2. Squarings xlviii
3. See Catriona Clutterbuck, 'Pilot and Stray in One': Sustaining Nothingness in the Travel Poems of Early Heaney, the Irish Review, Winter-Spring 2014-2015, Cork University Press, 2015.
   Also Joy or Night: Last Things in the Poetry of W.B.Yeats and Philip Larkin, Finders Keepers p 316 and Stepping Stones, Dennis O'Driscoll.

Part Two

Chapter Eight

1. Finders Keepers. Selected Prose 1971-2001. 'Mossbawn' and 'Something to Write Home About'.
2. Door Into The Dark. 1969.
3. 'The Cot' Seeing Things (S.T.1991). also Finders Keepers P52.
4. The Poetry of Seamus Heaney, Neil Corcoran, Faber and Faber 1998.
5. Stepping Stones P 171.
6. Churning Day (DN 1966).
7. Mother, DD.1969. Not included in Opened Ground, poems 1966-1996.
8. Irish Folk Ways. E.Estyn Evans.Routledge,1957. Now out of print. I have used the copy of my late brother-in-law, Colm Purcell, Galway.
9. The Making of a Poet, Michael Parker, Gill and MacMillan, Dublin 1993.
10. Ibid
11. Evans op cit.
12. Parker op cit
13. Ibid.
14. Something to Write Home About.
15. I treasure my copy of 'Death of a Naturalist' on which Seamus has written those lines 'Are your praties dry/ And are they fit for digging? /"Put in your spade and try", says Dirty-Face McGuigan... June 1977. I also have some tapes made during his time in Carysfort.
16. Finders Keepers P19 and Crossings xxxii in ST 1991.
17. Ibid.
18. Ibid.

Chapter Nine

1. Stepping Stones P5
2. Michael Parker P13
3. Helen Vendler P11
4. Ibid
5. Quoted Elmer Andrews P12. Elmer Andrews,Ed.,The Poetry of Seamus Heaney, Cambridge 1998. Also Poetry Ireland Review Issue 113, 2014. P 129, Michelle O'Sullivan.
6. Finders Keepers.
7. 'Docker' One of 24 poems omitted from 'Opened Ground'
8. Stepping Stones P130
9. Ibid
10. Veterans Dream, WO 1972
11. M.Curtis P10
12. 'Alphabets' Haw Lantern 1987
13. 'Damson' Spirit Level 1996
14. 'Thatcher' D.D. 1969
15. 'Veteran's Dream'. W.O. 1972
16. 'Midnight Anvil'. District and Circle 2006
17. D.D. 1969
18. The Cambridge Companion To Seamus Heaney. Ed Bernard O'Donoghue,Cambridge University Press 2009 P107
19. P.K. xvi Ed. Antoinnette Quinn
20. Ibid introduction xviii
21. E.E.Evans
22. Michael Parker P65
23. Bernard O'Donoghue op cit
24. Helen Vendler Ch.1
25. Ibid
26. E.Andrews

Chapter Ten

1. Parker P62
2. This poem is not included in 'Opened Ground', Poems 1966-1996, pubished in 1998.
3. Finders Keepers P23
4. Station Island vii
5. Not included in 'Opened Ground'
6. Feeling Into Words, F.K. P23.
7. Ibid
8. Elmer Andrews, editor, Icon Critical Guides, Cambridge 1998.

Part Three

Chapter Eleven

This chapter is entirely based on two works: Marianne Elliott, The Catholics of Ulster, Allen Lane, The Penguin Press, 2000.

> J.J. Lee, Ireland, Politics and Society, Cambridge University Press, 1989.

Tracing the development of the situation in which Seamus Heaney found himself in 1969 is difficult. Opinions, convictions and prejudices are dearly held and defended. Contradictions and disagreements have been activated with murderous results. Thousands are dead, injured or scarred. Personal beliefs and convictions are held and expressed with absolute certainty. The attention of the world has been focussed on Northern Ireland for over half a century. Seamus Heaney agonised over the situation, wrote about it and was respected as a spokesman of integrity. The evolution of the situation in Northern Ireland can be difficult even for an Irish person to comprehend. For anyone unfamiliar with Ireland and its history it can be incomprehensible.

I have attempted to present the bare bones as I have read professional historians and no personal opinion is expressed. I believe that some knowledge of Irish history is required to make some sense of a very involved and complicated situation.

Marianne Elliott's book is written from a Catholic standpoint, but with the pen of a highly respected historian and a citizen of Northern Ireland.

J.J.Lee is professor of history at University College Cork and universally respected and admired.

It is hoped that this chapter will enable a fuller understanding of the work of Seamus Heaney.

1. P 95 Elliott
2. 'The Human Chain' (HC 2010)
3. P85-89
4. P 130
5. P269
6. J.J.Lee P18
7. Elliott P128 8 ibid 9 Elliott P32

Chapter Twelve

1. Finders Keepers P24/25
2. Parker, op cit
3. Essay 'Belfast' in Finders Keepers
4. ibid
5. Deane S. quoted in Allen in O'Donoghue, op cit
6. David Wheatley, Chapter 8 in B. O'Donoghue, op cit P123
7. Neil Corcoran Chapter 11 in O'Donoghue.
8. Finders Keepers P25
9. Elmer Andews, Edna Longley, Ciaran Carson, David Lloyd.

Chapter Thirteen

1. Elmer Andrews, The Poetry of Seamus Heaney. London 1989
2. Stepping Stones P195
3. Ibid
4. Neil Corcoran, A Student's guide to Seamus Heaney. London 1986. This is the best volume on Seamus Heaney and I quote liberally on its contents.
5. Quoted in Andrew Murphy, Seamus Heaney. Northcote House 1996
6. Stepping Stones P110
7. Edna Longley, Poetry and Politics in Northern Ireland, in poetry in the Wars, Newcastle 1986. Also Michael Allen(ed), Seamus Heaney, Basinstoke 1997.
8. Andrew Murphy op cit

Chapter Fourteen

1. Elmer Andrews and Michael Allen.
2. Seamus Deane in Allen P71
3. Bernard O'Donoghue Introduction P7
4. Andrew Murphy P56
5. Deane in Allen P65
6. Elmer Andrews P166
7. Deane, Allen P66
8. Andrews P145 and 154
9. Stepping Stones.
10. Ibid P208
11. Andrews
12. Stepping Stones P197
13. Andrews P21
14. Jamie McKendrick Word Mad Flesh, Poetry Ireland 113
15. Andrews
16. Stepping Stones P425
17. Neil Corcoran in Bernard O'Donoghue P171
18. Stepping Stones
19. Finders Keepers P14
20. Seamus Deane, in Michael Allen
21. Deryn Rees-Jones, Poetry Ireland Review 2014 P82
22. Stepping Stones
23. Poem Carysfort 1988
24. Stepping Stones
25. E.E.Evans P163
26. Andrews

Chapter Fifteen

1. Seamus Heaney, Introduction 'Sweeney Astray'
2. Stepping Stones p151-153
3. Vendler p10
4. Dennis O Driscoll in Bernard O Donoghue,ed, p60
5. Vendler p5
6. Stepping Stones p467
7. Neill Corcoran. Ch3, p53
8. Quoted B. O Donoghue p8
9. Stepping Stones 262
10. Ibid 465
11. O Donoghue p8
12. Corcoran. Op cit
13. Stepping Stones 472
14. Ibid 471
15. Guinn Batten, Ch 12, O Donoghue,ed
16. Stepping Stones p471
17. Guinn Batten
18. Anne Stephenson in Curtis p137
19. Caitriona O Reilly, Poetry Ireland Review 113 p15/16
20. This is partly the source for the title of this book.
21. Stepping stones 425
22. Elmer Andrews p137
23. Stepping Stones p220
24. Kirkland in Michael Allen p262
25. Crediting Poetry p18
26. Elmer Andrews p116
27. Stepping Stones p471
28. Christian Wiman, 'Take Love', Poetry Ireland Review 113
29. Elmer Andrews p26/28

Clutterbuck, Irish Review, p106

Chapter Sixteen

1. Dennis O'Driscoll Introduction to Stepping Stones xii
2. Seamus Deane
3. Bernard O Donoghue P10
4. Helen Vendler, Strange Letters, Ch 6 Neill Corcoran
5. Patrick Crotty in Emer Andrews P75
6. P158
7. Elmer Andrews P73
8. Stan Smith The Chosen Ground, in Neill Corcoran
9. O Donoghue P66.
10. Rand Brand in O Donoghue P30

Chapter Seventeen

1. This is a reference to the story of the village folk who sold their souls to the devil. Shortly before the devil was due to collect, a group of tinkers (itinerant tinsmiths) came to the village. They constructed the tree-clock which never showed the correct time. The devil missed his deadline because he believed the clock.
2. Elmer Andrews
3. 'What is Heaney Seeing in Seeing Things?' Colby Quarterly March 1994.
4. Andrews P158
5. O'Donoghue P153
6. Ibid P63
7. Elmer Andrews P163
8. Helen Vendler

Chapter Eighteen

1. J.W. Foster P210 in Bernard O Donoghue op cit P210.
2. BOD P14
3. ibid P119
4. Foster
5. 'Heaney's Classics and the Bucolic', Bernard O Donoghue Chapter 7. The Cambridge Companion to Seamus Heaney, 2009'
6. ibid P117

Chapter Nineteen

1. A point made by Patrick Crotty and Helen Vendler
2. J.W.Foster, Crediting Miracles: Heaney after 50.
3. Elmer Andrews, Icon Books 1998
4. Richard Kirkland, Chapter 15, Michael Allen ed
5. F.K. P70
6. Mycenae Lookout. SL 1996
7. Bernard O Donoghue P14
8. GT P39
9. SS P466
10. Patrick Crotty, The Context of Heaney's Recepttion
11. Thomas Kinsella, quoted M.Parker P35
12. CP P29

SECONDARY SOURCES

Allen, M. ed. *New Casebooks, Seamus Heaney.* New York: St. Martin's Press. 1997.

Andrews, E. ed. *The Poetry of Seamus Heaney.* Cambridge: Icon. 1998

Carson, C. Sweeney Astray: Escaping from Limbo. In. Curtis, T. ed. *The Art of Seamus Heaney.* Dublin: Wolfhound Press, 2001.

Corcoran, N. Writing a Bare Wire: Station Island. In. Allen, M. ed. *New Casebooks, Seamus Heaney.* New York: St. Martin's Press. 1997.

Crotty, P. Selected Poems: All I Believed that Happened There Was Revision. In. Curtis, T. ed. *The Art of Seamus Heaney.* Dublin: Wolfhound Press, 2001.

Curtis, T. ed *The Art of Seamus Heaney.* Dublin: Wolfhound Press, 2001.

Curtis, T. A More Social Voice: Field Work. In. Curtis, T. ed. *The Art of Seamus Heaney.* Dublin: Wolfhound Press, 2001.

Davis, D. Door in the Dark. In. Curtis, T. ed. *The Art of Seamus Heaney.* Dublin: Wolfhound Press, 2001.

Deane, S. Seamus Heaney: The Timorous and the Bold. In. Allen, M. ed. *New Casebooks, Seamus Heaney.* New York: St. Martin's Press. 1997.

Doherty, T. Landscape: Seamus Heaney. In. Allen, M. ed. *New Casebooks, Seamus Heaney.* New York: St. Martin's Press. 1997.

Doherty, T. The Sign of the Cross: Review of the Government of the Tongue. In. Allen, M. ed. *New Casebooks, Seamus Heaney.* New York: St. Martin's Press. 1997.

Dunn, D. Quotidien Miracles: Seeing Things. In. Curtis, T. ed. *The Art of Seamus Heaney.* Dublin: Wolfhound Press, 2001.

Eagleton, T. Review of Field Work. In. Allen, M. ed. *New Casebooks, Seamus Heaney.* New York: St. Martin's Press. 1997.

Goodby, J. and Phillips, I. Not Bad: The Spirit Level. In. Curtis, T. ed. *The Art of Seamus Heaney.* Dublin: Wolfhound Press, 2001.

Groarke, V. ed. *Poetry Ireland Review.* Seamus Heaney Edition 113.

The Irish review. No's 49-50. Winter-Spring 2014/2015.

Hardy, B. Meeting the Myth: Station Island. In. Curtis, T. ed. *The Art of Seamus Heaney.* Dublin: Wolfhound Press, 2001.

Hughes, E. Representation in Modern Irish Poetry. In. Allen, M. ed. *New Casebooks, Seamus Heaney.* New York: St. Martin's Press. 1997.

Kendall, T. An Enormous Yes?: The Redress of Poetry. In. Curtis, T. ed. *The Art of Seamus Heaney*. Dublin: Wolfhound Press, 2001.

Kirkland, R. Paradigms of Possibility. In. Allen, M. ed. *New Casebooks, Seamus Heaney*. New York: St. Martin's Press. 1997.

Lloyd, D. Pap for the Dispossessed: Seamus Heaney and the Politics of Identity. In. Allen, M. ed. *New Casebooks, Seamus Heaney*. New York: St. Martin's Press. 1997.

Longley, E. North. In. Allen, M. ed. *New Casebooks, Seamus Heaney*. New York: St. Martin's Press. 1997.

Murphy, A. *Seamus Heaney. Writers and Their Work*. Plymouth: Northcote House. 2010.

O'Brien, C. A Slow North-East Wind: Review of North. In. Allen, M. ed. *New Casebooks, Seamus Heaney*. New York: St. Martin's Press. 1997.

O'Donoghue, B. Heaney's Ars Poetica: the Government of the Tongue. In. Curtis, T. ed. *The Art of Seamus Heaney*. Dublin: Wolfhound Press, 2001.

O'Donoghue, B. ed. *The Cambridge Companion to Seamus Heaney*. Cambridge: Cambridge University Press. 2009.

Parker, M. *Seamus Heaney, The Making of a Poet*. Dublin: Gill and MacMillan. 1993.

Phillips, H. Seamus Heaney's Beowulf. In. Curtis, T. ed. *The Art of Seamus Heaney*. Dublin: Wolfhound Press, 2001.

Ricks, C. Growing Up: Review of Death of a Naturalist. In. Allen, M. ed. *New Casebooks, Seamus Heaney.* New York: St. Martin's Press. 1997.

Ricks, R. The Month, the Meal and the Book: review of Fieldwork. In. Allen, M. ed. *New Casebooks, Seamus Heaney.* New York: St. Martin's Press. 1997.

Smith, S. The Distance Between: Seamus Heaney. In. Allen, M. ed. *New Casebooks, Seamus Heaney.* New York: St. Martin's Press. 1997.

Stevenson, A. The Peace Within Understanding: Looking at Preoccupations. In. Curtis, T. ed. *The Art of Seamus Heaney.* Dublin: Wolfhound Press, 2001.

Stevenson, A. Stations, Seamus Heaney and the Sacred Sense of the Sensitive Self. In. Curtis, T. ed. *The Art of Seamus Heaney.* Dublin: Wolfhound Press, 2001.

Tobin, D. Passage to the Center. *Imagination and the Sacred in the Poetry of Seamus Heaney.* Kentucky: Kentucky University Press. 1999.

Vendler, H. *Seamus Heaney.* Harvard: Harvard University Press. 1998.

Vendler, H. Second thoughts: The Haw Lantern. In. Curtis, T. ed. *The Art of Seamus Heaney.* Dublin: Wolfhound Press, 2001.

Lightning Source UK Ltd.
Milton Keynes UK
UKHW04f2243231018
331050UK00001B/2/P